MW00476579

EXAMIN...

OPTOMETRY

FOURTH EDITION

EXAMINATION REVIEW

OPTOMETRY

FOURTH EDITION

Linda Casser, O.D.
Director, Indianapolis Eye Care Center Indiana University School of Optometry Indianapolis, Indiana; Associate Professor Indiana University School of Optometry Bloomington, Indiana

Freddy W. Chang, O.D., Ph.D.
Chief, Optometry Section Veterans Administration Outpatient Clinic Los Angeles, California; Professor of Optometry Southern California College of Optometry Fullerton, California

Daniel R. Gerstman, M.S., O.D.
Associate Dean and Associate Professor Indiana University School of Optometry Bloomington, Indiana

Paul A. Pietsch, Ph.D.
Professor of Optometry Indiana University School of Optometry Bloomington, Indiana; Adjunct Professor of Anatomy Indiana University School of Medicine Bloomington, Indiana

Arthur Bradley, Ph.D.
Associate Professor Indiana University School of Optometry Bloomington, Indiana

APPLETON & LANGE
Norwalk, Connecticut

Copyright © 1994 by Appleton & Lange
Paramount Publishing Business and Professional Group
© 1989 by Appleton & Lange
Simon & Schuster Business and Professional Group

98 / 10 9 8 7 6 5 4 3

Prentice Hall International (UK) Limited, *London*
Prentice Hall of Australia Pty. Limited, *Sydney*
Prentice Hall Canada, Inc., *Toronto*
Prentice Hall Hispanoamericana, S.A., *Mexico*
Prentice Hall of India Private Limited, *New Delhi*
Prentice Hall of Japan, Inc., *Tokyo*
Simon & Schuster Asia Pte. Ltd., *Singapore*
Editora Prentice Hall do Brasil Ltda., *Rio de Janeiro*
Prentice Hall, *Englewood Cliffs, New Jersey*

ISSN 1073–5046

Acquisitions Editor: Jamie L. Mount
Production Service: Rainbow Graphics, Inc.
Designer: Penny Kindzierski

ISBN 0-8385-7449-1

90000

9 780838 574492

Contents

vi / Contents

Preface

We have written this book for the optometry student preparing to take national, state, or local examinations; for the optometrist seeking state licensure; and for those busy established practitioners who desire to keep abreast of the field as a whole through self-assessment.

The profession of optometry has undergone significant transformation and expansion of scope since the first edition of this book was written. New knowledge has been discovered, new technologies have come into being, new techniques have been devised, solutions to old problems have been developed, new and compelling reasons have been created for perfecting and applying traditional routines and procedures. Thus, for the fourth edition of this book to serve its intended audience and provide the basis of a comprehensive review of contemporary optometry, major revisions in orientation, as well as in content, have been undertaken.

In addition, major organizational changes have been made in the fourth edition. The chapter headings now directly correspond to the topical outlines of the Basic Science and Clinical Science sections of the National Board of Examiners in Optometry (NBEO) examination. This has entailed not only reorganization and revision of existing material but the addition of multiple new chapters. The relative size of individual chapters is consistent with the 1993 expansion of the NBEO Basic Science examination. To effectively address these new aspects, Dr. Arthur Bradley brings additional expertise as a fifth co-author, and the total number of questions has been expanded from 800 to 1000. To maximize the educational benefit of this volume, the explanatory answers have been retained and significantly expanded. The reference listings, found by chapter, have been updated and provide guidance to the reader for supplemental reading.

We believe, then, that the updating of material from the third edition to reflect new developments in optometry and related health care fields, combined with the reorganization of this volume as well as the addition of new material in expanded areas makes Optometry Examination Review, 4th edition, an excellent resource for its intended audience.

Appreciation is extended to the administration of the Indiana University School of Optometry for encouragement with this project, and to our many colleagues for expert advice. We also thank the individuals who were involved with the preparation of this manuscript.

We dedicate this edition to the late Ingeborg Schmidt, M.D., for her invaluable contributions to previous editions of this volume and to the profession of optometry.

1

Human Biology

DIRECTIONS (Questions 1–200): Each of the numbered items or incomplete statements in this section is followed by answers or completions of the statement. Select the ONE lettered answer or completion that is BEST in each case.

Gross Anatomy

1. How many cervical vertebrae do humans normally have?
   A. 4
   B. 5
   C. 6
   D. 7
   E. 8

2. Osteology is to bones as which of the following is to joints?
   A. kinesiology
   B. splanchnology
   C. arthrology
   D. myology
   E. neurology

3. What is the location of the azygous vein?
   A. right posterior mediastinum
   B. left posterior mediastinum
   C. left inferior quadrant of the abdominal cavity
   D. left side of the neck
   E. middle anterior mediastinum

4. What bone forms the superior rim of the bony orbit?
   A. frontal
   B. maxillary
   C. lacrimal
   D. great wing of the sphenoid
   E. lesser wing of the sphenoid

5. En route through the optic foramen, the optic nerve is accompanied by which of the following structures?
   A. ophthalmic division of the trigeminal nerve
   B. ophthalmic vein
   C. ophthalmic artery
   D. all of the above
   E. none of the above

6. The postganglionic parasympathetic fibers that innervate the lacrimal gland originate in what ganglion?
   A. semilunar
   B. pterygopalatine
   C. otic
   D. Edinger-Westphal
   E. ciliary

7. Which of these muscles does not originate on the anulus tendineus communis?
   A. lateral rectus
   B. superior oblique
   C. inferior oblique
   D. inferior rectus
   E. medial rectus

8. The central retinal artery usually branches from what artery?
   A. external carotid
   B. internal carotid

   C. posterior ciliary
   D. lacrimal
   E. ophthalmic

9. What does the thoracic duct primarily transport?
   A. arterial blood
   B. venous blood
   C. semen
   D. bile
   E. lymph

10. The nasolacrimal duct, which transports tear fluid away from the lacrimal sac, empties directly into the
    A. sphenoethmoidal recess of the nasal cavity
    B. superior meatus of the nasal cavity
    C. middle meatus of the nasal cavity
    D. inferior meatus of the nasal cavity
    E. antrium (of Highmore) of the nasal cavity

11. The spinal cord, per se, of most (95 percent) human beings termi-nates at about the level of which vertebra?
    A. cervical 2
    B. thoracic 2
    C. lumbar 2
    D. sacral 2
    E. coccygeal 2

12. The epiploic foramen communicates what with what?
    A. greater and lesser sacs of the peritoneum
    B. pyloric and fundic portions of the stomach
    C. pyloric stomach and the duodenum
    D. thoracic and abdominal cavities
    E. diploic veins of the skull and the superior sagittal sinus

13. The human vermiform appendix is an extension of the
    A. rectum
    B. sigmoid colon
    C. jejunum
    D. cecum/ascending colon
    E. descending colon

14. The common carotid artery shares the carotid sheath with the internal jugular vein and a nerve. What is the latter nerve?
    A. sympathetic chain
    B. phrenic
    C. recurrent laryngeal
    D. vagus
    E. mandibular division of the trigeminal (V2)

15. Which nerves form the roots of the brachial plexus?
    A. C1–C8
    B. T1–T8
    C. C1–C4
    D. C5–C8, T1
    E. L4, L5, S1–S3

16. In a normal human heart, blood being propelled out of the right ventricle passes through an orifice guarded by which valve?
    A. tricuspid
    B. mitral
    C. aortic semilunar
    D. pulmonary semilunar
    E. pyloric

Neuroanatomy/Neurophysiology

17. The medial geniculate bodies play a major role in relation to what form of stimulus?
    A. light
    B. sound
    C. odors
    D. tactile
    E. nociceptive

18. In the Warwick scheme of the oculomotor nuclear complex, the caudal central cells innervate what muscles?
    A. lateral rectus
    B. medial rectus
    C. levator palpebrae superioris
    D. superior rectus
    E. inferior rectus

19. If the medial rectus of the right eye contracts, which nucleus must fire to bring about contraction of the contralateral yoke muscle? Assume the Warwick plan for the IIIrd nuclear complex.
   A. caudal central of III
   B. trochlear
   C. dorsal lateral of III
   D. Perlia's
   E. abducens

20. If an eye is fully abducted, the firing of which nucleus will result in intorsion? Assume the Warwick plan for the IIIrd nuclear complex.
   A. dorsal lateral of III
   B. trochlear
   C. caudal central of III
   D. Perlia's
   E. abducens

21. Which cranial nerves decussate in the superior (anterior) medullary vellum?
   A. I
   B. II
   C. III
   D. IV
   E. V

22. The oculomotor nerve exits from the brain at what location?
   A. superior (anterior) medullary vellum
   B. interpeduncular fossa
   C. lower border of the pons
   D. immediately lateral to the decussation of the pyramids
   E. obex

23. Which of the following waves can be encountered in the electroencephalograms (EEGs) of human beings?
   A. alpha
   B. beta
   C. theta
   D. delta
   E. all of the above

24. Depolarization of the afferent innervating fibers of the superior semicircular duct of the inner ear depends on
   A. acceleration of endolymph toward the crista ampularis
   B. acceleration of endolymph away from the crista ampularis
   C. linear displacement of otoconia (otoliths) toward the macular kinocilia
   D. linear displacement of otoconia (otoliths) away from the macular kinocilia
   E. second order displacement of otoconia (otoliths) relative to the saccular stereocilia

25. From a functional standpoint, the semicircular canals of the inner ear pair up according to which of the following plans? (p = posterior; l = lateral; s = superior)
   A. p + p; l + l; s + s
   B. p + l; l + p; s + s
   C. l + l; s + p; p + s
   D. p + l; l + s; s + p
   E. none of the above

26. The surface location for the vestibular nuclei is the
   A. tectum
   B. lateral portion of the floor of the 4th ventricle
   C. lateral portion of the floor of the 3rd ventricle
   D. medial raphe of the floor of the 4th ventricle
   E. walls of ventricles I and II

27. Which of these choices is known to be a major, direct pathway between the vestibular and oculomotor nuclei?
   A. medial lemniscus
   B. lateral lemniscus
   C. lateral corticospinal tract
   D. medial longitudinal fasciculus
   E. superior longitudinal fasciculus

28. The cells of the Edinger-Westphal nucleus fall into what category?
   A. somatic motor
   B. preganglionic parasympathetic

    C. postganglionic parasympathetic
    D. postganglionic sympathetic
    E. preganglionic sympathetic

29. Axons from the Edinger-Westphal nucleus terminate in the
    A. ciliary ganglion
    B. intrinsic muscles of the eye
    C. superior cervical ganglion
    D. middle cervical ganglion
    E. tectum

30. Which nucleus is most directly involved in mediating ocular pain?
    A. Edinger-Westphal
    B. facial
    C. motor V
    D. mesencephalic V
    E. spinal V_1

31. The neuroanatomical structures within a facial colliculus are directly associated with the closure phase of blinking (via cranial nerve VII), and with what other action?
    A. abduction of the ipsilateral eye
    B. adduction of the ipsilateral eye
    C. adduction of the contralateral eye
    D. abduction of the contralateral eye
    E. bilateral sursumduction of both eyes

32. A patient complains of excruciating supraorbital pain. How do the neural signals mediating the latter pain reach the person's cerebral cortex?
    A. directly, without synapsing before reaching the postcentral gyrus
    B. via a synapsing relay in the thalamus
    C. via a synapsing relay in the supraoptic nucleus of the hypothalamus
    D. through the retrolenticular portion of the internal capsule
    E. via the loop of Meyer

33. Which of the following is neither an attribute nor is associated with the action potentials of mammalian nerves?
    A. all-or-none principle
    B. rate is directly proportional to stimulus intensity
    C. depolarization
    D. recovery period
    E. voltage change on the cell membrane

34. Which of the following is true of the membrane of a resting nerve fiber?
    A. is more positively charged exteriorly than interiorly
    B. has more sodium ions on its exterior than on its interior
    C. has more potassium ions on its interior than on its exterior
    D. all of the above
    E. none of the above

35. Saltatory conduction is directly involved in the excitability of
    A. smooth muscle
    B. Purkinje fibers in the heart
    C. skeletal muscle
    D. unmyelinated nerves
    E. myelinated nerves

36. What neurotransmitter substance serves the motor endplate of somatic motor nerves?
    A. acetylcholine
    B. dopamine
    C. norepinephrine
    D. epinephrine
    E. GABA

37. The immediate precursor of norepinephrine is
    A. epinephrine
    B. dopamine
    C. L-DOPA
    D. GABA
    E. tyrosine

Histology

38. In the stomach, which cells produce HCl?
- **A.** parietal
- **B.** mucous neck
- **C.** enterochromaffin
- **D.** zymogen chief
- **E.** surface cells

39. The epithelial lining of the small intestine is derived from the
- **A.** ectoderm
- **B.** endoderm
- **C.** mesoderm
- **D.** splanchnopleure
- **E.** somatopleure

40. When granules are used as the basis of classification, which one of the following cells is grouped with the lymphocyte?
- **A.** neutrophil
- **B.** eosinophil
- **C.** erythrocyte
- **D.** basophil
- **E.** monocyte

41. In a myofibril of skeletal muscle, the interval between successive Z lines is called the
- **A.** myosin or thick filament
- **B.** actin or thin filament
- **C.** sarcolemma
- **D.** sarcomere
- **E.** sarcoplasmic reticulum

42. The juxtaglomerular (JG) apparatus is found where in the kidney?
- **A.** thin loop of Henle
- **B.** afferent glomerular arteriole
- **C.** efferent glomerular arteriole
- **D.** proximal convoluted tubule
- **E.** distal convoluted tubule

43. Which of the following can produce progesterone?
A. pituitary gland
B. corpus luteum of the ovary
C. corpus albicans of the ovary
D. uterine endometrium
E. aerola of the mammary gland

44. Immediately after mitotic metaphase in humans, each sister cell normally contains a total of how many chromosomes?
A. 22
B. 23
C. 44
D. 46
E. 48

45. In humans, what is the site of most enzymatic breakdown of food-stuffs?
A. mouth
B. esophagus
C. stomach
D. duodenum
E. jejunum and ileum

46. In life, Haversian canals of bone contain
A. blood vessels
B. osteoblasts
C. osteocytes
D. osteoclasts
E. chondroclasts

47. Adipose is classified as what kind of tissue?
A. epithelial
B. connective
C. muscular
D. nervous
E. none of the above

48. The PMN or neutrophil may also be thought of as
A. macrophage
B. microphage
C. thrombocyte

    D. coprophage
    E. bacteriophage

49. A cubic millimeter (mm^3) of normal human blood contains roughly how many erythrocytes?
    A. 4–6 hundred million
    B. 4–6 million
    C. 4–6 hundred thousand
    D. 4–6 thousand
    E. 4–6 hundred

50. In a differential white count of normal human blood, how many eosinophils would you expect to find?
    A. 3%
    B. 30%
    C. 12%
    D. 16%
    E. 0.03%

51. The normoblast is a common microscopic finding in
    A. normal circulating blood
    B. white bone marrow
    C. red bone marrow
    D. germinal centers of lymph nodules
    E. germinal centers of the thymus gland

52. ATPase activity occurs in which of the following fractions of the myofibril?
    A. actin
    B. troponin
    C. light meromyosin
    D. heavy meromyosin
    E. tropomyosin

53. In electron micrographs, Nissl substance turns out to be
    A. artifact
    B. rough endoplasmic reticulum
    C. smooth endoplasmic reticulum
    D. Golgi complex
    E. mitochondria

54. The endothelium of the medium-sized or muscular artery is found on
   A. intima
   B. media
   C. adventitia
   D. internal elastic membrane
   E. external elastic membrane

55. The eyelashes (cilia) are a direct product of
   A. blood
   B. dermal connective tissue
   C. epithelium
   D. mesenchyme
   E. sebum

56. The human brain develops from
   A. ectoderm
   B. endoderm
   C. mesoderm
   D. mesenchyme
   E. neural crest

57. Osteoclasts are most closely associated with
   A. endochondrial ossification
   B. intramembranous ossification
   C. chondrogenesis
   D. bone resorption
   E. hydroxyapatite formation

58. In terms of function, the monocyte is most closely related to which of these cells?
   A. small lymphocyte
   B. medium-sized lymphocyte
   C. plasma cell
   D. mast cell
   E. macrophage

59. Which cells make blood platelets?
   A. plasma cells
   B. basophilic erythroblasts
   C. megakaryocytes

D. primitive reticular cells
E. Kupffer cells

60. Transitional epithelium lines which of these organs?
    A. pulmonary alveoli
    B. pancreatic duct
    C. islet of Langerhans
    D. urinary bladder
    E. gallbladder

61. Collagen fibrils are synthesized
    A. outside the cell
    B. within the rough endoplasmic reticulum of fibroblasts
    C. within the rough endoplasmic reticulum of epithelial cells
    D. within the rough endoplasmic reticulum of histiocytes
    E. within the rough endoplasmic reticulum of adipocytes

62. Spermatozoa develop where?
    A. epididymis
    B. prostate gland
    C. seminiferous tubules
    D. among the interstitial cells of the testes
    E. ejaculatory ducts

63. The organ of Corti is found in the
    A. cortex of the adrenal gland
    B. medulla of the adrenal gland
    C. middle ear
    D. inner ear
    E. nasopharynx

General Biochemistry

64. Which of the following statements is false about enzymes?
    A. They always contain derivatives of amino acids.
    B. They always contain peptide linkages.
    C. They always contain nucleotides.
    D. They often end with the suffix "ase."
    E. They are critical to most chemical reactions in the cell.

65. Which of these items contains the greatest number of phospho-lipid molecules?
   A. chromosomes
   B. sarcomere
   C. cell membrane
   D. polyribosomes
   E. nucleolus

66. If one strand of DNA contains the sequence A-A-A-C, its com-plement will ordinarily be
   A. T-T-T-G
   B. A-A-A-C
   C. U-U-U-C
   D. U-U-U-U
   E. T-T-T-U

67. The Embden-Meyerhof glycolytic pathway uses which of the fol-lowing as starting material?
   A. DNA
   B. ATP
   C. glucose
   D. alpha-keto glutaric acid
   E. pyruvic acid

68. Ribosomes are most directly involved in
   A. replication
   B. mitosis
   C. RNAase activity
   D. peptide synthesis
   E. hibernation

69. Chemically speaking, the opsins are most closely related to
   A. DNA
   B. myosin
   C. phospholipids
   D. ATP
   E. triglycerides

70. 11-*cis* retinal is most closely related to
   A. DNA
   B. beta-carotene

C. keratosulfate
D. glucuronic acid
E. alpha-keto glutaric acid

71. Present in the normal human lens, reduced glutathione is a
    A. dipeptide
    B. tripeptide
    C. polypeptide
    D. nucleotide
    E. nucleoside

72. Animal proteins are usually composed of how many different kinds of amino acids?
    A. 2
    B. 20
    C. 200
    D. 2000
    E. countless numbers

73. Which one of these amino acids contains an aromatic R group?
    A. glutamic acid
    B. lysine
    C. leucine
    D. phenylalanine
    E. glycine

74. Glucose is what kind of a sugar?
    A. triose
    B. pentose
    C. hexose
    D. septose
    E. none of the above

75. Which of these is the strongest type of bond?
    A. single covalent
    B. double covalent
    C. triple covalent
    D. hydrogen
    E. disulfide

76. ATP is what kind of a molecule?
   A. nucleotide
   B. peptide
   C. unsaturated fatty acid
   D. conjugated protein
   E. steroid

77. Where would you look to find histones?
   A. plasma membrane
   B. ergastoplasm
   C. mitochondria
   D. lysosomes
   E. chromatin

78. Which molecules bear the anticodons?
   A. DNA
   B. m-RNA
   C. t-RNA
   D. r-RNA
   E. enzymes

79. Introns are
   A. mitochondrial DNA
   B. code-containing sequences of mammalian DNA
   C. noncoding sequences of mammalian DNA
   D. proteins associated with mammalian DNA
   E. genetically engineered DNA

80. Which of the following occurs when animal cells are confronted with anaerobic conditions?
   A. They perish immediately.
   B. They accumulate lactic acid.
   C. They immediately cease all glucose metabolism.
   D. They produce ethanol.
   E. They accumulate pyruvic acid.

81. Krebs citric acid (or TCA) cycle occurs in what part of the cell?
   A. cytosol
   B. smooth endoplasmic reticulum
   C. Golgi complex

D. nucleus
E. mitochondria

82. The electron transport or respiratory chain occurs where in the cell?
    A. cytosol
    B. smooth endoplasmic reticulum
    C. Golgi complex
    D. nucleus
    E. mitochondria

83. Typically, DNA is produced from preexisting RNA in
    A. mammalian gametes
    B. retroviruses
    C. *E. coli*
    D. mammalian somatic cells
    E. mammalian rods and cones

84. The enzymes that copy DNA to make new DNA are classified into the category of
    A. DNAase
    B. DNA polymerase
    C. RNAase
    D. RNA polymerase
    E. reverse transcriptase

85. In humans and other higher organisms, DNA synthesis occurs only during which of these phases?
    A. S phase of the cell cycle
    B. G-1 phase of the cell cycle
    C. G-2 phase of the cell cycle
    D. prophase of mitosis
    E. metaphase of mitosis

86. What principally happens in the first step (reaction) in glycolysis via the Embden-Meyerhof pathway?
    A. Pyruvate is formed.
    B. A phosphate is removed from glucose.
    C. A phosphate is added to fructose.
    D. Glucose is split into two 3-carbon sugars.
    E. A phosphate is added to glucose.

87. Which of the following products of Krebs citrate, or TCA, cycle is not a tricarboxylic acid (i.e., not a TCA)?
   A. citrate
   B. *cis*-aconitate
   C. isocitrate
   D. succinate
   E. oxalosuccinate

88. The sugars for the nucleic acids can be produced metabolically by the
   A. urea cycle
   B. fatty acid cycle
   C. pentose pathway
   D. Krebs citrate or TCA cycle
   E. Embden-Meyerhof pathway

89. Chondroitin sulfate and keratan sulfate (keratosulfate), important mucopolysaccharides (glycosaminoglycans) of the corneal stroma, consist of monomeric units known as
   A. nucleic acids
   B. monosaccharides
   C. disaccharides
   D. polysaccharides
   E. polypeptides

90. Genes relate most directly to which of the following aspects of protein structure?
   A. primary
   B. secondary
   C. tertiary
   D. quaternary
   E. the entire structure

General Physiology

91. Which of the following terms refers to the liberation of potential energy?
   A. replication
   B. transcription

C. translation
D. catabolism
E. anabolism

92. A typical mammalian cell is isotonic to an NaCl solution of what percent concentration?
   A. 1.0
   B. 9.0
   C. 0.9
   D. 0.009
   E. 7.5

93. Dalton's Law of Partial Pressure, which applies to gaseous mixtures such as the air we breathe, predicts which of the following?
   A. Each gas in a mixture exerts its pressure in proportion to its percentage and independent of the other gases.
   B. Each gas in a mixture exerts a pressure whose magnitude depends on the specific nature of the other gases.
   C. A specific gas exerts increased pressure when it becomes part of a gaseous mixture.
   D. A specific gas exerts decreased pressure when it becomes part of a gaseous mixture.
   E. Each gas in a mixture exerts a pressure whose magnitude depends on the specific number of the other gases.

94. In angstrom units (A), what is the approximate thickness of the plasma membrane in a typical human cell?
   A. 0.7–1.0
   B. 7–10
   C. 70–100
   D. 700–1,000
   E. 7,000–10,000

95. How do the phospholipid molecules in the membrane of a living cell adhere with each other?
   A. covalent bonding
   B. ionic bonding
   C. hydrogen bonding
   D. hydrophobic interactions
   E. disulfide bridge formation

96. Water constitutes approximately what percentage of the normal, living human body?
   A. 99.99
   B. 90
   C. 60
   D. 20
   E. 0.99

97. Phagocytosis is to particles as which of the following is to liquids?
   A. pinocytosis
   B. diapedesis
   C. osmosis
   D. diffusion
   E. dialysis

98. These organelles are often said to be the respiratory centers of the mammalian cell.
   A. lysosomes
   B. microtubles
   C. Golgi bodies
   D. polyribosomes
   E. mitochondria

99. The fuel for the contraction of smooth muscle comes directly from the splitting of
   A. glucose
   B. creatine phosphate
   C. adenosine triphosphate
   D. adenosine diphosphate
   E. adenosine monophosphate

100. In terms of meters per second (m/sec), the fastest A fibers in human nerves show a conduction velocity of approximately
   A. 1
   B. 2
   C. 60
   D. 120
   E. 1,200

101. A single impulse on a motor nerve typically initiates a single muscle twitch. Poisoning which of the following will result in a series of tetanic contractions from a single impulse?
  A. acetylcholine
  B. acetylcholine esterase
  C. dopamine hydroxylase
  D. L-DOPA decarboxylase
  E. DNA polymerase

102. Synaptic vesicles, thought to house neurotransmitters or their immediate precursors, are found in the
  A. terminal of the preganglionic fiber
  B. membrane of the preganglionic fiber
  C. membrane of the postganglionic fiber
  D. synaptic cleft
  E. subsynaptic web

103. Which of the following statements is (are) generally true of hyperpolarization of the postganglionic membrane in a mammalian synapse?
  A. It tends to inhibit excitation.
  B. It is usually a graded response.
  C. It spreads with decrement from the site of initiation.
  D. It may be summed, both temporally and spatially.
  E. All of the above are true.

104. Serotonin, or 5-hydroxytryptamine (5-HT), synthesis begins with which amino?
  A. tryptophan
  B. tyrosine
  C. lysine
  D. glutamic acid
  E. any of the above

105. If a load is in excess of the lifting capacity of a contracting muscle, the muscle usually
  A. isotonically contracts
  B. isometrically contracts
  C. immediately cramps
  D. all of the above
  E. none of the above

106. The most significant difference between skeletal and smooth muscle exists in which of these respects?
A. myosin and actin
B. myofibrils
C. contractility
D. innervation
E. the use of ATP as a fuel

107. The osmotic pressure of human blood averages about what in terms of millimeters of mercury (mm Hg)?
A. 5700
B. 120
C. 80
D. 100 plus the person's age
E. 120/80

108. Clinically, the systolic pressure (in mm Hg) of a healthy young adult human at rest is approximately
A. 5700
B. 120
C. 80
D. 90
E. 120/80

109. A significant decrease in the specific gravity of human blood (normal range 1.052 to 1.061) most likely indicates
A. eosinophilia
B. anemia
C. leukopenia
D. hemophilia
E. leukemia

110. An increase in CO_2 in a tissue has what effect?
A. none
B. causes instant death
C. neutralizes the pH
D. elevates the pH
E. lowers the pH

111. The normal range of pH for circulating human blood is
  A. 6–8
  B. 8–9
  C. 7.3–7.5
  D. 6.5–7.0
  E. 12.6–13.2

112. The iron in hemoglobin makes possible a readily reversible combination of the protein molecule with
  A. oxygen
  B. carbon dioxide
  C. the rbc's membrane
  D. carbonic anhydrase
  E. none of the above

113. Fibrinogen is carried by
  A. platelets
  B. rbc's
  C. plasma
  D. neutrophils
  E. eosinophils

114. What is pulse pressure?
  A. the systolic pressure
  B. the diastolic pressure
  C. the difference between systolic and diastolic pressures
  D. ventricular systole
  E. ventricular diastole

115. The electrocardiogram (EKG) normally exhibits waves designated by convention as P, QRS complex, and T. Which of the following statements is true about the normal EKG?
  A. P precedes atrial contraction.
  B. R occurs just before ventricular contraction.
  C. T may be considered as the end of ventricular systole.
  D. The distance between P and R indicates the atrioventricular interval.
  E. All of the above are true.

116. The vagovagal reflex does what to the heart?
    A. slows it down
    B. speeds it up
    C. creates the rhythm of contraction
    D. terminates systole
    E. terminates diastole

117. Aldosterone is a hormone produced by the
    A. adenohypophysis
    B. neurohypophysis
    C. thyroid glands
    D. adrenal medulla
    E. adrenal cortex

General Microbiology

118. The eukaryotic cell is more complex than the prokaryotic cell at every level except the
    A. nucleus
    B. cell envelope
    C. plastids
    D. endoplasmic reticulum

119. Fibrils which extend outward from the bacterial cell and play a major role in adhering to surfaces in their environment are:
    A. monotrichous flagella
    B. pseudopods
    C. glycocalyx
    D. leptotrichous flagella

120. In a Gram stain, the gram-positive organism appears blue because the cell retains the
    A. crystal violet–iodine complex
    B. safranin dye
    C. carbolfuchsin dye
    D. methylene blue–chloride

121. An anaerobic organism introduced into wounds, and in the presence of necrotic tissue produces toxins which result in gangrene, is
   A. *Clostridium perfringens*
   B. *Escherichia coli*
   C. *Clostridium tetani*
   D. *Shigella sonnei*

122. The organism associated with toxic shock syndrome is
   A. *Streptococcus pneumoniae*
   B. *Staphylococcus aureus*
   C. *Salmonella* sp.
   D. *Neisseria* sp.

123. A gram-positive spore forming aerobic bacilli is
   A. *Streptococcus pyogenes*
   B. *Neisseria meningitides*
   C. *Morganella morganii*
   D. *Bacillus cereus*

124. Pseudomembranous colitis has been associated with the administration of antibiotics; however, the condition may be due to
   A. Metronidazole
   B. *Bacillus cereus*
   C. *Clostridium difficile*
   D. *Clostridium septicum*

125. A nonspore forming gram-positive bacilli that can produce a powerful exotoxin and which involves the respiratory tract, "club-shaped" in appearance, is
   A. *Corynebacterium diphtheria*
   B. *Staphylococcus epidermidis*
   C. *Listeria monocytogenes*
   D. *Enterobacter aerogenes*

126. Erysipelas in humans is caused by
   A. *Erysipelothrix rhusiopathiae*
   B. *Listeria monocytogenes*
   C. *Corynebacterium pyogenes*
   D. Group A beta-hemolytic streptococcus

127. A gram-positive spherical cell, usually appearing in grape-like clusters, coagulase-positive and responsible for abscess formation, a variety of pyogenic infections, and heat-stable enterotoxin, is
    A. *Streptococcus pyogenes*
    B. *Staphylococcus aureus*
    C. *Klebsiella pneumoniae*
    D. *Staphylococcus saprophyticus*

128. The formation of bubbles when a drop of hydrogen peroxide (H_2O_2) is placed on a slide with a small amount of bacterial growth indicates a positive test. That test is called the
    A. coagulase test
    B. synergy test
    C. serological test
    D. catalase test

129. A group A beta-hemolytic streptococcus is
    A. *Strep faecalis*
    B. *Strep pneumonia*
    C. *Strep pyogenes*
    D. *Strep agalactiae*

130. The most frequent cause of bacterial subacute endocarditis is
    A. *Strep pneumoniae*
    B. *Staph aureus*
    C. *Strep viridans*
    D. *Staph epidermidis*

131. Rheumatic fever is the most serious sequela to streptococcus infection, the onset of which is preceded by streptococcus of a specific group, which is
    A. group B
    B. group A
    C. group D
    D. group C

132. These are gram-positive diplococci. They are inhibited on solid media by optochin and are betahemolytic. The microorganisms are
    A. *Strep pneumoniae (Pneumococci)*
    B. *Strep viridans*

C. *Strep faecalis*
D. *Staph epidermidis*

133. The most common cause of urinary tract infection by a gram-negative rod that gives a positive spot indole test is
    A. *Enterobacter aerogenes*
    B. *Salmonella enteriditis*
    C. *Shigella dysenteriae*
    D. *Escherichia coli*

134. All of the following are true of *Pseudomonas aeruginosa* except
    A. oxidase positive
    B. ferments carbohydrates
    C. grows at 42°C
    D. sweet or grape-like odor

135. A gram-negative, motile, aerobic rod, some producing pyocyanin and pyoverdin, is
    A. *Pseudomonas mallei*
    B. *Pseudomonas cepacia*
    C. *Chromobacterium violaceum*
    D. *Pseudomonas aeruginosa*

136. This gram-negative bacilli or coccobacilli is nonmotile, nonfermentative, and oxidative-positive. It is a member of the normal flora of the upper respiratory tract and occasionally causes bacteremia, conjunctivitis, and keratitis. Most of the cases occur in the alcoholic population. The organism is
    A. *Moraxella lacunata*
    B. *Alcaligenes faecalis*
    C. *Moraxella liquefaciens*
    D. *Klebsiella pneumonia*

137. A gram-negative, pleomorphic bacteria that requires X and V factors, lacks hemolysis, and is found on the mucous membranes of the upper respiratory tract in humans, is
    A. *Hemophilus ducreyi*
    B. *Campylobacter coli*
    C. *Hemophilus influenzae*
    D. *Serratia marcescens*

138. The Koch-Weeks bacillus, a gram-negative, pleomorphic bacteria that has been associated with a highly communicable form of conjunctivitis, is known as
   A. Hemophilus aegytius
   B. Moraxella liquefaciens
   C. Hemophilus ducreyi
   D. Morganella morganii

139. This organism is a gram-negative, nonmotile diplococcus. The individual cocci appears kidney shaped. This organism attacks mucous membranes, producing acute suppuration. It is
   A. Brahamella catarrhalis
   B. Neisseria gonorrhoea
   C. Hemophilus ducreyi
   D. Neisseria meningitidis

140. This spiral, motile organism does not stain well with aniline dyes not successfully cultured on artificial media. It can be observed with the use of immunofluorescent stain or dark-field illumination. The organism is
   A. Treponema pallidum
   B. Leptospira–interrogans
   C. Borrelia recurrentis
   D. Borrelia burgdorferi

141. This organism is an obligate intracellular parasite, closely related to gram-negative bacteria, but lacks the mechanism for the production of metabolic energy and cannot synthesize ATP. The organism is
   A. Rickettsia rickettsii
   B. Lymphogranuloma venereum
   C. Mycobacterium leprae
   D. Chlamydiae trachomatis

142. This organism is cultured on Sabouraud's agar at room temperature. It may produce progressive systemic disease in debilitated or immunosuppressed patients. It ferments glucose and maltose and produces a pseudomycelium. The organism is
   A. Herpes simplex
   B. Francisella tularensis

C. *Candida albicans*
D. *Neisseria lactamica*

143. The smallest of the DNA-containing viruses is
    A. papovavirus
    B. parvovirus
    C. poxvirus
    D. adenovirus

144. This organism is an acid-fast bacilli. It possesses a thick, lipid-rich, and waxy cell wall. When grown in a liquid medium it forms a mold-like pellicle. In humans, it produces a chronic granulomatous infection of the lungs. The organism is
    A. *Mycobacterium tuberculosis*
    B. *Legionella pneumophilia*
    C. *Mycobacterium leprae*
    D. *Klebsiellae pneumoniae*

General Pharmacology

145. The concentration of a drug at the site of the target receptor depends on all of these factors except
    A. absorption
    B. protein binding
    C. metabolism
    D. distribution
    E. excretion

146. Which of the following drugs will decrease drug absorption by accelerating gastric emptying time?
    A. reserpine
    B. physostigmine
    C. metoclopramide
    D. diphenhydramine

147. The unionized form of a drug can rapidly pass through lipid membranes because it is
    A. water soluble
    B. bound to a carrier
    C. lipid soluble
    D. positively charged

148. Most lipid-soluble drugs are metabolized by enzymes whose major function is to convert the drug to
    A. a more polar form
    B. a more lipid form
    C. a precursor
    D. an insoluble form

149. A common characteristic of agonists and antagonists for a receptor is
    A. intrinsic activity
    B. efficacy
    C. affinity
    D. excitatory

150. One way to express the margin of safety of a drug is the Therapeutic Index, which is expressed as
    A. ED50/LD50
    B. LD1/ED99
    C. LD50/ED50
    D. ED1/LD99

151. The preferred route of administration for drugs which are rapidly metabolized by the liver is
    A. oral
    B. sublingual
    C. intraperitoneal
    D. rectal

152. All of the following are desirable properties for prolonged-release medication except
    A. insoluble form of the drug
    B. suspending in a viscous medium
    C. formulating with large particle size
    D. formulating with small particle size

153. All of the following are advantages of a pro-drug except
  A. prolong the release of the drug
  B. improve bioavailability
  C. mask unpleasant characteristics of a drug
  D. alter the solubility of a drug

154. The main disadvantage to the administration of a drug by the oral route is
  A. surface area for absorption is greater
  B. variable absorption pattern
  C. optimal absorption of weak acids
  D. the most economical

155. The process of biotransformation of a drug is referred to as
  A. changes in the chemical structure of the compound
  B. accumulation of the drug in muscles
  C. binding of the drug to plasma proteins
  D. binding of the drug to the receptor

156. Half-life (T − 1/2) of a drug refers to the
  A. time it takes for the drug to produce 50 percent of its effect
  B. time for 50 percent of the drug to be absorbed
  C. time it takes for 50 percent of the drug to be metabolized
  D. time it takes for the plasma concentration to be decreased by 50 percent

157. Emesis is contraindicated after the oral ingestion of poisons in all cases except where the patient
  A. has ingested a strong acid or alkali
  B. has ingested a pesticide
  C. has ingested a CNS stimulant
  D. has ingested a petroleum distillate

158. An example of pharmacokinetic drug interaction whereby a drug may increase the metabolism of other agents, thereby decreasing the therapeutic effect, is
  A. probenecid
  B. barbiturates
  C. cimetidine
  D. phenylbutazone

159. The autonomic nervous system innervates all the structures of the body except the
   A. skeletal muscle
   B. smooth muscle
   C. blood vessels
   D. glands

160. The parasympathetic nervous system is anatomically referred to as the
   A. craniosacral outflow
   B. lumbar-sacral outflow
   C. thoracolumbar outflow
   D. paravertebral chain

161. The neurotransmitter of the preganglionic autonomic fibers is
   A. acetylcholine
   B. norepinephrine
   C. epinephrine
   D. dopamine

162. The neurotransmitter at most of the postganglionic autonomic fibers of the sympathetic nervous system is
   A. acetylcholine
   B. norepinephrine
   C. epinephrine
   D. dopamine

163. The enzyme responsible for terminating the effect of the neurotransmitter at the postganglionic autonomic fibers of the parasympathetic nervous system is
   A. monoamine oxidase
   B. tyrosine hydroxylase
   C. cyclic AMP
   D. acetylcholinesterase

164. A direct-acting parasympathomimetic agent is
   A. propantheline
   B. mecamylamine
   C. albuterol
   D. bethanecol chloride

165. A short-acting reversible, indirect-acting parasympathomimetic agent is
  A. demecarium
  B. methoxamine
  C. pyridostigmine
  D. diisopropyl fluorophosphate

166. A direct-acting sympathomimetic agent that possesses primarily alpha activity at therapeutic concentration is
  A. terbutaline
  B. methoxamine
  C. phentolamine
  D. isoetharine

167. A potent nonselective beta adrenoceptor agonist is
  A. isoproterenol
  B. metaproterenol
  C. pirbuterol
  D. mephentermine

168. A selective alpha-2 agonist used in the treatment of hypertension is
  A. guanfacine
  B. methoxamine
  C. dobutamine
  D. terbutaline

169. An alpha-1 adrenergic blocking agent is
  A. terazosin
  B. terbutaline
  C. clonidine
  D. phentermine

170. A synthetic parasympatholytic agent is
  A. pralidoxime
  B. phentolamine
  C. propantheline
  D. phenmetrazine

171. Many anti-histaminic agents that block H-1 receptor also exhibit a significant anti-cholinergic effect. Which of the following is LEAST likely to produce this effect?
  A. diphenhydramine
  B. pyrilamine
  C. hydroxyzine
  D. promethazine

172. This beta-lactam compound is bactericidal but not active against gram-positive bacteria; anaerobic organism is resistant. It has excellent activity against *Pseudomonas aeruginosa*. It is
  A. penicillin G
  B. methicillin
  C. cefamandole
  D. aztreonam

173. A broad-spectrum antibiotic, bactericidal agent active against *Pseudomonas aeruginosa, Staphylococcus aureus, Enterobacteriaceae*, streptococcus, and anaerobic species, whose mechanism of action is the inhibition of DNA gyrase, is
  A. gentamicin
  B. ofloxacin
  C. rifamycin
  D. vancomycin

174. Which of the following agents is antipyretic and analgesic but only possesses weak antiinflammatory activity?
  A. acetaminophen
  B. indomethacin
  C. phenylbutazone
  D. ibuprofen

175. A sedative hypnotic that possesses a selective anticonvulsant effect and is especially useful in grand mal epilepsy is
  A. pentobarbital
  B. secobarbital
  C. phenobarbital
  D. meprobamate

176. An atypical antidepressant agent is
   A. trazodone
   B. amphetamine
   C. Tranylcypromine
   D. imipramine

177. A class I-A antiarrhythmic agent with significant anticholinergic effect and alpha adrenergic blocking effect is
   A. lidocaine
   B. flecainide
   C. quinidine
   D. amiodarone

178. The chronic use of some diuretics used in hypertensive management produces potassium loss, resulting in hypokalemia. Which of the following is a potassium sparing diuretic?
   A. chlorothiazide
   B. chlorthalidone
   C. spironolactone
   D. hydrochlorothiazide

179. An antiviral agent used in life- and sight-threatening infections due to cytomegalovirus and in cytomegalovirus retinitis, but is very toxic, is
   A. acyclovir
   B. ganciclovir
   C. ribavirin
   D. zidovudine

General Pathology

180. All of the following systemic conditions may produce generalized fluid retention except
   A. congestive heart failure
   B. systemic hypertension
   C. nephrotic syndrome
   D. cirrhosis

181. All of the following are properties of acute inflammation except
  A. blood flow is accelerated in the early stages
  B. blood flow is decreased in the early stages
  C. leucocyte migration
  D. exudation of fluid and plasma proteins

182. All of the following are local clinical signs of acute inflammation except
  A. heat
  B. swelling
  C. normal function
  D. redness

183. The term stasis in acute inflammation is due to all of the following except
  A. increased permeability of the microvasculature
  B. outpouring of protein-rich fluid into extravascular tissues
  C. transient vasoconstriction
  D. increased blood viscosity

184. The most important feature of the inflammatory reaction at the cellular level is the
  A. increase in protein-rich exudation
  B. accumulation of leukocytes
  C. release of histamine
  D. increase in mitosis

185. All of the following are chemical mediators of inflammation except
  A. histamines
  B. serotonin
  C. epinephrine
  D. platelet-activating factors

186. All of the following systemic factors will influence wound healing except
  A. nutrition
  B. hematologic deficiencies
  C. active metabolites of arachidonic acid
  D. glucocorticoids

187. All of the following local factors influence wound healing except
   A. increased blood circulation
   B. previous tissue injury
   C. foreign bodies
   D. infection

188. Cellulitis, caused by hemolytic streptococci, is largely due to the production of
   A. beta-lactamase
   B. exotoxin
   C. hyaluronidase
   D. protease

189. The formation of multinucleated giant cells in macrophage clusters are called
   A. neoplastic giant cells
   B. giant cell arteritis
   C. Hodgkin's giant cells
   D. Langhan's giant cells

190. The lymphocyte that is responsible for antibody production and delayed hypersensitivity is
   A. T-cells
   B. A-cells
   C. B-cells
   D. S-cells

191. Carcinoma is a malignant tumor of
   A. mesenchymal origin
   B. peritoneal origin
   C. epithelial origin
   D. melanocytes

192. Cardiac hypertrophy at necropsy is best evaluated by
   A. ventricular wall thickness
   B. measurement of heart size from chest x-ray
   C. heart weight relative to body size
   D. thickness of atrium

193. Toxic myocarditis may result from exposure to all of the following chemical agents except
 A. Adriamycin
 B. 5-Fluorouracil
 C. amphetamines
 D. bleomycin

194. In chronic renal failure, serum levels of all of the following are increased except
 A. phosphates
 B. sulfates
 C. calcium
 D. aldosterone

195. This clinical syndrome may occur in the third trimester of pregnancy; with proteinuria, edema, and hypertension may develop
 A. preeclampsia
 B. systemic amyloidosis
 C. diabetic nephropathy
 D. allergic nephritis

196. A common form of hamartoma found in the kidney is
 A. tubular adenomas
 B. medullary fibromas
 C. leiomyomas
 D. angiomyolipomas

197. The microorganism that causes a pneumonia with a fairly low attack rate and significant mortality, is spread by aerosols of contaminated water from air conditioning cooling towers, and does not stain with the Gram stain is
 A. *Mycoplasma pneumoniae*
 B. *Legionella pneumophila*
 C. *Streptococcus pneumoniae*
 D. *Hemophilus influenzae*

198. A lymphocytic thyroiditis that is characterized by thyroid enlargement, lymphocytic infiltration of the gland, and the presence of thyroid auto-antibodies is
 A. Hashimoto's thyroiditis
 B. infectious thyroiditis

C. Riedel's thyroiditis
D. focal lymphocytic thyroiditis

199. An endocrine disorder that produces hypertension, potassium depletion, metabolic alkalosis, and suppresses plasma renin activity is
A. hyperaldosteronism
B. hypothyroidism
C. hyperadrenocorticism
D. hyperparathyroidism

200. Pheochromocytomas may be associated with all of the following except
A. medullary carcinoma
B. parathyroid hyperplasia
C. mucosal neuroma
D. pituitary adenoma

Answers and Discussion

Gross Anatomy

1. **(D)** The human vertebral column (spinal column) consists of 7 cervical, 12 thoracic, 5 lumbar, 5 sacral, and 3 to 5 coccygeal vertebrae. All mammals, excluding sloths but including giraffes, have 7 cervical vertebrae. The first cervical vertebra is called the atlas because the head rests directly on it. The second cervical vertebra, most often called the axis, is sometimes referred to as the epistropheus. A cervical vertebra can be distinguished from thoracic or lumbar vertebrae by a foramen in the transverse process (f. transversarium or vertebral f.) which transmits the vertebral artery, the principal artery of the posterior portion of the brain.

2. **(C)** Kinesiology is the study of locomotion and the structures involved; splanchnology of the viscera; myology of muscle, per se; neurology denotes both the study of the nervous system and the clinical practice involving diseases of the nervous system. The prefix *arthro-* (and arth-) means joints. Thus, *arthr*itis is joint inflammation; *arthro*scopy is endoscopic examination of the interior of a joint, usually with an *arthro*scope.

3. **(A)** The azygous and hemiazygous veins straddle the vertebral column, on the right and left sides of the posterior mediastinum, respectively. The azygous vein, a direct tributary of the superior vena cava, originates in the abdominal cavity opposite the first and second lumbar vertebrae, enters the thorax via the aortic hiatus, and directly or indirectly drains much of the posterior aspect of the mediastinum. The main tributaries of the azygous vein are

the right intercostal veins, right bronchial veins, the hemiazygous vein, and the accessory azygous vein. The latter two drain much of the left posterior mediastinum.

4. **(A)** The rim of the orbit is made up of portions of the frontal (superior), zygomatic (lateral-inferior), and maxillary (medial-inferior) bones. The lacrimal bone, with the fossa for the lacrimal sac, lies in the orbit's inferior-medial corner. The great(er) and lesser wings of the sphenoid lie inside the orbit.

5. **(C)** The ophthalmic veins (superior and inferior) and V-1 (ophthalmic nerve or ophthalmic division of the trigeminal nerve) reach the orbit via the superior orbital fissure. The superior orbital fissure also transmits the oculomotor (III), trochlear (IV), and abducens (VI) nerves. The latter three cranial nerves innervate the extraocular muscles.

6. **(B)** The preganglionic parasympathetic fibers for the lacrimal gland originate in the salivatory nucleus (superior salivatory according to some authors), exit the brain stem with the facial nerve (VII), pass through the geniculate ganglion without synapsing, and there part company with VII to become a part of the greater superficial petrosal nerve. The greater superficial petrosal nerve joins the deep petrosal nerve (the latter carrying postganglionic sympathetic fibers from the carotid plexus) to form the nerve of the pterygoid canal (Vidian) nerve. Named as such because it courses through the pterygoid canal, the nerve in question enters the pterygopalatine (sphenopalatine) fossa where its preganglionic parasympathetic components finally synapse. The sympathetic components of the Vidian nerve pass through the pterygopalatine ganglion without synapsing. Leaving the pterygopalatine ganglion, the sympathetic and parasympathetic fibers destined for the lacrimal gland first enter the main trunk of the maxillary nerve (V-2). Passing through the zygomatic and zygomaticofacial nerves, the autonomic nerve fibers under consideration transfer via a communicating branch to the lacrimal nerve, a branch of V-1, before terminating in the lacrimal gland.

7. **(C)** Also spelled *annulus*, the a. tendineus communis is a fibrous ring at the optic foramen representing the common origin of the four recti and the superior oblique muscles. The inferior

oblique, the correct answer here, arises from the orbital surface of the maxilla, just lateral to the lacrimal groove. The inferior oblique lies in the medial-inferior aspect of the front of the orbit. The levator palpebrae superioris, which inserts into the upper lid, arises just above the anulus on the under surface of the lesser wing of the sphenoid bone.

8. **(E)** The central retinal artery is the first and smallest branch of the ophthalmic artery; it occasionally arises from the lacrimal artery. The ophthalmic artery branches from the internal carotid inside the skull. The ophthalmic artery's dozen branches can be divided into two groups: orbital and ocular; the latter supply mainly the eye and the former, the eye's adnexa. The central retinal artery, of course, belongs to the ocular group.

9. **(E)** The thoracic duct is the common trunk of all lymphatics in the body. With its origin in the upper abdomen as the cisterna chyli, the thoracic duct passes through the diaphragm behind the aorta, courses through the posterior mediastinum into the root of the neck, and ends in the left subclavian vein. Lymph from the intestines often has a high fat content (i.e., is chylous). The lymphatic capillaries from the intestines are called lacteals because the chylous lymph within them takes on a lactescent, or milky, appearance.

10. **(D)** In each nasal cavity, superior, middle, and inferior conchae (or turbinates) subdivide the space into superior, middle, and inferior meatuses. (Meatus is the singular.) The superior and middle conchae are parts of the ethmoid bone. The inferior concha is a bone of itself.

11. **(C)** The plane of L2 is roughly two-fingers' breadth above the umbilicus or navel. At the level in question, the spinal cord proper ends in a so-called conus medullaris, while a non-neural filum terminale extends from the conus to the first segment of the coccyx. The plane of L2 has clinical significance, for below this level a needle can be injected into the vertebral canal to tap cerebrospinal fluid or inject local anesthetic with reduced risk of debilitating injury.

12. **(A)** The epiploic foramen is also called the mouth of the lesser sac (or omental bursa) of the peritoneal cavity. The greater sac is what one encounters upon opening the peritoneal cavity. Usually hidden by the overhanging liver, the epiploic foramen can be found by first finding the free border of the lesser omentum on the lesser curvature of the stomach.

13. **(D)** The vermiform appendix opens into the cecum, a cul-de-sac off the beginning of the ascending colon, at the ileo-cecal junction. The appendix can be long or short and, within limits set by its length, can occupy virtually any location in the abdomen. But in a well-known study of some 10,000 cases, about 64 percent had the appendix tucked behind the cecum; in some 32 percent it extends infero-medially; other locations accounted for the balance.

14. **(D)** The carotid sheath is part of the deep fascia of the neck. The sympathetic trunk is imbedded in the posterior wall of the carotid sheath but not actually within the sheath's lumen. The carotid sheath is continuous with the fibrous pericardium.

15. **(D)** The brachial plexus is formed from the ventral (anterior) divisions (rami) of cervical nerves 5–8 and thoracic nerve 1 (i.e., C5–T1). The cervical plexus is formed from C1–C4. L4–L5 and S1–S3 constitute the lumbosacral plexus.

16. **(D)** Blood being propelled from the right ventricle is on its way to the lungs and thus passes through the semilunar valve of the pulmonary artery. The aortic semilunar valve has a corresponding function on the left side of the heart where it guards the ascending aorta and regulates blood flow from the left ventricle. The tricuspid valve guards the right atrioventricular opening and when closed prevents the regurgitation of blood from the right ventricle back into the right atrium. The mitral or bicuspid valve does a similar thing, but at the left atrioventricular canal.

Neuroanatomy/Neurophysiology

17. **(B)** The medial geniculate body, or nucleus (MGB or MGN), connects to the primary auditory cortex via the auditory radia-

tions. It is part of the thalamus. Much of its direct input is supplied from the inferior colliculi in the midbrain. The principal pathway of the latter signals can be seen on the surface of the brainstem in the form of the brachium of the inferior colliculus.

18. **(C)** Warwick based his now widely accepted map on Wallerian degeneration within the oculomotor nuclei of monkeys after experimental destruction of the innervation of each extraocular muscle. Destruction of the levator palpebrae superioris produced degeneration on both sides of the caudal central nucleus of the oculomotor complex (nerve III). The dorsal lateral nucleus of the IIIrd nuclear complex appears to innervate the ipsilateral (same sided) inferior rectus. An intermediate lateral nucleus innervates the ipsilateral inferior oblique. A ventral lateral nucleus innervates the ipsilateral medial rectus. A dorsal median nucleus supplies the contralateral superior rectus muscle.

The lateral rectus is supplied by the ipsilateral abducens nerve (cranial nerve VI). The trochlear nerve (IV) innervates the superior oblique muscle of the contralateral eye.

19. **(E)** A question of this sort should be approached with the Yoke Table (with cranial nerve *nuclei* included):

LR	*(VI)*	MR	*(ventral lateral III)*
SR	*(dorsal medial III)*	IO	*(intermediate lateral III)*
SO	*(IV)*	IR	*(dorsal lateral III)*

20. **(B)** See answers **18** and **19**.

21. **(D)** Decussate means to cross to the other side. Trochlear fibers (IV) can be traced as they cross to the opposite side in the superior medullary vellum. Shortly after decussating, the trochlear fibers exit the brain stem. The latter location is just below the inferior colliculus.

22. **(B)** The interpeduncular (ip) fossa lies between the cerebral peduncles (basis pedunculi, pes pedunculi, crus cerebri). The anterior boundary of the ip fossa is formed by the mammillary bodies, representing the posterior, inferior portion of the hypothalamus. The posterior boundary of the ip fossa is formed by the superior border of the pons.

23. **(E)** The EEG, brain waves (or rhythms), detectable at scalp (but measurable on the cerebrum—deep EEG) are an indirect result and algebraic sum of the electrical activity within and among the cells of the central nervous system. Four sorts have been identified, mainly on the basis of different frequencies and wave forms: alpha, beta, theta, and delta brain waves.

Alpha waves have a frequency of 8 to 13 Hz (cycles per second) and an amplitude of around 50 μV; they are typically recorded during quiet wakefulness (e.g., from electrodes over the occipital lobe, the patient resting with eyes closed) but are quickly replaced by asynchronous discharges during alerting (e.g., suddenly opening the eyes with lights on).

Beta waves exhibit variable amplitudes and are often defined as brain waves with a frequency greater than 13 Hz. Their typical range is 14 to 25 Hz. Beta waves are most readily recorded over the frontal parietal regions of the scalp when the CNS is active or under conditions of psychological distress. Their presence during sleep (REM sleep) may signal dreaming.

Theta waves show frequencies of 4 to 7 Hz. They are recorded from the temporal and parietal regions of children but occur in adults during emotional stress or disappointment.

Delta waves are very slow (less than 3.5 Hz) and are of moderately high amplitude (>50 μV). They occur in infants, during very deep sleep (Stage 4), and in organic brain diseases.

The EEG changes dramatically during epileptic seizures. In the tonic phase (spastic) of a grand mal seizure, the EEG is characterized by relatively high voltages (100 to 200 μV) and frequencies of 50 Hz or more; in the clonic phase (convulsive), the amplitudes remain high but the frequency falls dramatically. In petit mal seizures, the waves take on a highly characteristic form (fast spike followed by a slow "hump") but are of low frequencies and relatively high amplitudes (>50 μV). The EEG of psychomotor epilepsy also has a characteristic wave form and is of low frequency and relatively high amplitude.

24. **(B)** Orientation of the hair cells in the crista ampularis determines whether maximum stimulation occurs with the endolymph directed toward or away from the ampulla. In the cristae of both the superior and posterior ducts, maximum stimulation obtains with acceleration *away* from crista. The opposite is true of the lateral (horizontal) canal, where the rule is *toward*.

25. (C) Humans have three pairs of semicircular canals. They all work together to register changes in position of the head in the three spatial dimensions. Strictly speaking, the canals are channels within the petrous portion of the temporal bone, the sense organ, the crista ampullaris, being at one end of a membranous duct within the canal, most precisely referred to as the semicircular duct. The semicircular canals do contain fluid—perilymph. But it is the endolymph within the semicircular duct that directly mediates the stimulation of the crista (see answer **24**).

26. (B) The zone for the vestibular nuclei is at the junction of the floor and wall of the 4th ventricle's rhomboid fossa. There are four vestibular nuclei: superior, inferior, medial, and lateral. They register and relay signals carried from the vestibular portions of the inner ear over the vestibular division of cranial nerve VIII (auditory, acoustic or cochleo-vestibular).

27. (D) The medial longitudinal fasciculus may be abbreviated MLF. Concurrent with signals through the MLF, some communication to extraocular nuclei (III, IV, and V) arrives over a route other than the MLF. The additional pathway(s) may be through the reticular formation. (Some authorities regard the reticular formation as a kind of on-off switch—facilitator and inhibitor—for much of the CNS.)

28. (B) They also fall into the generic category, visceral motor neurons. Fibers from the Edinger-Westphal nucleus exit the brain stem as part of cranial nerve III. Whether sympathetic or parasympathetic, preganglionic fibers synapse, and terminate, in peripherally situated ganglia. The smooth muscle or gland cells innervated by visceral motor nerves are thus supplied by postganglionic fibers.

29. (A) The postganglionic parasympathetic fibers to the intrinsic eye muscles reach the eyeball via the short ciliary nerves. After penetrating the back of the eyeball, the nerves work their way forward in the uveal tract. Note that sympathetic fibers in the ciliary ganglion (or any other parasympathetic ganglion) are postganglionic fibers merely in transit and do not synapse there.

30. (E) This is also known as the descending nucleus of the trigeminal. The inbound trigeminal fibers en route to the spinal nucleus of V collectively form what is called the tract of the spinal V. The latter tract terminates as its fibers synapse in the spinal nucleus of V, those from the ophthalmic nerve (V1) at a more superior level than those of the maxillary nerve (V2) and the mandibular nerve (V3). The spinal tract of V lies on the surface of the brain stem. V1 fibers do not extend below the obex; i.e., the level of closure of the fourth ventricle. Trigeminal tractotomy (to relieve severe facial pain) below the level of the obex does not obliterate sensations from the eye and therefore spares the blink reflex (necessary to spread tears).

31. (A) The facial colliculus contains the abducens nucleus, which innervates the ipsilateral lateral rectus, an important abductor of the eye. The facial colliculus also contains the internal genu of the facial nerve, from which its name derives. The latter fibers supply the muscles of facial expression, of which the orbicularis oculi (the eyelid closer) is a member.

32. (B) Olfaction (smell) being the one major exception, all sensory input to the cerebrum relays there via the thalamus. This includes vision and hearing. The LGB (LGN) and MGB (MGN), in the optic and auditory systems, respectively, while sometimes called the metathalamus, are nevertheless bona fide thalamic nuclei.

33. (B) This is characteristic of so-called graded responses to subthreshold stimuli. Graded responses can summate. Summation can result in the cell's discharging an action potential (i.e., an impulse, which does obey the all-or-none principle).

34. (D) These conditions are typically true of resting cells in general: slightly positive exterior, more Na^+ outside and K^+ inside. When irritated, the exterior in the vicinity of the irritation (stimulus) typically depolarizes; more Na^+ then appears on the interior and K^+ on the exterior of the membrane.

35. (E) Saltatory means *leaping,* which the impulses on typical mammalian myelinated nerve fibers seem to mimic as they move from one node of Ranvier to another, reminiscent of the ignition of a string of firecrackers. Saltatory conduction is very efficient in terms of energy requirements. Nerve fibers lacking in myelin sheaths, and therefore without nodes of Ranvier, cannot execute saltatory conduction.

36. **(A)** Acetylcholine is the neurotransmitter at the junction between somatic motor nerves and the skeletal muscles they innervate. After entering and stimulating the postsynaptic membrane, acetylcholine is split into acetate and choline. The enzyme that does the splitting is acetylcholine esterase. Thus, acetylcholine esterase activity helps ready the postsynaptic membrane for another chemical salvo.

37. **(B)** Norepinephrine (noradrenaline) is the principal adrenergic neurotransmitter of the central nervous system (CNS). Its synthetic sequence is as follows: (phenylalanine); tyrosine; L-DOPA; dopamine; norepinephrine. The amino acid, tyrosine, is taken as the starting point in the biogenesis of norepinephrine. Tyrosine may be obtained from the diet or be converted by the body from the essential amino acid, phenylalanine (thus, phenylalanine is represented in parentheses). Dopamine, the immediate precursor of norepinephrine, can act as a neurotransmitter in certain neurons. Cells of the adrenal medulla, and thus outside the CNS, have a methylase enzyme that can affix a methyl (CH_3) to norepinephrine and convert it to epinephrine (adrenaline).

Histology

38. **(A)** Hydrochloric acid is one of the most important products of the stomach, as far as digestion is concerned, and its contributions are many. The stomach can be divided, histologically, into three parts: cardiac (nearest the esophageal sphincter), gastric (or fundic), and pyloric, around the pyloric sphincter. The parietal cells that produce HCl are found in the gastric glands (of the gastric stomach).

39. **(B)** Endoderm lines the primitive gut and is thus the source of the lining of the entire gastro-intestinal tract from the pharynx to the rectum. Portions of the mouth (stomadeal) and anal canal (proctodeal) develop from ectoderm. The linings of the larynx, trachea, bronchi, and lungs are also derived from endoderm.

40. **(E)** By convention, the leukocytes (white blood cells) are grouped as granulocytes and agranulocytes. The granulocytes (typically produced in red marrow or myelogenous connective tissue) are neutrophils, eosinophils, and basophils. Mature forms of these cells have lobed, or polymorphic, nuclei. The agranulocytes, lymphocytes, and monocytes may have slightly bent, but not permanently lobed, nuclei. A few so-called azurophile granules (purple in blood stains) actually do occur in the cytoplasm of most agranulocytes.

41. **(D)** The sarcomere shortens in contraction. It elongates during relaxation. *Sarco-* means muscle; *mere* means piece. The so-called "muscle piece" is regarded by many authorities as the structural and functional unit of the myofibril.

42. **(B)** JG cells store renin. Renin is an enzyme that, in the plasma, causes the release of angiotensin I into the blood. In the lung alveolar air converts angiotensin I to angiotensin II, the active form, which is both a vasoconstrictor and a trigger for the release of aldosterone, the hormone from the adrenal cortex that promotes reabsorption of Na^+ by the kidney's distal convoluted tubule.

43. **(B)** Progesterone maintains the endometrium. Menstruation ensues upon the withdrawal of progesterone. During early pregnancy, chorionic gonadotropin delays the degeneration of the corpus luteum and this organ continues for a while to produce progesterone while the placenta fully develops. Eventually, the placenta becomes the supplier of progesterone and thus a major contributor during pregnancy to the maintenance of the endometrium.

44. **(D)** Human chromosomes once were miscounted and earlier texts erroneously placed the number at 48. Now it is known that the diploid number for humans (the chromosomes one finds in normal, resting somatic cells) is 22 pairs of so-called autosomes plus two X chromosomes if the individual is female and an X and a Y if a male. The haploid number, which one finds in germ cells (sperm or egg), is 23: 22 autosomes and a sex chromosome, either X or Y. All mature human ova have an X chromosome (because the oögonia, the starting cell in oögenesis, have only XX pairs), but the sperm can have either an X or a Y. The latter is the basis for the well-known fact that, in humans, the sex of the embryo is an active, direct function of the father.

45. (D) In the strict sense of the word, digestion denotes the rendering of foodstuffs into a form that can a) be absorbed from the lumen of the alimentary canal and b) be utilized by the body's metabolic pathways. For much of our foodstuffs, digestion translates into the chemical reduction of polymers into their monomeric units, a process that depends on enzymes. Prior to the arrival in the lumen of the duodenum, foodstuffs undergo predigestion—the preparation, physical and chemical, for the actual digestion. The exocrine pancreas produces most of the important digestive enzymes (proteases for proteins, lipases for lipids, amylases for carbohydrates, and nucleases for nucleic acids). Pancreatic juices are delivered to the lumen of the duodenum, the main arena of digestion, via the pancreatic duct. Absorption of most digestive breakdown products occurs in the jejunum, with special substances passing out of the gut at other locations.

46. (A) Haversian canals exist in compact (or cortical) bone but not trabecular (spongy or cancellous) bone. Compact bone is made up of lamellae. The lamellae surrounding Haversian canals are called Haversian lamellae. Haversian lamellae plus the centrally situated Haversian canal constitute Haversian systems.

47. (B) The fat in adipose tissue is intracellular. Unless artifactually expelled, the fat is actually part of (a lipid inclusion in) the cytoplasm of fat cells (sometimes referred to as adipocytes). When the lipid is reduced to small amounts in their cytoplasm, fat cells (adipocytes) resemble fibroblasts.

48. (B) Microphages phagocytose microorganism. Macrophages engulf particles, such as dust, bile salts, or dead cells and cell parts. Some macrophages, such as the Kupffer cells in the sinusoids of the liver, are fixed in position. (Fixed macrophages in endothelial-lined sinusoids, such as the liver, thymus, lymph nodes, or spleen—along with the endothelial cells—constitute what some authors call the reticulo-endothelial, or R-E system.) Other macrophages, such as the dust cells one can find in most human lungs, can migrate, sometimes out of the body, or appear in body fluid.

49. **(B)** The cubic millimeter (mm^3) has become the standard hematologic unit of measurement. White blood cells number on the approximate order of 6,000 to 10,000 per mm^3. For blood platelets (thromboplastids) the figure is some 150,000 to 300,000 per mm^3, depending on the counting procedure.

50. **(A)** Specific relative values for white blood cells vary among textbooks. Therefore, the following percentages should be regarded as orders of magnitude: neutrophils, 50–75; eosinophils, 2–5; basophils, 0.5–1; lymphocytes, 20–45; monocytes, 3–8.

51. **(C)** The mammalian normoblast looks like an erythrocyte with a nucleus. Granulocytes and red blood cells are generally thought to be products of red bone marrow (myeloid connective tissue) and agranulocytic leukocytes (lymphocytes and monocytes) products of lymphatic tissue (lymphoid connective tissue). However, some experiments have indicated that a cell with the potency to produce all the blood cells actually circulates in the blood. See also answer **40.**

52. **(D)** This enzyme is located in the cross bridge between the thick (myosin) filament and thin filament; "mer" means piece. The meromyosins, heavy and light—large proteins in their own right—are "pieces" of myosin, the complex protein of the myofibril's thick filament. Actin, troponin, and tropomyosin contribute to the myofibril's thin filament.

53. **(B)** The rough ER, sometimes called ergastoplasm, contains ribosomes, the protein manufacturing machinery of the cell. The presence of Nissl substance indicates that the neuron is heavily engaged in protein synthesis. One sign of neuronal degeneration is chromatolysis—breakdown of Nissl substance.

54. **(A)** All blood vessels, from the lowly capillaries to the aorta, are lined by endothelium. A single, very flat layer of cells, endothelium belongs to what the histologist classifies as simple squamous epithelium.

55. (C)   Hair is an epidermal appendage, and the epidermis is made of epithelium. Like sweat glands, hair, hair follicles, and nails, epidermal appendages develop from ectoderm, which grows in from the exterior surface of the embryo during intrauterine life. A dermal (connective tissue) papilla does develop in the bulb, at the base of the hair follicle. Blood vessels in the dermal papilla nourish the hair. If the dermal papilla dies, the hair follicle degenerates, the hair ceases growing and is eventually sloughed and not replaced, as in balding.

56. (A)   The earliest forerunner (anlage) of the central nervous system is a thickening, the medullary plate, in the ectoderm of what will become the embryo's back. The plate curls into a tube (neural tube), and the tube sinks into the underlying mesoderm to complete development remote from the exterior of the body.

57. (D)   Osteoclasts can be seen microscopically in the immediate vicinity of active bone resorption. They are multinucleated cells. Osteoblasts manufacture the raw materials for bony matrix. Osteoblasts become the osteocytes, the cells of mature bone. Osteocytes are within the lacunae (small spaces) of the bony matrix. Numerous canniculi, minute channels in the bony matrix, interconnect the lucunae and serve as nutrient passageways to each individually trapped osteocyte.

58. (E)   The monocyte of blood is a circulating form of macrophage. It is also classified as an agranulocyte. Its numbers increase in the tissue during chronic inflammation.

59. (C)   Megakaryocytes are large, multilobed cells normally found in the red bone marrow of adults. During embryonic life, they exist in the liver and spleen, the homeopoietic (blood-forming) organs in the embryo. Normally, the liver and spleen do not retain their blood cell forming functions postpartum. However, if the need arises, the spleen can quickly resume homeopoiesis.

60. (D)   Transitional epithelium lines the ureter as well as the urinary bladder. The surface cells (those closest to the urine) exhibit a crust-like exterior, called, in fact, the crusta. These surface cells flatten out when the organ distends, assuming a squamous appearance. As the organ empties, the cells assume a cuboidal shape.

The name derives from the capacity of the surface cells to make a transition from squamous to cuboidal or vice versa.

61. **(A)** Fibroblasts make and put out (by exocytosis) procollagen molecules. The latter are triple helices of polypeptides, both of whose ends are amputated outside the cell by extracellular procollagen peptidase enzymes to produce tropocollagen units. Tropocollagen units join to make collagen fibrils.

62. **(C)** The seminiferous tubule is the site of spermatogenesis, the production of sperm cells. The following constitute the cell population of the seminiferous tubule: spermatogonia (which multiply mitotically); primary spermatocytes (derived from spermatogonia but engaged in the first meiotic division); secondary spermatocytes (the daughters of primary spermatocytes); spermatids (the haploid daughters of secondary spermatocytes and thus the immediate result of the second meiotic division); and spermatozoa or sperm (which, without further cell division, differentiate directly from the spermatids). Meiosis, which is often called maturation division, involves one round of chromosomal replication but two rounds of cell division. In mitosis, each round of chromosomal replication precedes each division, thus preserving diploidy (2N). Fertilization unites the haploid (N) sperm with the N ovum to reestablish 2N.

63. **(D)** The inner ear consists of the snail shell-like cochlea, for hearing, and the vestibular organ, which is involved in balance. The organ of Corti, whose most important elements are so-called hair cells, lies within the cochlear duct (scala media), bathed in endolymph, and upon the basilar membrane. The hairs of hair cells (cilia) are embedded in an overhanging flap, the tectorial membrane. Cochlear nerve fibers are wound around the hair cells. Vibrations of the basilar membrane, set up by rhythmic shock waves within fluids of the inner ear (and set to the tempo of the beating ear drum), can mechanically stimulate hair cells in the organ of Corti by creating a sort of clothes line effect on their hairs, a shearing action that depolarizes the hair cells' membrane. Sufficiently depolarized, the hair cells can detonate impulses within cochlear nerve fibers wrapped about them.

General Biochemistry

64. (C) Nucleotides are the building blocks (monomers) of polynucleotides, the strands constituting the nucleic acids. Enzymes are proteins. Proteins consist of polypeptides, derivatives of amino acids (peptides), linked head-to-tail by specialized bonds called peptide linkages.

65. (C) Phospholipids represent the principal structural elements of all membranes. Phospholipids possess a hydrophilic (water-loving) head and a hydrophobic (water-fearing) tail. When phospholipids are immersed in an aqueous solution the tails pack together to minimize the surface in contact with water. The interaction among hydrophobic surfaces is sometimes referred to as hydrophobic bonding.

66. (A) In DNA, the complementing rule is A-T, G-C, or vice versa. In RNA, U takes the place of T. If the sequence in the question were serving as a template for RNA, the answer would be U-U-U-G.

67. (C) Reactions involving glucose and its derivatives are directly and indirectly responsible for putting a third phosphate onto the tail of ADP to make ATP (adenosine *di*-phosphate to adenosine *tri*-phosphate), sometimes metaphorically called the "high octane" fuel of the body. Glycolytic products (from pyruvic acid) feed Krebs citric acid (TCA) cycle. The citric acid cycle generates H^+ (protons) which fuel the respiratory chain (electron transport chain) and which, in the presence of oxygen, generate water. When oxygen is in short supply, electron transport falters, H^+ is not withdrawn, and the citric acid cycle clogs up and shuts down. Under anaerobic conditions, the Embden-Meyerhof pathway generates lactate (lactic acid), which cannot be used in the citric acid cycle.

68. (D) Ribosomes are a sort of cytological platform on which messenger (m) RNA can be placed. With mRNA seated, individual transfer (t) RNAs, with a particular amino acid attached, can drag specific monomers of future polypeptides into position on the ribosome. A particular t-RNA can complement a specific triplet sequence of bases (a codon) within the m-RNA. In this way, a particular amino acid is placed at a specific location in the polypeptide chain. The peptide linkages in the latter are formed enzymatically.

69. **(B)** Like myosin, an opsin is a protein. DNA consists of polynucleotide chains. ATP (adenosine triphosphate) is a nucleotide with a chain of three phosphate groups attached to it. Choices C and E fall into the category of lipids.

70. **(B)** A beta-carotene molecule is two potential retinoid molecules fused tail-to-tail. 11-*cis* retinal is the so-called chromophore of the visual pigments. Retin*al* is an abbreviation for retinaldehyde; the terminal carbon atom in the molecule's tail has attached to it a double bonded oxygen (carbonyl) and a hydrogen. The alcoholic congener of retin*al*, retin*ol*, whose tail terminates in a CH_2OH, is more commonly known as Vitamin A. The prefix 11-*cis* refers to a permanent kink in retinal at the 11th carbon (which shares a double bond with carbon 12 of the tail). When rhodopsin (the visual pigment of the rod) absorbs light, the tail straightens out, the retinal pulls away from the opsin, and the entire pigment begins to break down. With no permanent kinks in its tail, a retinoid is called *all-trans*.

71. **(B)** In its reduced form, glutathione (GSH) consists of GYL-CYS-gammaGLU. A free SH (sulfhydryl) group in CYS can allow for oxidation by forming S-S (disulfide bridges) between two glutathiones to produce GSSG. Reversible formation of GSSG may "sop up" free energy that might otherwise be available to create undesirable cross-linkages among proteins, as in aging or cataract formation; i.e., glutathione, via oxidation and reduction (redox reactions), may play a protective role in tissues such as the crystalline lens.

72. **(B)** Although many more than 20 natural and synthetic amino acids exist, not all can fit together end-to-end to form the polypeptide chains of proteins. The 20 amino acids commonly found in protein chains may be thought of as having a head, body, and tail. The head of one can react with the tail of another in what is called a peptide linkage—polypeptides, when several join in a chain. The body also has a so-called R group, projecting off one side. The R is different for each amino acid. The heads, bodies (less the

R), and tails are identical. Thus, variations in the number and sequence of Rs make one polypeptide different from another while the central chains differ only in length.

73. **(D)** The R of PHE contains a phenyl group; i.e., a benzene or aromatic ring. R groups may be acidic, basic, or neutral. Some Rs are rather bulky (e.g., lysine) while others are relatively small. The R of glycine consists of only a single hydrogen atom.

74. **(C)** Glucose contains six carbon atoms. Ribose and deoxyribose of RNA and DNA are 5 carbon sugars; i.e., they are pentoses. During its metabolism, the original glucose frame is split into two triose skeletons.

75. **(C)** Single, double, and triple covalent bonds share one, two, or three pairs of electrons, respectively. The greater the number of shared pairs, the stronger the bond. Also, the greater the number of shared pairs, the more restricted the movement of the two atoms, relative to each other.

76. **(A)** To illustrate the answer: A-A-A-A-A-A would represent a polynucleotide from which six adenosine monophosphate (AMP) molecules could be derived. Placing another phosphate on an AMP would yield an ADP, adenosine diphosphate. (See also answer **67**.)

77. **(E)** Chromatin consists of DNA and proteins. Among the proteins of chromatin, the histones have been the most extensively studied class and may be the most important. Some investigators believe that histones determine which genes in the nucleus will be available for transcription (making of m-RNA and thus the reading of the genetic code) and which will be sequestered (i.e., kept out of action).

78. **(C)** There is a specific t-RNA, each with its own anticodon, for each amino acid. Although enzymes must act to forge the peptide linkages, the match between anticodon and the codon in m-RNA is what accounts for a particular amino acid occupying a specific location along a polypeptide chain; see also answer **68**.

79. (C) Exons are the coding sequences of mammalian DNA. In bacteria, the genes are continuously encoded. But since the late 1970s it has been known that the genes of eucaryotic cells (cells with nuclei) can be discontinuous; i.e., the chain of DNA is made up of some base sequences that carry the code for a particular polypeptide (exons) interspersed by introns. The piece of RNA initially made on a discontinuous gene (in primary transcription) must undergo secondary cutting and splicing before it can serve as the m-RNA template for a specific polypeptide.

80. (B) Under aerobic conditions (plentiful oxygen), gylcolysis yields pyruvate (pyruvic acid), which can be utilized to keep metabolism going and large amounts of ATP coming. Under anaerobic conditions, the cell manufactures lactate (lactic acid), which is structurally very similar to pyruvate but which, in mammals, cannot be further acted upon chemically until aerobic metabolism resumes. If it is not removed by the circulation, lactic acid can build up in the tissues. Lactic acid might be regarded as a molecular manifestation of oxygen debt. (See answer **67**.)

81. (E) TCA is an abbreviation for *tri*-carboxylic acid cycle. (Note that the suffix *ate* means acid.) In essence, what occurs in the Krebs cycle is that the carbon atoms of the original glucose (identified as acetate in some texts) are joined to a *di*-carboxylic acid (oxaloacetic acid) to form the tricarboxylic acid, citrate. (The Krebs cycle is also called the Citric Acid Cycle.) After a series of reactions, the TCAs are converted back to DCAs (and eventually oxaloacetate again); hence, "cycle." (See answer **67**.)

82. (E) Both the Krebs cycle and electron transport occur in the mitochondria. One might say that the former feeds the latter—as long as the cell is operating aerobically.

83. (B) Unlike mammalian genes (DNA), those of resting retroviruses are made of a single strand of RNA. Retrovirus particles carry an enzyme, reverse transcriptase, so called because it can use a strand of RNA as a template to make a new strand of DNA. When the retrovirus infects a cell, it first makes an RNA-DNA hybrid, using its reverse transcriptase. The hybrid then makes a single strand of DNA (a DNA transcript). The strand of DNA serves as a template for a complementary DNA strand. The result is a double-stranded segment of viral DNA. If the latter becomes incorporated into the host cell's chromosomes, it can use the cell's genetic machinery to manufacture new viral particles with single-stranded RNA as the viral gene.

84. **(B)** A DNAase enzyme breaks down DNA molecules. RNA and DNA strands are polymers of nucleotides, polynucleotides. Thus, the enzymes that help fuse the nucleotide chains together are called polymerases.

85. **(A)** G-1 (or gap 1) follows mitosis; the S phase, when the genes replicate, follows G-1 and is itself followed by G-2 (second gap in turnover); mitosis (sometimes called M) follows G-2. More compactly put: G-1, S, G-2, M, G-1, S, G2, M . . . as long as the cell continues to grow.

86. **(E)** Phosphates are added and subtracted during various steps in the pathway, with a net gain of two ATP molecules for each entering glucose. The extra phosphates can be furnished from inorganic sources.

87. **(D)** The tricarboxylic acids (tricarboxylates or TCAs) are citrate (citric acid), cis-aconitate, isocitrate, and alpha-keto-glutarate. The dicarboxylic acids (DCAs) are succinyl CoA, succinate, fumarate, malate, and oxaloacetate. There are typically 9 steps per cycle, ideally in the order presented, with two cycles occurring for each glucose originally taken into the cell.

88. **(C)** Also called the hexose monophosphate pathway, or pentose shunt (as well as the phosphogluconate pathway), the pentose (phosphate) pathway begins with action of the enzyme glucose 6-phosphate dehydrogenase, which sets the stage for the eventual conversion of the original 6 carbon molecule into a 5 carbon or pentose sugar, as ribose and its congeners are.

89. **(C)** In other words, two monosaccharides fuse to form the simplest unit of structure of a glycosaminoglycans (new name for mucopolysaccharide). The glycosaminoglycans, in general, consists of a hexose (like galactose or glucuronic acid) linked to a hexosamine (amino sugar).

90. **(A)** Primary structure refers to the specific amino acid sequence. Secondary, tertiary, and quaternary structures refer to progressively more complex organization of the chains. Proteins can also conjugate with other kinds of molecules to make, for example, glycoproteins (sugar + protein), lipoproteins (lipid + protein).

General Physiology

91. **(D)** *Catabolism* is breaking down, chemically, which must happen to fuel molecules, if free energy is to be liberated from them. *Anabolism* is building up, which the body must do to renew tissues, restore fuel stocks, or assemble new biopolymers.

92. **(C)** The correct choice, 0.9, is the numerical value of mammalian physiological saline. Values greater than 0.9 would represent a hypertonic condition for a mammal. Concentrations below 0.9 are hypotonic.

93. **(A)** Appreciate that Dalton's law extends to air in the alveolar spaces of the lung. Air is a variable gaseous mixture. But, minus water vapor, air typically exhibits (by volume): 78.03 percent nitrogen; 20.94 percent oxygen; 0.99 percent rare gases; and 0.04 percent carbon dioxide.

94. **(C)** Å is the abbreviation for an angstrom. An Å is 0.1 of a nanometer (nm) and roughly the diameter of an atom. The micron (micrometer or μm) of light microscopy contains 10,000 Å. Also, $Å = 10^{-10}$ m (meters).

95. **(D)** Hydrophobic interactions, or bonds, represent attempts of molecules to minimize the hydrophobic surface exposed to a polar solvent. The molecules do this by pressing firmly together. If the polar solvent is withdrawn, the interaction ceases. Thus, membranes whose phospholipids adhere because of hydrophobic bonding could not exist without water. (See answer **65**.)

96. **(C)** In a molecule of water, the oxygen atom (of the H_2O) is displaced to one side and the two hydrogens to the other. The asymmetry imparts dipolarity to the molecule, the O side being elec-

tronegative and the H side electropositive. The polarity makes waters highly interactive with other polar molecules, including itself.

97. (A) Pino (from *pineos*) means to drink. A pinosome is a fluid-filled vacuole formed by pinocytosis. Along with phagocytosis, pinocytosis is classified under endocytosis, the process whereby the cell engulfs and incorporates materials too large for dissuasion.

98. (E) See answer 81. Lysosomes are bags of enzymes that can degrade proteins. Microtubules are minute tubes seen in certain circumstances with the electron microscope. Golgi bodies are membranous structures that are involved in assembling supermolecular complexes. Polyribosomes are assemblages of ribosomes, whose presence usually indicates that the cell is engaged in protein synthesis.

99. (C) ATP is the general service fuel for the body. See comments to 67. Special fuels exist (e.g., GTP or UTP), but they are usually produced from ATP.

100. (D) Nerve fibers can be classified according to fiber diameter, myelination, conduction velocity, threshold to electrical stimulation, and the character of their electrical record. Three broad, overlapping categories exist: A, B, and C. The A fibers are myelinated, have a fiber diameter of 1 to 22 μm, and a conduction velocity of 5 to 120 m/sec. B fibers are lightly myelinated, have a fiber diameter < 3 μm, and conduct at 3 to 15 m/sec. C fibers have a diameter < 2 μm, are said to be unmyelinated, and conduct at some 0.6 to 2 m/sec. The spike potential of the A fiber is much shorter than that of B or C. Thresholds also vary among the three types. Subcategories of A fibers exist. In human nerves, the A fibers that conduct at 120 m/sec typically innervate skeletal muscles. Preganglionic autonomic fibers fall into the B category. Postganglionic autonomics are C fibers, as are the afferents conveying the vaguely localized pain or pressure sensations from the viscera.

101. (B) Without the AChase enzyme to split it, ACh would continue to irritate the postsynaptic membrane. The muscle would continue to contract, until exhausted. In nerve-to-nerve contact, where AChase has been poisoned, the postsynaptic neuron would continue to receive stimulation. The neural gate would remain open when it should close. Strychnine can have this effect.

102. **(A)** An impulse arriving at the axon terminal appears to cause synaptic vesicles to attach to the presynaptic membrane, discharge their contents into the synaptic cleft and, possibly, recycle their own membranes into the plasma membrane of the presynaptic cell.

103. **(E)** In other words, they are not impulses in the general meaning of the term. In contrast, the impulse per se does not occur unless the stimulus reaches threshold. But when it exists, the impulse obeys the all-or-none law.

104. **(A)** 5-HT appears to be an important neurotransmitter, and it exists in comparatively high concentration in the hypothalamus, midbrain (mesencephalic) raphe, basal ganglia, pineal body, and elsewhere in the central nervous system. The 5-HT pathway begins with the amino acid, tryptophan, which is first hydroxylated (an OH is put onto it) at its number 5 carbon to produce 5-hydroxytryptophan; the latter is decarboxylated (has a molecule of CO_2 enzymatically plucked from it) to produce the amine, 5-hydroxytriptamine—5-HT—or serotonin.

105. **(B)** Isotonic contraction occurs when the muscle changes its overall length. In isometric contraction, the muscle's length remains constant, while the tone increases.

106. **(D)** The contractile apparatus of smooth, skeletal, and cardiac muscle is the myofibril, which contains the contractile proteins, actin, and myosin. The latter proteins are arranged somewhat differently in smooth versus the other types of muscle. The different arrangement imparts a different microscopic appearance to smooth versus skeletal and cardiac muscle. However, contractility depends on the sliding of actin on myosin; i.e., although the details differ, the underlying principle (actin sliding) is basically similar in all muscle, smooth versus skeletal versus cardiac.

107. (A) Osmotic pressure of blood should not be confused with blood pressure. Osmotic pressure is a function of the concentration of a fluid; i.e., of the osmolality.

108. (B) Systolic pressure is the pressure measured on the walls of the arteries during systole; i.e., contraction of the heart, especially the ventricles. Diastolic pressure is the pressure measured at diastole, the relaxation of the heart; 80 mm Hg is the value for normal diastolic pressure.

109. (B) The specific gravity of plasma is about 1.026 and erythrocytes (rbc's), 1.093. Given that the rbc's make up 45 percent of the hematocrit (Hct), a drop in the relative abundance of rbc's (tantamount to anemia) will produce a proportional decrease in the specific gravity of the blood.

110. (E) The pH of the body depends mainly on three buffer systems: bicarbonate buffer, phosphate buffer, and protein buffer. Although not especially powerful, the bicarbonate system is the body's most important one because its two main components, HCO_3^- ion and CO_2, can be regulated physiologically: HCO_3^- ion is removed by the kidney and CO_2 is expired by the lung.

111. (C) A drop in the pH of body fluids produces acidosis. A rise in pH produces alkalosis. Severe acidosis can induce coma. Alkalosis can induce muscular spasms (tetany).

112. (A) An average-sized human body contains some 4 grams of iron, half of which, in life, is bound to hemoglobin. Men excrete about 1 mg of iron daily, mainly via defecation. In women of child-bearing age, menstruation ups the average daily loss to about 2 mg per day.

113. (C) The plasma carries both fibrinogen and prothrombin. Platelets can release thromboplastin, an enzyme that converts prothrombin to thrombin. Thrombin, in turn, converts fibrinogen to fibrin, which can trap blood cells to form a clot.

114. (C) Measured at the brachial artery, the pulse pressure of humans is usually about 40 mm Hg. Pulse pressure is strongly influenced by the stroke volume output of the heart (how much blood the heart thrusts out during a beat) and by the total distensibility (compliance) of the arteries.

115. (E) The EKG arises from potential differences between excited and unexcited portions of the heart. The P wave occurs just before the onset of atrial contraction. The QRS complex occurs just before the onset of ventricular contraction. In the normal EKG, the T wave is considered to represent ventricular repolarization.

116. (A) The vagovagal reflex can prevent the heart from beating itself to death. When triggered, the vagovagal reflex can cause the heart to stop, momentarily (exhibit bradycardia). Following a short pause, the heart usually resumes beating at a reduced rate. The vagovagal reflex can be elicited, among other things, by pressure on the eyeball, under which circumstance it is called the oculocardiac reflex. The input (afferent arc) for the latter is via visceral afferents from ocular blood vessels which travel in branches of V1.

117. (E) Aldosterone is produced by the zona glomerulosa of the adrenal cortex. Necessary to sustain life, aldosterone promotes the exchange of K^+ for Na^+ in the distal convoluted tubule of the kidney. The latter exchange eliminates excess K^+ from the body while retaining a normal Na^+ level.

General Microbiology

118. (B) The prokaryotic cell is simpler than the eucaryotic cell at every level except the cell envelope, which is more complex in the prokaryotic cell.

119. (C) Glycocalyx are a loose network of fibrils which extend out from the bacterial cell and play a major role in adhering to surfaces in their environment.

120. (A) The gram-positive organism appears blue in gram staining because the cell retains the crystal–violet iodine complex. Gram-negative organisms are decolorized by alcohol.

121. (A) *Clostridium perfringens*, an anaerobic organism, is the most common of the species in the presence of necrotic tissue to cause gas gangrene.

122. (B) *Staph aureus* is associated with toxic shock syndrome. Most strains of *S. aureus* isolated from patients with toxic shock syndrome produce a toxin called Toxic Shock Syndrome Toxin 1 (TSST-1).

123. (D) *Bacillus cereus* is a gram-positive spore forming aerobic bacillus. These are saprophytic organisms prevalent in soil, water, air, and on vegetation. They produce an enterotoxin that can cause food poisoning.

124. (C) Pseudomembranous colitis has been associated with *Clostridium dificile*. There is almost always a prior history of antibiotic therapy. The most common antibiotics used are ampicillin and clindamycin.

125. (A) *Corynebacterium diphtheriae* is a non-spore forming gram-positive bacilli that can produce a powerful exotoxin which affects the respiratory tract, causing diphtheria in humans.

126. (D) Group A beta-hemolytic streptococcus causes erysipelas in humans. If the portal entry is the skin, erysipelas results, with massive brawny edema and a rapidly advancing margin of infection.

127. (B) *Staph aureus* is a gram-positive cocci and is coagulase positive. It is a major pathogen for humans. They are usually arranged in grape-like clusters.

128. (D) The liberation of O_2 when hydrogen peroxide is placed on a slide with bacterial growth is the catalase test. *S. aureus* produces an enzyme, catalase, which converts hydrogen peroxide to oxygen and water.

129. (C) *Strep pyogenes* is a group A beta-hemolytic streptococcus. It is usually sensitive to bactracin. Large zones of beta hemolysis are produced when cultured on sheep blood agar plates.

130. **(C)** *Strep viridans* is the most frequent cause of subacute bacterial endocarditis. They are the most prevalent members of the upper respiratory flora.

131. **(B)** Group A streptococcus infection precedes the onset of rheumatic fever, 1 to 4 weeks earlier. This is the most sequelae to hemolytic streptococcal infection.

132. **(A)** *Strep pneumoniae* is gram-positive diplococci, lancet-shaped. They are arranged in chains, possessing a capsule of polysaccharide that permits typing with specific antisera.

133. **(D)** *Escherichia coli* is the most common cause of urinary tract infection by a gram-negative rod. It tests positive for indoles, lysine decarboxylase, and mannitol fermentation.

134. **(B)** *Pseudo aeruginosa* grows at 42°C, is oxidase positive, and produces a "sweet, grape-like" odor. It does not ferment carbohydrates but many strains oxidize glucose.

135. **(D)** *Pseudo aeruginosa* is a gram-negative, motile, obligate aerobic rod. *Ps. aeruginosa* forms smooth, round colonies with fluorescent greenish color. It often produces the nonfluorescent pigment, pyocyanin.

136. **(A)** *Moraxella lacunata* is a gram-negative bacillus or coccobacillus: nonmotile, nonfermentative, and oxidative positive; causes bacteremia, conjunctivitis, and endocarditis.

137. **(C)** *Hemophilus influenzae* is a gram-negative pleomorphic bacteria that requires an enriched media. It is differentiated from related gram-negative bacilli by its requirement for X and V factors.

138. **(A)** *Hemophilus aegyptius,* also known as the Koch-Weeks bacillus, is sometimes referred to as *H. influenzae* biotype 111. It has been associated with a highly communicable form of conjunctivitis

139. (B) *Neisseria gonorrhoea* is a gram-negative, nonmotile diplococcus. The individual cocci appears kidney shaped. When the organism occurs in pairs, the flat or concave sides are adjacent.

140. (A) *Treponema pallidum* is a spiral, motile organism which does not stain with aniline dyes and is not successfully cultured on artificial media. The organisms are actively motile and rotate steadily around their central axis filament.

141. (D) *Chlamydia trachomatis* is an obligate intracellular parasite. It lacks the mechanism for the production of metabolic energy and cannot synthesize ATP.

142. (C) *Candida albicans* is an oval budding yeast that produces a pseudomycelium. It is cultured on Sabouraud's agar. It may produce progressive systemic diseases in the immunocompromised patient.

143. (B) Parvovirus is the smallest DNA-containing virus. It has no envelope but has cubic symmetry with 32 capsomers. It contains a single-stranded DNA.

144. (A) The most frequent source of infection from this organism is the patient who excretes large numbers of the organism from the respiratory tract. The number of active cases of tuberculosis is on the rise in the United States, particularly in urban areas, in prison populations, and among the immunocompromised. Some of the newly emergent strains of tuberculosis are resistant to conventional drug therapy.

General Pharmacology

145. (B) The concentration of a drug attained at the site of the target receptor depends on the amount of the drug administered and the extent and rate of its absorption, distribution, metabolism, and excretion.

146. (D) Reserpine, physostigmine, and metoclopramide will accelerate the gastric emptying rate and thus decrease the absorption of drugs that are absorbed in the stomach; e.g., digoxin. However, they may enhance the absorption of drugs in the small intestine.

147. **(C)** The unionized form of a drug molecule can rapidly cross lipid membranes while the ionized form of the drug tends to cross barriers that favor water-soluble compounds.

148. **(A)** The lipid-soluble drugs are converted to a more polar form, or water soluble, so that the metabolites can be eliminated by the kidneys.

149. **(C)** Agonists and antagonists have affinity for the receptor. Those drugs that mimic the effects of the neurotransmitter are referred to as agonists. Compounds that do not possess intrinsic activity but produce their effects by inhibiting the action of the agonist are called antagonists.

150. **(C)** The Therapeutic Index is expressed as the ratio of the median lethal dose (LD50) to the median therapeutic dose (ED50), which is indication of the selectivity of the drug in producing the desired effect.

151. **(B)** Drugs that are destroyed by gastrointestinal acidity or subjected to substantial presystemic metabolism may be formulated to be administered by sublingual or buccal route.

152. **(D)** By choosing a relatively insoluble form of the drug, formulating with large particle size, and suspending in a viscous medium, slow release can be produced.

153. **(A)** Prodrugs have been used advantageously to:
—Improve bioavailability.
—Mask unpleasant characteristics of drugs.
—Alter drug solubility.
—Provide site specific delivery of drugs.

154. **(B)** The disadvantages of administering a drug by the oral route are destruction of the drug by the stomach acidity and enzymes and variable patterns of absorption

155. (A) Biotransformation of a drug is the conversion of the drug by enzymes to a more polar form so that it can be readily excreted by the body. In some instances, the metabolite or the biotransformed drug may be pharmacologically active.

156. (D) The half-life is the time it takes for the plasma concentration of the drug to be reduced by 50%. This is a function of the combined rates of metabolism and excretion.

157. (B) Emesis should be considered if the patient has ingested potentially dangerous compounds such as pesticides. If the patient has ingested a corrosive poison, emesis increases the likelihood of gastric perforation and further necrosis of the esophagus.

158. (B) Many drugs, when administered chronically to animals and humans, increase the activity of drug metabolizing enzymes and, as a result, decrease the effect of the drug. A well-known example of such a drug is phenobarbital.

159. (A) The autonomic nervous system innervates the heart blood vessels, glands, and smooth muscle. All of these organ systems are under involuntary control and are thus controlled by the autonomic nervous system. The skeletal muscles are under voluntary control.

160. (A) The parasympathetic nervous system is anatomically referred to as the craniosacral division of the autonomic nervous system because it is made up of the cranial and sacral nerves.

161. (A) The neurotransmitter of the preganglionic fibers of both the sympathetic and the parasympathetic nervous systems of the autonomic nervous system is acetylcholine.

162. (B) The neurotransmitter of the majority of postganglionic fibers of the sympathetic nervous system is norepinephrine.

163. (D) Destruction of neurotransmitter, acetylcholine following each impulse at the postganglionic sites of the parasympathetic nervous system and all the preganglionic site is carried out by the enzyme acetylcholinesterase.

164. (D) Bethanecol is a direct-acting parasympathomimetic agent that acts more selectively on the gastrointestinal tract and the urinary bladder than does acetylcholine. It is resistant to breakdown by cholinesterases.

165. (C) Pyridostigmine is a "reversible" cholinesterase inhibitor used in the symptomatic treatment of myasthenia gravis. Pyridostigmine is a close congener of neostigmine.

166. (B) Methoxamine is a direct-acting sympathomimetic agent with relatively specific alpha-1 selective activity. It causes a dose-related increase in peripheral vascular resistance.

167. (A) Isoproterenol is a potent nonselective beta adrenergic agonist with low affinity for alpha adrenergic receptors. Isoproterenol relaxes almost all varieties of smooth muscle when the tone is high.

168. (A) Guanafacine is an alpha-2 adrenergic agonist that is more selective for alpha-2 receptors than is clonidine. Guanafacine lowers blood pressure by stimulating central alpha-2 receptors.

169. (A) Terazosin is a selective alpha-1 adrenergic antagonist. It is less potent than prazosin, the prototype of alpha-1 adrenergic antagonist. Terazosin is more soluble in water than prazosin.

170. (C) Propantheline is one of the more widely used synthetic antimuscarinic agents. Its pharmacological properties are similar to methantheline, a synthetic parasympatholytic agent, but it is two to five times more potent.

171. (B) Many of the histamine-1 antagonists tend to inhibit responses to acetylcholine that are mediated by muscarinic receptors. Among the first generation antihistamines, pyrilamine is one of the least likely to produce the anticholinergic effect.

172. (D) Aztreonam is a monocyclic beta-lactam (monobactam) compound. The antimicrobial activity of aztreonam differs from other beta-lactam antibiotics in its ability to be effective against *Enterobacteriaceae* and *Pseudomonas aeruginosa* but ineffective against gram-positive bacteria and anaerobic organisms.

173. **(B)** Ofloxacin is a member of the class of synthetic antimicrobial agents known as the fluoroquinolones. These agents have a broad spectrum of activity including *Pseudomonas aeruginosa, Staphylococcus aureus, Enterobacteriaceae,* and *Streptococcus.* The mechanism of action is the inhibition of the enzyme, DNA gyrase.

174. **(A)** Acetaminophen has antipyretic and analgesic effects that are similar to those of aspirin. However, they have only weak antiinflammatory effects.

175. **(C)** Phenobarbital, a sedative-hypnotic, but exerts maximal anticonvulsant action at doses below those required for hypnosis. Phenobarbital is an effective agent for generalized tonic-clonic and partial seizures.

176. **(D)** Trazodone is an atypical antidepressant. It is thought to potentiate the actions of serotonin. Unlike the tricyclic antidepressants that possess significant anticholinergic properties, the anticholinergic effects produced by trazodone are very mild.

177. **(C)** Quinidine has significant anticholinergic actions, blocking the effects of vagal stimulation or parasympathetic effect. Quinidine also has alpha adrenergic blocking properties.

178. **(C)** Spironolactone, an aldosterone antagonist is used in the treatment of hypertension and in the management of refractory edema. It is administered in conjunction with thiazide diuretics to prevent the excessive loss of potassium ions.

179. **(B)** Ganciclovir, an antiviral agent is active in vitro against all herpes viruses, including cytomegalovirus. Because of its toxicity ganciclovir's use has been limited to life- or sight-threatening infections with cytomegalovirus.

General Pathology

180. **(B)** The primary causes of generalized fluid retention include increased hydrostatic pressure, viz congestive heart failure, cirrhosis, and nephrotic syndrome.

181. **(B)** Properties of acute inflammation are vasodilatation and changes in blood flow, leukocyte migration, and exudation of fluid and plasma proteins.

182. **(C)** Local signs of acute inflammation are heat, swelling, redness, and loss of function. The redness and heat are due to increased blood flow to the area. The swelling is due in part to vasodilatation and cellular edema, pain, and loss of function.

183. **(C)** Stasis in acute inflammation is due to increased permeability of the microvasculature, outpouring of protein-rich fluid into the extravascular tissue, and increased blood viscosity.

184. **(B)** The most important feature of the inflammatory response is the accumulation of leukocytes. It is associated with the initial phagocytosis of foreign material. It is also important against microbial invaders.

185. **(C)** The chemical mediators of inflammation are histamines, serotonin, bradykinin, and platelet-activating factors together with various proteolytic enzymes resulting in the production of polypeptides.

186. **(D)** The systemic factors that will influence wound healing are nutrition, hematologic deficiencies, glucocorticoids, age, the adequacy of blood supply, and certain systemic diseases; e.g., diabetes.

187. **(A)** The local factors that may influence would healing are previous tissue injury, foreign bodies, and infection. The presence of a single suture was found to enhance the invasiveness of staph. 10,000 times.

188. **(C)** Hemolytic streptococcus produces cellulitis due to the production of hyaluronidase or "spreading factor" which breaks down hyaluronic acid in the ground substance of the connective tissue.

189. **(D)** Langhan's giant cells are multinucleated giant cells in macrophage clusters. The adjacent cells in the macrophage clus-

ters often fuse to form multinucleated giant cells containing up to 50 to 100 nuclei.

190. **(A)** T-cell lymphocytes are responsible for the antibody production and in mediating the various phenomena associated with cell-mediated immunity or delayed hypersensitivity.

191. **(C)** Malignant tumors of epithelial or organ parenchymal origin are referred to as carcinomas. Tumors that are clearly carcinomas, but lack defining characteristics, are referred to as undifferentiated or anaplastic carcinomas.

192. **(C)** Cardiac hypertrophy is best evaluated by heart weight provided that the excess weight is not due to epicardial fat and that heart weight is relative to the patient's body size.

193. **(D)** Toxic injury to heart muscle is known to be produced by cyclophosphamide, adriamycin (doxyrubicin), 5-Fluorouracil, and amphetamines. Bleomycin, unlike other antibiotic members of its class, seldom causes stem cell suppression of bone marrow elements.

194. **(C)** Phosphates begin to increase, leading to increased entry of calcium into bone, resulting in a decrease in serum calcium ions. The chronically damaged kidney also fails to convert 25-hydroxy vitamin D to the metabolically active 1,25-dihydroxy vitamin D, resulting in the defective absorption of calcium from the intestinal tract.

195. **(A)** Preeclampsia may occur in the third trimester of pregnancy, in which proteinuria, edema, and hypertension may occur. If the condition becomes more severe with decreased renal function, convulsion, and perhaps death, it is referred to as eclampsia.

196. **(D)** Angiomyolipomas are a common form of hamartoma found in the kidney. They consist of circumscribed but not encapsulated masses of blood vessels, smooth muscles, and fat cells in varying proportions. They are clinically insignificant but are the commonest lesions of tuberous sclerosis.

197. (B) *Legionella pneumophilia* is the microorganism with a fairly low attack rate and significant mortality and does not stain with Gram stain.

198. (A) Hashimoto's thyroiditis is characterized by thyroid enlargement, lymphocytic infiltration of the gland, and the presence of thyroid antibodies.

199. (A) Hyperaldosteronism is characterized by hypertension, potassium depletion, metabolic alkalosis, and suppression of plasma renin activity.

200. (D) Pheochromocytoma may be associated with the familial form of medullary carcinoma which has an autosomal dominant mode of inheritance and parathyroid hyperplasia or adenoma and multiple mucosal neuromas. Pituitary adenomas have been reported to be associated with Addison's disease.

References

1. Anderson JE. *Grant's Atlas of Human Anatomy.* 8th ed. Baltimore: Williams and Wilkins; 1983.
2. Carpenter M, Sutin J. *Human Neuroanatomy.* 8th ed. Baltimore and London: Williams and Wilkins; 1983.
3. Cotran RS, Kumar V, Robbins SL. *Robbins Pathologic Basis of Disease.* 4th ed. Boston: WB Saunders; 1989.
4. Darnell JE, Lodish H, Baltimore D. *Molecular Cell Biology.* 2nd ed. New York: Freeman; 1990.
5. Gilman AG, Rall TW, Nies AS, Taylor P. *Goodman and Gilman's Pharmacological Basis of Therapeutics.* 8th ed. New York: Pergamon Press; 1990.
6. Graig CR, Stitzel RE. *Modern Pharmacology.* 2nd ed. Boston: Little, Brown and Co; 1986.
7. Guyton A. *Textbook of Medical Physiology.* 8th ed. Philadelphia: WB Saunders; 1991.
8. Jawetz E, Melnick JL, Adelberg EA, Brooks GF, Butel JS, Ornston LN. *Medical Microbiology.* 18th ed. Norwalk, Ct: Appleton & Lange; 1989.
9. Kelly DE, Wood RL, Enders AC. *Bailey's Textbook of Microscopic Anatomy.* 18th ed. Baltimore: Williams and Wilkins; 1984.
10. Kissane JM. *Anderson's Pathology.* Vol 1 and 2, 9th ed. Philadelphia: WB Saunders; 1990.
11. Netter FH. *Atlas of Human Anatomy.* Summit, NJ: Ciba; 1989.
12. Stedman TL. *Stedman's Medical Dictionary.* 25th ed. Baltimore: Williams and Wilkins; 1990.
13. Stryer L. *Biochemistry.* 3rd ed. New York: Freeman; 1988.
14. Wheater PR, Burkitt HG, Daniels VG. *Functional Histology.* 2nd ed. London and New York: Churchill Livingstone; 1987.
15. Williams PL, Warwick R, Dyson M, Bannister LH. *Gray's Anatomy.* 37th ed. London and New York: Churchill Livingstone; 1989.

2

Ocular/Visual Biology

Anatomy of the Eye, Ocular Adnexa, and Visual Pathways

201. What mechanism accounts for most (70 percent) of the sodium ion content of aqueous humor?

   A. diffusion
   B. secretion
   C. pinocytosis
   D. phagocytosis
   E. osmosis

202. The cells most actively involved in the production of aqueous humor belong to
   A. posterior iridial epithelium
   B. unpigmented ciliary epithelium
   C. pigmented ciliary epithelium
   D. retinal pigment epithelium
   E. hyalocytes

203. The efferent fibers that serve the ciliary body leave the brain stem at which of the following locations?
   A. lower border of the pons, medially
   B. lower border of the pons, laterally
   C. interpeduncular fossa
   D. superior medullary vellum
   E. inferior medullary vellum

204. The main group of zonule fibers arise where?
   A. pars plana ciliaris
   B. pars plicata ciliaris
   C. Bruch's membrane
   D. anterior vitreous
   E. line of Schwalbe

205. The external surface of the suprachoroidea comes into direct contact with
   A. Bruch's membrane
   B. retinal pigment epithelium
   C. episclera
   D. stromal layer of the sclera
   E. lamina fusca of the sclera

206. The outer portion of the human ciliary muscle is formed by
   A. skeletal (or striated) muscle
   B. Müller's circular smooth muscle
   C. Brücke's longitudinal smooth muscle
   D. radially oriented smooth muscle
   E. radially oriented skeletal (or striated) muscle

207. The pupillary membrane is produced from
   A. neural ectoderm
   B. surface ectoderm

    C. mesenchyme
    D. endoderm
    E. somites

208. The vascular tunic of the eye is often referred to as the
    A. retina
    B. cornea
    C. sclera
    D. uvea
    E. episclera

209. In terms of ml, how much aqueous humor is normally contained in the anterior chamber?
    A. 0.025
    B. 0.25
    C. 2.5
    D. 25
    E. 250

210. The posterior wall of the anterior chamber angle is formed by
    A. Schwalbe's line
    B. canal of Schlemm
    C. trabecular apparatus
    D. pars plana of the ciliary body
    E. iris and lens

211. The protein content of the lens exceeds that of which of these items?
    A. lacrimal gland parenchyma
    B. belly of the lateral rectus muscle
    C. corneal epithelium
    D. all of the above
    E. none of the above

212. What is the yoke muscle of the left lateral rectus?
    A. right lateral rectus
    B. right medial rectus
    C. left medial rectus
    D. right superior oblique
    E. right inferior oblique

213. Which muscles can synergistically aid the medial rectus muscle in the adduction of the eyeball?
    A. superior and inferior recti
    B. superior and inferior obliques
    C. superior rectus and superior oblique
    D. inferior rectus and inferior oblique
    E. medial and lateral recti

214. What are the glands of Zeis?
    A. palpebral sweat glands
    B. sebaceous glands of the eyelashes
    C. oil-producing glands in the tarsal plate
    D. goblet cells in the conjunctival fornices
    E. sebaceous glands of the ordinary hair follicles in the palpebral skin

215. Destruction of the cervical sympathetic trunk would most likely manifest itself in
    A. Horner's syndrome
    B. Bell's palsy
    C. Argyll Robertson pupil
    D. Bumke's pupil
    E. Munchausen (Münchhausens) syndrome

216. Which of the following terms histologically classifies the normal conjunctiva?
    A. epidermis
    B. mucous membrane
    C. lamina propria
    D. amorphous membrane
    E. avascular membrane

217. The posterior conjunctival arteries branch from the
    A. episcleral branches of the anterior ciliary arteries
    B. perforating branches of the palpebral arcades
    C. recurrent branches of the long posterior ciliary arteries
    D. major arterial circle of the iris
    E. minor arterial circle of the iris

218. The anterior conjunctival arteries are given off by the
- **A.** episcleral branches of the anterior ciliary arteries
- **B.** perforating branches of the palpebral arcades
- **C.** recurrent branches of the long posterior ciliary arteries
- **D.** major arterial circle of the iris
- **E.** minor arterial circle of the iris

219. Most blood from the uvea drains out of the eyeball via
- **A.** venae comitantes of the episcleral arteries
- **B.** venae comitantes of the central retinal arteries
- **C.** venae comitantes of the anterior ciliary arteries
- **D.** venae comitantes of the palpebral arteries
- **E.** vortex veins

220. Aqueous humor in the canal of Schlemm drains into what venus plexus (or plexuses)?
- **A.** deep scleral
- **B.** intrascleral
- **C.** episcleral
- **D.** all of the above
- **E.** none of the above

221. Which choice best denotes the arteries that form the major arterial circle of the iris?
- **A.** anterior ciliary
- **B.** long posterior ciliary
- **C.** anterior ciliaries and long posterior ciliary
- **D.** long and short posterior ciliary
- **E.** temporal and nasal branches of the central retinal

222. Where are the palisades of Vogt?
- **A.** limbal conjunctiva
- **B.** optic disc
- **C.** inner aspect of Bruch's membrane
- **D.** outer aspect of Bruch's membrane
- **E.** just lateral to the central meniscus of Kuhnt

223. What is the origin of the postganglionic sympathetic cells associated with active pupillary mydriasis?
    A. superior cervical ganglion
    B. Edinger-Westphal nucleus
    C. cilo-spinal center of Budge
    D. ciliary ganglion
    E. hypothalamus

224. The lateral half of the right lateral geniculate body (nucleus) receives signals about objects in which portion(s) of the visual field quadrant(s) of the left eye?
    A. superior nasal
    B. inferior nasal
    C. superior temporal
    D. inferior temporal
    E. all quadrants

225. Concerning the previous question, the homonymous field sector(s) of the right eye is (are) what?
    A. superior nasal quadrant
    B. inferior nasal quadrant
    C. superior temporal quadrant
    D. inferior temporal quadrant
    E. all quadrants

226. The lateral half of the right lateral geniculate body signals what portion of the primary visual cortex?
    A. upper lip of the right calcarine fissure
    B. lower lip of the right calcarine fissure
    C. upper lip of the left calcarine fissure
    D. lower lip of the left calcarine fissure
    E. the occipital pole, bilaterally

227. All optic radiations eventually enter the occipital lobe, but those fibers of the radiations known as the loop of Meyer also extend into which other lobe of the cerebrum?
    A. parietal
    B. temporal
    C. frontal
    D. limbic
    E. prefrontal

228. In what gyrus does the loop of Meyer terminate?
- **A.** lingual
- **B.** cuneate
- **C.** cingulate
- **D.** lingual and cuneate
- **E.** postcentral

229. A bitemporal heteronymous hemianopsia is most consistent with which of these postmortem findings?
- **A.** left occipital lobotomy
- **B.** right occipital lobotomy
- **C.** total destruction of both occipital lobes
- **D.** complete destruction of the optic chiasm
- **E.** mid-sagittal incision through the optic chiasm

230. Which portion of the binocular visual maps onto the occipital pole of the cerebrum?
- **A.** upper peripheral
- **B.** lower peripheral
- **C.** upper and lower peripheral
- **D.** central
- **E.** none of the above

231. The band of Gennari occupies what layer of the cerebral cortex?
- **A.** II
- **B.** III
- **C.** IV
- **D.** V
- **E.** VI

232. The two occipital lobes intercommunicate most directly via which of these structures?
- **A.** superior longitudinal fasciculus
- **B.** cerebral peduncle
- **C.** genu of the corpus callosum
- **D.** splenium of the corpus callosum
- **E.** posterior commissure

233. Which of these values is the nearest approximation of the number of fibers in the human optic nerve?
    A. hundred thousand
    B. one million
    C. one hundred million
    D. one billion
    E. one trillion

234. Just deep to the corneal epithelium lies
    A. corneal endothelium
    B. corneal stroma
    C. Descemet's membrane
    D. Bowman's layer
    E. Schwalbe's line

235. The external nuclear layer of the retina contains nuclei of
    A. rods and cones
    B. rods but not cones
    C. cones but not rods
    D. bipolar cells
    E. amacrine cells

236. Müller cells of the retina are generally classified as
    A. glia
    B. neurons
    C. macrophages
    D. connective tissue
    E. mesenchymal derivatives

237. Hassal-Henle warts of the cornea can be found microscopically by following
    A. epithelium
    B. Bowman's layer
    C. stroma
    D. Descemet's membrane
    E. endothelium

238. The lateral terminations of both Bowman's and Descemet's membranes can be used to mark the
    A. anterior boundary of only the pathologist's limbus
    B. anterior boundary of only the histologist's limbus

    C. anterior boundary of both the pathologist's and histologist's limbus

    D. posterior boundary of only the pathologist's limbus

    E. posterior boundary of only the histologist's limbus

239. The surface area of the drainage angle of the eye is significantly increased by

    A. trabecular meshwork

    B. canal of Schlemm

    C. iridial epithelium

    D. corneal endothelium

    E. pars plicata ciliaris

240. Kuhnt's central meniscus at the optic nerve head is made up of

    A. a stratified layer of astrocytes

    B. a stratified layer of oligocytes

    C. myelinated optic nerve fibers

    D. unmyelinated optic nerve fibers

    E. cartilage

Ocular and Visual Pathway Development

241. The optic vesicles are outgrowths of the

    A. roof of the diencephalon

    B. floor of the diencephalon

    C. lateral walls of the diencephalon

    D. lateral walls of the mesencephalon

    E. roof of the telencephalon

242. The crystalline lens develops from

    A. surface ectoderm

    B. neural ectoderm

    C. mesoderm

    D. endoderm

    E. neural crest

243. The retinal pigment epithelium develops from
   A.   optic stalk
   B.   outer layer of the optic cup
   C.   inner layer of the optic cup
   D.   fetal fissure
   E.   neural crest

244. Rods and cones develop from which portion of the optic anlage?
   A.   optic stalk
   B.   outer layer of the optic cup
   C.   inner layer of the optic cup
   D.   fetal fissure
   E.   neural crest

245. The process by which the lens placode becomes the lens vesicle is
   A.   involution
   B.   evolution
   C.   replication
   D.   evagination
   E.   invagination

246. In the early stages of ocular development the space between the two layers of the optic is in direct communication with the
   A.   1st ventricle of the brain anlage
   B.   2nd ventricle of the brain anlage
   C.   3rd ventricle of the brain anlage
   D.   lateral ventricles of the brain anlage
   E.   cerebral or Sylvian aqueduct (iter) of the brain anlage

247. Developmentally and histologically, which of the following does not belong on a list with the others?
   A.   corneal stroma
   B.   iridial stroma
   C.   sclera
   D.   Bruch's membrane
   E.   lens fibers

248. The fetal hyaloid artery occupies principally the
   A.   primary vitreous body
   B.   secondary vitreous body

C. tertiary vitreous body
D. adult vitreous body
E. all of the above

249. In the human fetus, myelination of the optic nerve fibers begins at the optic chiasm and progresses distally to reach the lamina cribrosa between the
A. 7th month and 8th month
B. 3rd month and 4th month
C. 7th week and 8th week
D. 3rd week and 4th week
E. 1st month and 8th month

250. In the human fetus, when do the eyelids open (i.e., when is the palpebral fissure fully patent)?
A. 7th month
B. 7th week
C. 7th day
D. 9th month
E. the eyelids are always separated

251. In the normal human ERG, which wave's amplitude, expressed in millivolts, is below zero?
A. A
B. B
C. C
D. D
E. all of the above

252. Y retinal ganglion cells exhibit which of these features?
A. rapid conduction
B. slow conduction
C. do not project to the LGB
D. prolonged responses
E. axons show only hyperpolarization

253. With reference to neurons of the visual cortex, the term "simple cell" implies that
- **A.** the attending electroretinogram (ERG) contains only one component
- **B.** the attending electroencephalogram (EEG) consists of a single sine wave
- **C.** if the cell discharges in response to a slit of light of specific orientation in its receptive field, the cell will stop discharging if the slit is tilted
- **D.** the cell discharges only if diffuse light is presented in its receptive field
- **E.** the cell sustains its discharge when a slit of light is moved, providing that the target retains its axis of orientation

254. Meibomian glands produce what portion of the precorneal tear film?
- **A.** tear fluid proper
- **B.** oily layer
- **C.** mucoid layer
- **D.** sweat
- **E.** none of the above

255. Closing the eyelids is best explained by
- **A.** gravity
- **B.** relaxation of the orbicularis oculi
- **C.** contraction of the orbicularis oculi
- **D.** elastic recoil of the tarsal plate
- **E.** contraction of the levator palpebrae superioris

256. The sensory signals for tactile blinking are carried on branches of which cranial nerve?
- **A.** II
- **B.** III
- **C.** IV
- **D.** V
- **E.** VI

257. Sneezing can be induced by bright light as part of the dazzle response. What cranial nerve carries the afferent signal?
   A. olfactory
   B. optic
   C. glossopharyngeal
   D. vagus
   E. trigeminal

258. Normally, the osmotic pressure of human tears is isotonic to an NaCl solution of what percent?
   A. 9.0
   B. 0.9
   C. 0.09
   D. 7.0
   E. 0.7

259. The normal pH range of human tear fluid averages
   A. 10.6–12.0
   B. 7.3–7.7
   C. 1.1–4.7
   D. 8.0–8.25
   E. 0.1–0.2

260. The Schirmer test measures what feature of human tears?
   A. osmotic pressure
   B. molarity
   C. pH
   D. rate of formation
   E. pK

261. Organic solvents can rapidly penetrate and thereby seriously damage the corneal epithelium because of which component of the cells' membranes?
   A. phospholipids
   B. ATPase enzymes
   C. proteins
   D. sugars
   E. electrolytes

262. To what does Hering's law refer?
   A. innervation of the muscles used in conjugate eye movements
   B. strength of contraction of the intraocular muscles
   C. plane of the eyeball defined by the horizontal and vertical axes (X-Z)
   D. plane of the eyeball defined by the sagittal and vertical axes (Y-Z)
   E. nystagmus

263. The main fuel for ocular motility is
   A. ATP
   B. ADP
   C. UTP
   D. CTP
   E. GTP

264. In mm Hg, what is the usual range of human intraocular pressure?
   A. 80–90
   B. 1–10
   C. 10–22
   D. 1.0–2.2
   E. 0.1–0.22

265. Inhibition of corneal ATPase activity would have what effect on hydration of the corneal stroma?
   A. none
   B. rapid drop
   C. rapid rise
   D. slow decrease
   E. slow increase

266. The vitreous humor normally transmits what percentage of visible light?
   A. 20
   B. 45
   C. 4.5
   D. 100
   E. 90

267. Which of the following pathways can be employed by the crystalline lens in the metabolism of glucose?
   A. glycolytic
   B. citric acid (Krebs) cycle
   C. hexose monophosphate (pentose)
   D. sorbitol
   E. all of the above

268. Relative to the others on the list, which of these vitamins is usually in the highest concentration in the normal human lens?
   A. A
   B. B
   C. C
   D. D
   E. E

269. A Mittendorf dot is
   A. an organelle of the visual cell's myoid
   B. a form of drusen
   C. a sign of corneal vascularization
   D. a remnant of the tunica vasculosa lentis
   E. a foreign body giant cell in the vitreous body

270. Which of the following Brodmann map areas is an integral part of the occipital eye fields?
   A. 17
   B. 19
   C. 8
   D. 22
   E. 4

271. Most of the time, in what condition are the pupils of a normally sleeping person?
   A. constricted (miotic)
   B. vigorous hippus
   C. full mydriasis
   D. partial mydriasis
   E. Argyll Robertson

272. The human lateral geniculate body (equivalent to both the dorsal and ventral LGNs of many experimental animals) exhibits six layers of neurons. Which layers receive signals from the opposite retina?
    A. all 6
    B. 1–3
    C. 2, 3, 5
    D. 2, 4, 6
    E. 1, 4, 6

273. In the Dratz-Hargrave model of rhodopsin, the opsin weaves back and forth several times through the membrane of the outer segment disc; hydrophobic segments of the protein lie within the disc membrane's structure and hydrophilic portions (head, loops, and tail) protrude either to the external (cytoplasmic) or internal surfaces of the disc. Relative to the disc membrane, where is the rhodopsin's chromophore (11-*cis* retinal)?
    A. embedded with the hydrophobic portions of the opsin within the disc membrane's structure
    B. on the exterior of the disc attached to a free end of the opsin
    C. on the interior of the disc attached to a free end of the opsin
    D. on the exterior of the disc attached to a hydrophilic loop of the opsin
    E. on the interior of the disc attached to a hydrophilic loop of the opsin

274. 11-*cis* retinal is most accurately classified as what kind of congener or derivative of vitamin A?
    A. alcohol
    B. acid
    C. aldehyde
    D. ester
    E. isomer

275. Which sectors of the visual field maps contain the physiological blind spot?
    A. only the nasal inferior quadrants
    B. only the temporal inferior quadrants
    C. superior and inferior temporal quadrants
    D. superior and inferior nasal quadrants
    E. temporal crescents

Ocular Pharmacology

276. For a drug to pass through the cornea effectively, it must have
  A. polar groups
  B. a negative charge
  C. biphasic solubility
  D. a positive charge

277. When a drug in solution is instilled topically in the eye, most of the absorption into the vascular system occurs through
  A. nasolacrimal duct
  B. conjunctival vasculature
  C. lid vasculature
  D. limbal arcades

278. The advantage of using an ointment vs an ophthalmic solution in the eye is that it
  A. does not interfere with vision
  B. is less comfortable on application
  C. has less retention time
  D. has longer retention time

279. A direct-acting cholinergic agent used in glaucoma therapy is
  A. epinephrine
  B. pilocarpine
  C. physostigmine
  D. timolol

280. A sympathomimetic agent used topically to dilate the pupil is
  A. tropicamide
  B. pilocarpine
  C. cyclopentolate
  D. phenylephrine

281. A 4-year-old child is suspected of accommodative esotropia. The cycloplegic of choice is
  A. homatropine
  B. atropine
  C. scopolamine
  D. tropicamide

282. A 24-year-old white male complains of flashes and floaters. He reveals in his medical history that he is hypertensive and that he is under the care of his family physician. The mydriatic of choice should be
    A. epinephrine
    B. ephedrine
    C. tropicamide
    D. phenylephrine

283. To obtain maximum mydriasis, a synergistic effect is achieved with
    A. tropicamide and phenylephrine
    B. tropicamide and homatropine
    C. phenylephrine and epinephrine
    D. ephedrine and phenylephrine

284. Which of the following is not a systemic side effect of atropine?
    A. flushing of the cheeks
    B. dryness of mouth
    C. thirst
    D. bradycardia

285. A patient with open angle glaucoma is also asthmatic and hypertensive. The antiglaucoma drug of choice should be
    A. betaxolol
    B. epinephrine
    C. pilocarpine
    D. levobunolol

286. A patient with open angle glaucoma is also hypertensive. The antiglaucoma drug of choice should be
    A. betaxolol
    B. epinephrine
    C. timolol
    D. albuterol

287. A nonselective beta adrenergic antagonist used topically in the treatment of chronic open angle glaucoma is
A. metoprolol
B. metipranolol
C. atenolol
D. betaxolol

288. A patient with an anisocoria also reports that she experiences decreased sweating on the same side with the smaller pupil and you also observe ptosis on the same side with the miotic pupil. You instill 1 drop 1% phenylephrine in each eye. The pupil dilates significantly and the ptosis is gone. The location of the lesion is
A. central
B. preganglionic
C. postchiasmal
D. postganglionic

289. A patient with narrow anterior chamber angles is dilated with phenylephrine. You want to reverse the mydriasis with minimum risk of causing a pupil block. Your drug of choice should be
A. dapripazole
B. pilocarpine
C. clonidine
D. echothiophate

290. Which of the following is a prodrug used to lower intraocular pressure spike following ocular surgery?
A. carbachol
B. epinephrine borate
C. apraclonidine
D. timolol

291. Which of the following anesthetics also produces mydriasis?
A. benoxinate
B. cocaine
C. proparacaine
D. tetracaine

292. An agent used in the treatment of vernal and giant papillary conjunctivitis, whose mechanism of action is inhibiting the degranulation of sensitized mast cell, is
    A. chlorpheniramine
    B. flurbiprofen
    C. antazoline
    D. cromolyn sodium

293. The importance of using Rose bengal as a dye in certain ocular disease is because it
    A. stains devitalized tissue
    B. penetrates the intact corneal epithelium
    C. stains collagen
    D. is mucolytic

294. The antiinflammatory agent with the least potential of increasing intraocular pressure in susceptible patients when administered topically is
    A. fluorometholone
    B. dexamethasone
    C. prednisolone
    D. betamethasone

295. The agent that is indicated for inhibitation of ocular surgical miosis is
    A. prednisolone
    B. flurbiprofen
    C. phenylbutazone
    D. propine

296. All of the following are adverse effects of corticosteroids except
    A. increase the rate of epithelial regeneration
    B. inhibit the rate of wound healing
    C. impair fibroelastic and keratolytic activity
    D. increase intraocular pressure

297. A nonsteroidal drug that has provided a greater reduction of signs and symptoms in giant papillary conjunctivitis is
    A. suprofen
    B. flurbiprofen

C. diclofenac sodium
D. sulindac

298. Which of the following is a broadspectrum antimicrobial agent, is bactericidal, acts by inhibiting DNA gyrase, and is a topical ophthalmic agent?
A. nalidixic Acid
B. cephalothin
C. netilmicin
D. ciprofloxacin

299. A recently introduced combination antibacterial agent for topical application reported to be as effective as Neosporin and slightly better than chloramphenicol in the treatment of bacterial conjunctivitis but not against *N. gonorrhea*. This agent is
A. norfloxacin
B. neomycin—polymyxin B
C. trimethorprim—polymyxin B
D. gramicidin—polymyxin B

300. A patient has conjunctivitis due to the chlamydia specie. The drug of choice should be
A. oral ampicillin
B. oral spectinomycin
C. oral tetracycline
D. oral prednisone

301. Which of the following exhibits greater potency against *Pseudomonas aeruginosa* but is less potent against *Serratia marcescens*?
A. kanamycin
B. gramicidin
C. polymyxin B
D. tobramycin

302. Which of the following agents may be utilized for the prophylaxis of ophthalmia neonatorum in lieu of silver nitrate?
A. bacitracin
B. prednisolone
C. gramicidin
D. erythromycin

303. An antiviral that exhibits selective toxicity is
A. acycloguanosine
B. trifluorothymidine
C. iododeoxyuridine
D. cytosine arabinoside

304. An antifungal agent with a broad spectrum of action is
A. amphotericin B
B. ketoconazole
C. nystatin
D. polymyxin B

305. A fluorinated pyrimidine that possesses antifungal activity and is effective against cryptococcus species and candida species is
A. nystatin
B. amphotericin B
C. polymyxin B
D. 5-flucytosine

Answers and Discussion

Anatomy of the Eye, Ocular Adnexa, and Visual Pathways

201. (B) Active transport, i.e. In contrast, diffusion accounts for the return of aqueous humor to the blood. The latter event occurs via the canal of Schlemm.

202. (B) The inner, nonpigmented ciliary epithelium shows large concentrations of Na-K activated ATPase activity. As indicated in the answer to the previous question, the production of aqueous humor is an active event. ATP serves as the fuel for the process in question.

203. (C) They are the preganglionic parasympathetic components of cranial nerve III. As is true of autonomic nerves in general, preganglionics serve their effector organ indirectly; i.e., via their synapse with postganglionic neurons. The specific fibers at issue originate in the E-W nucleus and synapse with cells in the ciliary ganglion.

204. (A) By convention, the ciliary end of the zonule (of Zinn or suspensory ligament of the lens) is the origin. The lens capsule end is the insertion. The activity of the ciliary muscle effects the changes in tension on the zonules.

205. (E) From outside in, the choroid is made up of these four layers: 1) suprachoroid, 2) blood vessel or vascular layer, 3) choriocapil-

97

laris, and 4) Bruch's membrane. The suprachoroidea is in contact with the inner surface of the sclera. (The sclera is made up of three layers; from inside out: lamina fusca, sclera proper, and episclera.) Bruch's membrane, the inner layer of the choroid, is apposed to the retinal pigment epithelium.

206. (C) In the conventional wisdom, the ciliary muscle is made up of three parts: 1) outer, longitudinal, or meridional (Brücke's muscle); 2) middle radial or oblique; and 3) inner circular (Müller's ciliary muscle—not to be confused with Müller's palpebral muscle). The primate ciliary muscle, histologically, is smooth muscle. Birds have striated ciliary muscles.

207. (C) These remnants of the fetal vascular tunic (persistent pupillary membrane) are present in 95 percent of newborn babies. They appear in some 20 percent of adults. Some authorities attribute many permanent so-called "floaters" to them. As is true of blood vessels in general, the embryonic source of the pupillary membrane is mesenchyme.

208. (D) By convention the eye has been divided into three principal coats or tunics: 1) outer (fibrous); 2) middle (vascular, also uvea and uveal tract); 3) inner (nervous or neural). The uvea, or uveal tract, consists of the choroid, the stroma of the ciliary body, and the stroma of the iris. Rich in blood vessels, the uvea is often called the vascular coat. It is also traversed by fine nerve fibers en route to and from the front or back of the eyeball.

209. (B) The anterior chamber is deepest centrally and becomes shallower peripherally, towards the drainage angle. The volume of the posterior chamber, into which the aqueous humor is introduced, is about 0.06 ml. Normally, the pupil represents the portal through which the aqueous circulates in moving from the posterior to the anterior chamber.

210. (E) On the other hand, the anterior wall of the anterior chamber is the corneal endothelium, except at the drainage angle. There it is the trabecular meshwork. Laterally (peripherally), the anterior chamber is formed by the anterior extreme of the stroma of the ciliary body.

211. (D) Protein contributes to 33 percent of the total weight of the lens. This value is almost double that of other bodily tissues, including skeletal muscle. Normally, some 85 percent of the lens proteins are water-soluble. The latter are known as crystallins, of which three types exist in humans: alpha-, beta-, and gamma-crystallin. The water-insoluble fraction (15 percent) of lens proteins, known as lens albuminoids, increases with age and also in senile cataracts.

212. (B) The yoke table should be memorized: LR-MR; SR-IO; SO-IR. Questions involving conjugate movements of the eyes should be answered by referring to the yoke table. It can also be helpful to place the corresponding cranial nerves in the yoke table: LR(VI)–MR(III); SR(III)–IO(III); SO(IV)–IR(III).

213. (A) Working together (synergistically), the SR and IR cancel each other's movements on the horizontal axis; i.e., they mutually prevent elevation and depression (sursumduction and desursumduction). A parallel but opposite situation exists with the two obliques which, when acting together, can assist the LR in abduction of the eye.

214. (B) Sebaceous glands secrete oil. Their secretion is of the holocrine type. A holocrine secretion consists of sloughed, whole cells.

215. (A) Horner's syndrome, which might well be called sympathetic paralysis (paresis or palsy) of the eye and adnexa, consists of 1) *ptosis,* droop of the upper lid, due to flaccid paralysis of Müller's (superior) palpebral muscle (smooth muscle and, therefore, autonomically innervated); 2) *miosis,* resulting from paralysis of the dilator muscle of the iris and consequent removal of competition for the sphincter of the iris; 3) *anhidrosis* (absence of sweating), owing to the fact that sweat glands are sympathetically innervated; 4) *enophthalmus,* apparently sunken eyeball, possibly a consequence of flaccidity of both the inferior and superior palpebral muscles.

Concerning the alternate (incorrect) choices, Bell's (or facial) palsy affects cranial nerve VII. Argyll Roberston pupil is a loss of the light reflexes, both direct and consensual, but with normal pupillary constriction during the "near" or accommodative response. Classical Argyll Roberston pupil is thought to be an important indicator of neurosyphilis. Bumke's pupil is psychogenically induced widening of the pupil. Munchausen syndrome is defined as repeated (possibly obsessive) fabrication of disease symptoms to gain medical attention.

216. **(B)**   Unlike true skin (integument), whose outer layer is dead, mucous membranes such as the conjunctiva are normally covered by living cells. Like the interior surfaces of lips, the surface of the conjunctiva must be kept wet in order to remain viable. Of course, tears produce the moisture for the conjunctiva.

217. **(B)**   As Duke-Elder observes, the bulbar conjunctiva is the only superficial tissue whose constituent vessels are externally visible. The conjunctival vessels lie in the lamina propria of the conjunctiva. Unless inordinately thickened, the overlying conjunctival epithelium is transparent. (See also answer **218.**)

218. **(A)**   The conjunctival arteries come from two sources: 1) the palpebral branches of the nasal and lacrimal arteries of the lid and 2) the anterior ciliary arteries which, in the posterior part of the orbit, branch from the ophthalmic artery and also from the ophthalmic artery's muscular branches. Thus, the conjunctiva is supplied by arteries that come off their parent vessels at some distance from each other—eyelids versus the orbit, respectively.

219. **(E)**   The blood vessels of the eyeball can be divided into two systems: a) retinal, represented by the central retinal artery and vein and b) ciliary. Concerning the ciliary veins, most authorities recognize three systems: 1) vortex venous system, 2) anterior ciliary venous system, and 3) posterior ciliary venous system. The vortex system drains virtually the entire choroid, including the choriocapillaris, most of the ciliary body, and much of the iris, and collects into four large veins—the vortex veins—one serving the venous drainage of each quadrant of the eyeball. Situated just behind the equator of the eyeball, each vortex vein traverses an oblique channel, the vortex canal, through the sclera. Most uveal blood leaves the eyeball via the vortex veins.

Although much smaller than the vortex system, the anterior ciliary venous system plays a crucial rule in aqueous drainage, and thus in the regulation of intraocular pressure. The anterior ciliary venous system drains the anterior and outer parts of the ciliary body. Emissary veins from the system connect to the efferent channels of the canal of Schlemm; the ciliary system also helps drain the episcleral venous plexus.

The posterior ciliary system is small, inconstant, and is usually assigned minor functional importance.

220. (D) Dye particles placed in the anterior chamber of experimental animals can be traced into the plexuses enumerated in A, B, and C. Nevertheless, most aqueous humor appears to flow from the canal of Schlemm into the deep scleral plexus. A part of the anterior ciliary venous system (see answer **219**), the deep scleral plexus interconnects with the intrascleral and episcleral plexuses. An aqueous vein may arise from either Schlemm's canal, directly, or secondarily from the deep scleral plexus to convey aqueous humor into the episcleral veins.

221. (C) The long posterior ciliary artery reaches the major arterial circle of the iris via the uvea. The anterior ciliary artery ends by bifurcating into a smaller episcleral branch and a larger perforating branch, the latter piercing the eyeball to reach the base of the iris where the major arterial circle resides.

222. (A) These are akin to the ridges that produce fingerprints; i.e., as interdigitations between the epithelium and underlying connective tissue. The palisades of Vogt appear as radially arranged ridges 1–2 mm apart between the sclera and cornea. As is true of dermal pegs in the integument, the dermal papillae within the palisades contain small blood vessels and lymphatics.

223. (A) All sympathetic nerve fibers to the eye and its adnexa originate (have their karyosomes in) the superior cervical ganglion. The preganglionic sympathetic nerves serving active mydriasis arise in the intermediate gray horn of lower cervical and upper thoracic segments of the spinal cord. Known as the ciliospinal center of Budge, the absolute extent of the latter may vary somewhat around levels C8-T1.

224. (C) First of all, remember that fibers from the nasal hemiretina cross to the opposite side of the brain, whereas those from the temporal hemiretina remain on the same side. Now the lateral half of the LGB receives fibers from below the equator, nasal hemiretina from the contralateral eye, and temporal hemiretina from the ipsilateral eye. Of course, the opposite is true for the medial half of the LGB. As far as the fields are concerned, what lies up in the field for optical reasons projects down on the retina and thus out on the LGB. We might put the rule as follows: *field-retina-LGB: up-down-out* (or *down-up-in*). Setting these facts together, we can conclude that the lateral half of the right LGB "sees" what is in the superior temporal quadrant of the left eye's visual fields.

225. (A) See also answer **224.** The temporal (T) hemiretina of one eye is homonymous (pairs) with the nasal (N) hemiretina of the contralateral eye. Using a prime sign to denote opposite side, we might state the rule: T + N'. If we divide the retina into superior (S) and inferior (I) halves, then we can state the rule for the quadrants of a retina: TS + NS' TI + NI'. We can use the same designations for the visual fields. But appreciate that, for optical reasons (and the 180° rotation of the projection), the field's S is the retina's I.

Etymologically, hoMON'ymous means bearing the same name; i.e., belonging to the same family or group. In the case of the retinas (or visual fields), the homonymous pairs receive projections from the same half of the binocular field when the eyes are working together. Heteronymous is the opposite term. Thus, N + N' and T + T' are heteronymous. One might say that the two nasal (or temporal) halves of the retina "look" in opposite directions.

The adjective homonymous is most often used in reference to partial blindness (hemianopsia or hemianopias) involving (or potentially involving) homonymous (T + N') fields of the two eyes. Homonymous hemianopsias occur when the lesions lie posterior to the optic chiasm. A bitemporal hemianopsia (tunnel vision) is heteronymous and is most common in lesions of the middle of the optic chiasm, where the sets of nasal fibers (carrying temporal information) cross to the opposite side of the brain.

226. (B) Thus the lower lip of the calcarine fissure registers signals about the upper visual fields; vice versa for the upper lip. Extending the rule in answer **224,** we can include the visual cortex (also called area 17, calcarine cortex, and striate cortex). Thus, *field-retina-LGB-17: up-down-out-down* (or *down-up-in-up*).

227. **(B)** The portion of the optic radiations known as Meyer's temporal loop must swoop around the inferior horn of the lateral ventricle, in the temporal lobe, before turning posteriorly towards the occipital lobe. The development of Meyer's loop is related to the downward and forward growth of the temporal lobe in the fetus.

Synonyms for optic radiations, incidentally, are geniculocalcarine or geniculostriate pathways; geniculo- from the lateral geniculate body, calcarine from the calcarine fissure, striate from the term striate cortex, an alternative for primary visual cortex.

228. **(A)** The lower lip of the calcarine fissure is formed by the lingual gyrus. The cuneate gyrus forms the upper lip. The loop of Meyer, of course, terminates in the former.

229. **(E)** Nasal fibers with signals about the temporal fields cross (decussate) at the optic chiasm. A bitemporal field defect generally implicates the nasal fibers from both eyes. Both sets lie close together as they cross to the other side. Temporal fibers (thus nasal fields) do not ordinarily decussate.

230. **(D)** The cortical map area for central field is on the posterior surface of the occipital lobe; i.e., the occipital or posterior pole of the cerebrum. The anterior extreme of the primary visual (striate) cortex registers signals from the temporal extremes of the fields.

231. **(C)** In the conventional wisdom, the cerebral cortex (like the LGB) exhibits six layers. Gennari's band or line appears as a white stripe (or stria) that can be seen with the naked eye in a fresh slice through the visual cortex. The stripe accounts for the term striate cortex, frequently used to denote the visual cortex. (Many authorities also refer to the striate cortex as area 17—from Brodmann's map of the cerebral cortex). Microscopically, Gennari's band is confined strictly to the primary visual cortex and serves as a marker to delineate the latter from the immediately adjacent area 18.

232. **(D)** The corpus callosum is a massive commissure between the two cerebral hemispheres. Its genu is situated in the anterior part of the cerebrum. The splenium lies in the occipital lobe and thus

forms a potentially important bridge between the two sides of visual receiving station.

233. **(B)** About half (53 percent) of the optic nerve fibers cross at the optic chiasm while roughly the other half (47 percent) stay on the same side. Optic nerve fibers are the axons of retinal ganglion cells. Those that synapse in the LGB make up the retinogeniculate pathways or the anterior segment of the primary visual pathways.

234. **(D)** From out to in, the five main layers of the cornea are 1) epithelium, 2) Bowman's layer (membrane), 3) stroma (or tunica propria), 4) Descemet's membrane, and 5) endothelium. Tear fluid bathes the epithelium. Aqueous humor wets the endothelium.

235. **(A)** By convention, the retina is divided into ten principal layers. From outside in, they are 1) pigment epithelium, 2) receptor layer, 3) external limiting membrane, 4) outer nuclear layer (nuclei of rods and cones), 5) outer plexiform layer (synaptic), 6) inner nuclear layer (nuclei of horizontal, bipolar, amacrine, and Müller cells), 7) inner plexiform layer (synaptic), 8) ganglion cell body layer, 9) optic fiber layer (axons of retinal ganglion cells), and 10) inner limiting membrane.

236. **(A)** Müller cells are regarded as the main glial cells of the retina. Their nuclei lie in the inner nuclear layer. But their cytoplasm is extensively distributed through the retina and serves to pack intracellular spaces.

237. **(D)** Hassal-Henle warts or bodies are endothelium-covered bumps at the limbal extreme of Descemet's membrane. The warts in question increase in size and number with age. Like Descemet's membrane, they are acellular.

238. **(C)** The limbus is the junction of the cornea and sclera. Some controversy exists about its exact limits. However, in both major definitions—the pathologist's and the histologist's limbi—the limbus starts at the terminations of Bowman's and Descemet's membranes. The peripheral edge of the corneal stroma is curved and fits into a complementary groove in the anterior extreme of

the sclera. In the histologist's limbus, the latter curve extends between the terminal points of Bowman's and Descemet's membranes. In the pathologist's plan, the anterior boundary of the limbus is a perpendicular line extending between the termination points of Bowman's and Descemet's membranes; the posterior limit is parallel to and 1.5 mm behind the anterior limit and passes through the scleral spur. The pathologist's definition places the aqueous drainage system at the limbus. The histologist's plan excludes much of the drainage apparatus but takes into account the important structural and functional difference between the corneal stroma and the sclera. Thus the two systems have their advantages and disadvantages.

239. (A) The trabecular meshwork extends from the end of Descemet's membrane to the scleral spur and stroma of the ciliary body and is also attached to the stroma of the iris. Some authors divide trabecular apparatus into three parts: iris processes (or pectinate ligament), uveal trabeculae (attached to the ciliary body), and corneoscleral trabeculae.

240. (A) Astrocytes (astroglia), the main constituents of Kuhnt's central meniscus, are glia. Glia (astroglia, oligodendroglia, and microglia) are the support cells of the central—not the peripheral—nervous system and exist in the optic nerve because, developmentally and microscopically, the optic nerve and the retina are direct extensions of the brain. (See also the next answer.)

Ocular and Visual Pathway Development

241. (C) The embryonic brain vesicle (encephalon) first divides into three parts: forebrain (prosencephalon), midbrain (mesencephalon), and hindbrain (rhombencephalon). Very soon thereafter, the forebrain gives rise to a telencephalon (forerunners of the cerebrum)—a pair of anteriorly directed bulges—and a diencephalon. The hindbrain also subdivides into a metencephalon (forerunner of the pons and cerebellum) and myelencephalon (future medulla).

The diencephalon is the posterior portion of the forebrain. It is identifiable early in embryonic life by virtue of the optic vesicles growing off its lateral walls.

242. (A) The lens begins as a placode or thickening in the surface ectoderm and invaginates into the optic cup, rounding up eventually into a hollow vesicle. The space in the lens rudiment is eventually obliterated.

243. (B) The leading edge of the optic vesicle, after reaching the surface ectoderm (and inducing the differentiation of the lens placode) invaginates, forms the inner layer of the optic cup, and gives rise to the neural retina. The cavity of the original optic vesicle is eventually obliterated as the inner layer collapses onto and apposes the outer layer. The outer layer of the cup is destined to become the retinal pigment epithelium. The inner layer produces the other layers of the retina. The lip of the cup marks the site of the future ora serrata. Cells on both the outer and inner edges of the rim grow forward to produce the two layers of epithelium of both the ciliary body and the iris. Invading mesenchymal cells (possibly of mesectodermal origin—see answer **247**) surround the outer layer of the optic cup (future retinal pigment epithelium) and cover the future ciliary and iris (iridial) epithelium; these mesenchymal cells produce the uvea (middle or vascular tunic). A subsequent mesenchymal invasion forms the outer tunic (sclera). The dogma is that iridial muscles are derived from the cells (ectoderm) that grow forward from the rim optic cup.

244. (C) See answer **243**. *Anlage* (pl. anlagen) is the embryonic rudiment of an organ. Thus the neural tube is the *anlage* of the central nervous system. The two surfaces of the rim of the optic cup are the *anlagen* of the iris and the ciliary epithelia.

245. (E) The answer is effectively given in **242** but much development depends on the processes denoted by the alternative choices. *Involution,* retrogression, is an important and often essential feature of organ development (e.g., see **248** below). Many developmental events mimic biological *evolution. Replication* of genes, chromosomes, and cells occurs in growth and differentiation. *Evagination,* the opposite of *invagination,* occurs normally in some instances but can result in developmental anomalies.

246. (C) The 3rd ventricle is the space of the diencephalon. The diencephalon, in turn, is the source of the optic vesicle. As development progresses, the lumina of the optic stalk and optic vesicle are obliterated.

247. **(E)** Research in more recent years has provided evidence to the effect that cranial neural crest cells (of neuroectodermal origin) join with mesenchyme of mesodermal origin to form mesectoderm. The latter mixture, as mesenchyme—morphologically speaking—produces much of the connective tissue of the eye, the histological category into which fall the items in A–D. The lens, however, is of ectodermal origin and, as already indicated, is produced from the lens placode (see answer 242). The term lens "fiber" means lens "cell," incidentally; the usage is similar to that with muscle, where muscle *fiber* is tantamount to muscle *cell*.

248. **(A)** Vitreal development is closely associated with the advent, differentiation, and disappearance of the hyaloid artery and its branches. The hyaloid vessels develop in the primary vitreous body, involute in the secondary vitreous body, and are ideally gone from the tertiary vitreous body, being represented there as the centrally located Cloquet's canal.

249. **(A)** Only after myelination can the optic nerve fibers propagate impulses efficiently enough to serve in vision. Note, though, that the optic vesicle is already visible in the human embryo at 26 days after fertilization. Myelination in the CNS, including the optic nerve, is provided by oligodendroglia (oligocytes). The latter glial cells are the CNS cousins of the Schwann cells that form the myelin sheaths in the PNS (peripheral nervous system).

250. **(A)** During the 10th week of development in humans, the rudiments of the eyelids have fused to form the lid adhesion. The developing lids normally remain sealed until the 7th month when separation, or lid dysjunction, occurs. The lid adhesion may be essential for normal palpebral morphogenesis (organ differentiation).

251. **(A)** ERG is the universally recognized abbreviation for electroretinogram, which is a record of light-evoked retinal action currents. The normal ERG typically exhibits four waves which, in order of appearance, are most often designated A, B, C, and D. The A wave is a quick pulse of negative millivoltage and repre-

sents electrophysiological activity in the membranes of the stimulated photoreceptor cells. The B wave, which typically peaks at or above 0.6 millivolts, is generally believed to represent principally the inner nuclear layer. The C wave, a relatively broad band of millivoltage (peak at about 0.5 mV), is thought to be initiated by the photoreceptors but to be principally a function of the retinal pigment epithelium. The D wave occurs upon withdrawl of the stimulus. Because the recordings are made at the surface of the eye, electroretinography can be a noninvasive procedure.

252. (A) Three physiologically distinct retinal ganglion cells have been identified in the mammalian retina: X, Y, and W. The Y cells conduct more rapidly than the X variety. W cells conduct relatively slowly and project only to the pretectal area and the superior colliculus.

253. (C) Complex cells of the visual cortex are those that continue firing, until the orientation of the stimulus is made more complicated. Hypercomplex cells continue to show activity when changes in the stimulus cause the complex cells to cease.

254. (B) Meibomian glands exists in the tarsal plates of the eyelids. Modified sebaceous glands, they (with some help from the accessory sebaceous glands of Zeis) are the principal source of the oily layer of the tear film. The tear fluid proper is produced by the main lacrimal gland and the accessory lacrimal glands (of Krause and of Wolfring). The mucoid, or deep layer of the tear film, is produced by goblet cell of the conjunctiva.

255. (C) The orbicularis oculi muscle, like all muscles of facial expression, is innervated by cranial nerve VII, the facial nerve. Thus, one consequence of Bell's facial palsy can be the inability to close the eyelid on the affected side of the face. Of course, blinking is essential for the spreading of the tear film (see also answer 254).

256. (D) The trigeminal nerve (cranial nerve V) is the general somatic sensory nerve for most of the face, the exceptions being skin inside the tragus and on the concha (outer ear), innervated by sensory portions of cranial nerves VII and X, respectively. The name *trigeminal* derives from the fact that the nerve in question

consists of three divisions (has three origins): ophthalmic (V-1), maxillary (V-2), and mandibular (V-3). V-1 innervates the eye and the ocular adnexa.

257. **(B)** Light is the stimulus. Thus the sensory information is delivered to the central nervous system by the optic nerve; i.e., cranial nerve II. The circuitry is unknown.

258. **(B)** This is true of most body fluids. As indicated above (**254**), glands produce the components of the tear film. However, the gland cells obtain NaCl from the blood plasma.

259. **(B)** The pH of tears is a function of its composition. In mEq/L (milequivalents per liter), the major electrolyte content of human tears is: bicarbonate ion 26, Cl⁻ 135, K⁺ 15–29, Na⁺ 142. Tears also contain glucose (2.5–4.1 mg/100 ml). Of the proteins present, 60 percent is albumin and 21 to 25 percent of total protein is the antibacterial agent, lysozyme. Immunoglobins are also found among tear proteins.

260. **(D)** The Schirmer test measures tear formation. The test is conducted with a 30 × 5 mm rectangle of No. 41 Whatman filter paper. A 5 mm tab, folded over at one end, is placed in the inferior conjunctival sac for 5 minutes. The moist area, minus the tab, is then measured. The normal range for young adults is 10–25 mm.

261. **(A)** Organic solvents disrupt cell membranes by dispersing, hydrophobically, interacting components. The cell membranes in question belong principally to the corneal epithelium of which there are three layers: 1) surface cell layer, 2 strata of squamous but living cells; 2) wing cell layer, 2 to 3 tiers of polygonal cells, some of which, in profile, resemble a hovering bat; 3) basal cell layer, a single layer of tall cells whose basement membrane closely adheres to Bowman's layer.

262. **(A)** Herring's law is applicable to conjugate eye movements. Also called the law of equal innervation, it states that in all voluntary conjugate eye movements, equal and simultaneous innervation flows from the oculogyric centers to the muscles responsible for establishing the direction of the gaze.

263. (A) ATP is the general fuel for all muscular activity. Ocular motility is a direct function of the collective activities of the extraocular muscles. The extraocular muscles are derived embryologically from the myotomes of somites and, consequently, look and act like somitic muscles in general.

264. (C) Some authors give 15–16 mm Hg as the most commonly measured intraocular pressure. At any rate, the continuous production and elimination of aqueous humor is closely associated with changes in intraocular pressure. Intraocular hypertension can occur as a result of 1) blockage in the aqueous outflow and drainage system; 2) increased extraocular venous pressure, reflected to the venus plexi at the limbus, and 3) accelerated aqueous production, secondary to high blood pressure.

265. (C) When ATPase inhibitors (such as oubain) were placed in the conjunctival sac or injected into the anterior chamber of rabbits, the challenged corneas underwent rapid over-hydration. The corneal stroma has a higher Na^+ content than plasma, aqueous, and tears. With the sudden failure of the sodium pump, which would occur following inhibition of the associated ATPase, the osmotic environment would demand a rapid and immediate inrush of water to establish equilibrium between the corneal stroma and its environment. Over-hydration can cause disruption of the internal organization of the cornea and an attending loss of transparency.

266. (E) Although the vitreous humor (or body) is 98–99.7 percent water, its rheological (physical) state in healthy young adults is 80 percent gel ("solid") and 20 percent sol (liquid). The gel vitreous humor resembles the matrix of loose fibrous connective tissue: randomly arranged collagen fibrils in an amorphous ground substance of Na-hyaluronate (hyaluronic acid) molecules. The sol (liquid) vitreous humor contains hyaluronate but lacks collagen fibrils.

267. (E) In the lens, some 80 percent of glucose appears to be metabolized through the Embden-Meyerhof glycolytic pathway, with the end-product being lactic acid. Most of the lactic acid is removed mainly via the aqueous humor, which serves as the circulatory medium for the lens. Some 5 percent of the glucose in the lens is used in the citric acid cycle (TCA or Krebs). The hexose monophosphate, or pentose pathway, is reported to use some 15 percent of the lens glucose. The hexose monophosphate is the source of ribose sugars (for nucleic acid synthesis) and also contributes to other metabolic needs of the lens. The sorbitol pathway can come into play when excess glucose accumulates in the lens (as in diabetes mellitus).

268. (C) Vitamin C is ascorbate (ascorbic acid). While uncertainty exists about the precise role of ascorbate in lens metabolism, circumstantial evidence suggests that it may assist oxidation-reduction (redox) reactions, alone or in conjunction with glutathione.

269. (D) The Mittendorf dot is one of the congenital anomalies that can degrade the transparency of the lens. Generally on the back of the lens, and also known as spurious posterior polar cataract, the Mittendorf dot is an unresorbed vestige of the embryonic tunica vasculosa lentis. Like the fetal hyaloid artery, the tunica vasculosa usually disappears during the 7th intrauterine month.

270. (B) The occipital eye fields lie in Brodmann map areas 18 and 19. This cortical territory is associated with involuntary, smooth, and conjugate pursuit movements of the eyes. The other type of conjugate eye movement, saccadic (jerky or stepwise), can be either involuntary (as in the correctional phase of nystagmus) or willful (as in the learned, stepwise excursions of the eyes during reading). The frontal eye fields, in Brodmann area 8, is the territory of the cerebral cortex implicated in saccades.

271. (A) Pupils can contract to a diameter of less than 1 mm and dilate to over 9 mm. During sleep, the pupils can transiently widen during dreams or following loud noises or other sensory stimulation (e.g., tickling the feet). But extensive, permanent pupillary dilation in a nonconscious person is an indication of parasympathetic collapse and is usually a sign of life-threatening brain damage. The normally constricted pupils at sleep may be regarded as indicative of sympathetic relaxation. Since the sphincter of the iris is parasympathetically innervated, its contraction is unchecked when the sympathetically innervated dilator muscle relaxes.

272. **(E)** Thus, LGB layers 1, 4, and 6 receive fibers from the nasal hemiretina of the opposite (contralateral) eye. Layers 2, 3, and 5 receive fibers from the temporal hemiretina of the eye on the same (ipsilateral) side. The layers are numbered from inferior to superior. The perikaryia (cell bodies) of cells in layers 1 and 2 are much larger than those of the other layers. For this reason, 1 and 2 are called the magnocellular layers and 3 through 6 are called the parvocellular layers.

273. **(A)** The phospholipids of the disc membrane set the stage for the entire molecular assembly and, in the cell (aqueous environment), determine which parts of the visual pigment reside in the interior or exterior.

274. **(C)** Retin*al* could also be called vitamin A aldehyde. Dietary vitamin A is the alcohol version (retinol) of the class (retinoids). The differences involve the terminal group on the molecule: CHO on retinal, CH_2OH for the tail of retinol. 11-*cis* retinal, the chromophore of visual pigment molecules, is a geometric isomer of *all trans* retinal. The latter configuration is assumed by retinal following the light-induced dissociation of each visual pigment molecule into one opsin (protein) and one chromophore (retinal).

275. **(C)** The blind spot corresponds to the optic disc; i.e., to the optic nerve head, where the retina lacks visual receptors. The optic disc is ovoid, lies somewhat displaced off-center but on the equator and in the nasal hemiretina. Therefore, when projected on a visual field map, the blind spot lies in the temporal field of each eye. Harrington and Drake note that the normal blind spot is very constant: its center is 15.5° temporal to the fixation point and 1.5° below the horizontal meridian, its height is 7.5°, and its width is 5.5°.

Ocular Pharmacology

276. **(C)** Compounds that are capable of exhibiting biphasic solubility can penetrate the cornea very effectively. This is dictated by the structure of the cornea, in which the epithelium and endothelium favor lipophilic substances while the stroma favors hydrophilic substances.

277. (A) Most of the drug that enters the systemic circulation when it is instilled topically is absorbed through the nasolacrimal duct.

278. (D) Ointments are suspensions in a thick oleaginous base. As a result of the increased viscosity, it is retained in the cul-de-sac for a longer period of time—until the base melts. Thus, contact time between the drug and the ocular tissues is increased.

279. (B) Pilocarpine, a direct-acting cholinergic or parasympathetic agent, when instilled topically, can reduce the intraocular pressure in patients with glaucoma. It acts by increasing the outflow facility.

280. (D) Phenylephrine is a direct-acting sympathomimetic agent used to produce mydriasis. It is predominantly an alpha-1 adrenoceptor stimulator. It produces mydriasis by stimulating the dilator muscle of the iris.

281. (B) Atropine is indicated for cycloplegic refraction in children less than 5 years of age in whom accommodative esotropia is suspected. Atropine, being the most potent of the cycloplegics, is required because children of that age have the greatest amount of accommodation.

282. (C) In patients with known hypertension, tropicamide is the mydriatic of choice because it does not possess the ability to cause an increase in the blood pressure, which is a contraindication for this patient.

283. (A) In order to obtain maximum mydriasis for internal examination of the eye, both tropicamide and phenylephrine must be instilled topically. The resulting maximum mydriasis obtained is due to the synergistic effect of tropicamide and phenylephrine.

284. (D) Atropine is an anticholinergic drug that blocks the cholinergic or parasympathetic receptors. The adverse effects from systemic absorption of atropine are dry mouth, flushing of the cheeks, thirst, and tachycardia.

285. (A) Patients who have been diagnosed as glaucomatous but in addition are asthmatics should not be prescribed a nonselective beta blocker because it can be fatal. However, a cardioselective beta adrenergic blocker such as betaxolol should be the drug of choice.

286. **(C)** Patients who have glaucoma and are hypertensive may be safely prescribed a nonselective beta blocker such as timolol (Timoptic). In addition to the intraocular pressure lowering effects, timolol can also decrease blood pressure and heart rate, which will benefit the hypertensive patient.

287. **(B)** Metipranolol is a nonselective beta adrenergic blocker used topically to treat chronic open angle glaucoma. Its pharmacological profile is very similar to the other nonspecific beta blockers. However, it is available in an 0.3 percent ophthalmic solution.

288. **(D)** Phenylephrine 1% will dilate the sympathetically denervated pupil if the lesion involves the postganglionic neuron of the sympathetic nervous system. The resultant effect of the postganglionic lesion is the development of denervation hypersensitivity.

289. **(A)** Dapriprazole is an alpha blocker indicated for the reversal of mydriasis by phenylephrine, an alpha-1 agonist. It has been shown that reversal of phenylephrine mydriasis with pilocarpine can precipitate a pupil block glaucoma.

290. **(C)** Apraclonidine, an alpha-2 agonist, is indicated in the prevention of postsurgical intraocular pressure spikes after laser trabeculoplasty, iridotomy, and YAG capsulotomy.

291. **(B)** Cocaine, a local anesthetic, is also an indirect-acting adrenergic agonist. On topical instillation, it produces anesthesia and mydriasis. It produces mydriasis by inhibiting the reuptake of norepinephrine.

292. **(D)** Cromolyn sodium is used in the treatment of vernal conjunctivitis and giant papillary conjunctivitis. It acts by inhibiting the degranulation of mast cells and thus prevents the release of histamine and other chemical mediators of inflammation.

293. **(A)** Rose Bengal selectively stains devitalized corneal and conjunctival epithelium a brilliant red color that lasts for hours. It

stains cells and their nuclei. The most important clinical application is in the diagnosis of keratoconjunctivitis sicca.

294. **(A)** Fluorometholone, a steroidal antiinflammatory agent, is less likely to produce an increase in intraocular pressure when administered topically. It has been shown that in patients treated with dexamethasone and fluorometholone suspensions, fluorometholone demonstrated a lower propensity to increase IOP than dexamethasone.

295. **(B)** Flurbiprofen, a nonsteroidal antiinflammatory agent, has been shown to inhibit the miosis during the course of cataract surgery. Its mechanism of action is thought to be through the inhibition of the enzyme cyclooxygenase.

296. **(A)** Corticosteroids decrease the rate of epithelial regeneration wound healing, fibroblastic and keratolytic activity, and a propensity to increase IOP in susceptible individuals.

297. **(A)** Suprofen, a nonsteroidal antiinflammatory agent, has been shown to be effective in the management of giant papillary conjunctivitis. In studies, it has been shown to produce a greater decrease in signs and symptoms in GPC.

298. **(D)** Ciprofloxacin is a broad spectrum bactericidal agent effective against both gram-positive and gram-negative microorganisms. It is one of the newer antibiotics of the fluoroquinolone class. Its mechanism of action is through the inhibition of the enzyme DNA gyrase.

299. **(C)** Topical trimethoprim—polymyxin B (Polytrim) is indicated in the treatment of surface ocular infections caused by susceptible strains. It was reported to be as effective as Neosporin.

300. **(C)** Tetracyclines are currently the treatment of choice in chlamydial infections. However, they are contraindicated in children less than 12 years of age and in pregnant mothers.

301. **(D)** Tobramycin, an aminoglycoside antibiotic, has been shown to be more effective against *Pseudomonas aeruginosa* than gentamicin in vitro but less effective against *Serratia marcescens* than gentamicin.

302. (D) Erythromycin is effective for prophylaxis for gonococcal ophthalmia neonatorum. It is less irritating and more effective than silver nitrate.

303. (A) The affinity of acyclovir for herpes virus-encoded thymidine kinase is greater than for the mammalian thymidine kinase.

304. (B) Ketoconazole, an imidazole antifungal agent, is highly active against a broad spectrum of fungi. It is the drug of choice for the treatment of nonmeningeal blastomycosis, histoplasmosis, and coccidioidomycosis in patients who are immunologically competent.

305. (D) Flucytosine is a fluorinated pyrimidine. It has clinically useful activity against *Cryptococcus neoformans, Candida species, Torulopsis glabrata,* and the agents of chromomycosis.

References

1. Allinson RW, Geibee DS, Bieber S, Hodes BL. *Reversal of Mydriasis by Dapriprazole.* Ann Ophthalmol 1990;22:131–138.
2. Bartlett JD, Jaanus SD. *Clinical Ocular Pharmacology.* 2nd ed. Boston: Butterworths; 1989.
3. Carpenter M, Sutin J. *Human Neuroanatomy.* 8th ed. Baltimore and London: Williams and Wilkins; 1983.
4. Duke-Elder S. *System of Ophthalmology.* vol. II. St. Louis: CV Mosby; 1961.
5. Gilman AG, Rall TW, Nies AS, Taylor P. *The Pharmacological Basis of Therapeutics.* 8th ed. New York: Pergamon Press; 1990.
6. Harrington DO, Drake MV. The Visual Fields: *Text and Atlas of Clinical Perimetry.* 6th ed. St. Louis: CV Mosby; 1990.
7. Hart WM. *Adler's Physiology of the Eye.* 9th ed. St. Louis: CV Mosby; 1992.
8. Hogan MJ, Alvarado JA, Weddell JE. *Histology of the Human Eye.* Philadelphia: WB Saunders; 1971.
9. Jakobiec FA. *Ocular Anatomy, Embryology and Teratology.* Philadelphia: Harper and Row; 1982.
10. Lamberts DW, Potter DE. *Clinical Ophthalmic Pharmacology.* Boston: Little, Brown and Co; 1987.
11. Martin JH. *Neuroanatomy.* New York: Elsevier; 1989.
12. Stedman TL. *Stedman's Medical Dictionary.* 25th ed. Baltimore: Williams and Wilkins; 1990.
13. Stryer L. *Biochemistry.* 3rd ed. New York: Freeman; 1988.

3

Theoretical, Ophthalmic, and Physiological Optics

Geometrical Optics

306. An opaque object 14 cm high is placed 30 cm in front of an extended source of light 20 cm high. Where must a screen be placed so that none of it is in total shadow?
  A. beyond 61 cm behind the object
  B. beyond 70 cm behind the object
  C. beyond 61 cm behind the source
  D. all of the above
  E. none of the above

307. If a plane mirror moves towards a man, his image
    A. moves away from the mirror at twice the rate
    B. moves toward the mirror at the same rate
    C. moves toward the mirror at twice the rate
    D. remains stationary
    E. none of the above

308. The top of a vertical plane mirror 2½ ft high is 4½ ft from the floor. The eye of a person standing in front of the mirror is 5 ft from the floor and 3½ ft from the mirror. What are the distances from the wall on which the mirror hangs to the nearest and farthest points on the floor that are visible in the mirror?
    A. 47 in. and 482 in.
    B. 28 in. and 378 in.
    C. 14 in. and 189 in.
    D. 56 in. and 756 in.
    E. none of the above

mirror Pwr
-2n/r

309. An object is placed between two mirrors that are inclined at an angle of 31 degrees. Where must the object be placed to form 12 images?
    A. only in the central 10 degrees
    B. only within 6 degrees of either mirror
    C. only on the bisector of the angle
    D. only in the central 19 degrees
    E. none of the above

310. Determine the angle of deviation for a ray that is incident at 25 degrees on a plane-refracting surface separating air from plastic index 1.49.
    A. 13° 27′
    B. 16° 33′
    C. 29° 59′
    D. 8° 31′
    E. none of the above

Right Answer

311. Determine the critical angle of refraction for diamond glass of index 2.4173 when in contact with water.
    A. 57° 46′
    B. 33° 28′
    C. 39° 23′

D. 61° 27′

E. none of the above

312. A glass cube 2 in. on a side has a critical angle of 38° 7′ when in contact with air. A ray of light incident on one side at 45° passes through the cube and out the opposite side. What is the lateral displacement of the ray?
    A. 0.182 in.
    B. 1.456 in.
    C. 0.728 in.
    D. 0.364 in.
    E. none of the above

313. An object is observed through a tank of water with vertical plane glass walls. The line of sight is normal to the sides of the tank, and the object is 20 cm from one side and 60 cm from the opposite side. What is the apparent location of the object? (Neglect the effect of the thin glass walls.)
    A. 50 cm from the near side
    B. 40 cm from the near side
    C. 38 cm from the near side
    D. 80 cm from the near side
    E. none of the above

314. A prism made of glass whose critical angle is 38° 41′ in air is found to have a minimum deviation of 46° 16′. Find the largest apical angle a prism made of the above glass may have and still allow light to pass through it.
    A. 67° 22′
    B. 144° 44′
    C. 38° 41′
    D. 77° 22′
    E. none of the above

315. Light is incident normally on a 27° prism of index 1.49. What is the total deviation produced?
    A. 56° 11′
    B. 15° 34′
    C. 22° 33′
    D. 42° 34′
    E. 18° 50′

316. The distance between a point object and the eye of an observer is 75 cm. A plate of glass 25 cm thick, index 1.500, is interposed midway between the object and eye with its two parallel surfaces perpendicular to the line of sight. Find the curvature of the wave front spreading out from the object when it reaches the eye.
  A. −1.50 D
  B. −3.33 D
  C. −1.87 D
  D. −5.00 D
  E. −2.33 D

317. Light falling on a concave surface separating glass of index 1.500 from air is convergent towards a point 25 cm beyond the vertex. The curvature of the surface is 4.00 D. Find the point where the refracted rays cross the optical axis.
  A. +12.5 cm
  B. +11.1 cm
  C. −40.00 cm
  D. +6.25 cm
  E. +33.2 cm

318. A small air bubble in a glass sphere of 2-in. radius, viewed so that the bubble and the center of the sphere are in line with the eye, appears to be 3/4 in. from the point of the surface nearest the eye. What is its actual distance, assuming an index of 1.500 for the glass?
  A. 0.947 in.
  B. 0.615 in.
  C. 1.90 in.
  D. 0.475 in.
  E. 1.25 in.

319. The power of a planoconvex lens whose index is 1.490 is +10.00 D in air. When submerged in liquid of index 1.650, its power is
  A. +2.25 D
  B. +1.60 D
  C. −2.50 D
  D. −1.60 D
  E. −3.27 D

320. The angular distance of a star from the optical axis of a curved refracting surface that separates air from glass of index 1.750 is 10.5 degrees. The surface is convex and has a curvature of 10 diopters. Find the linear displacement of the star's image from the axis.

    A. 48.1 mm
    B. 13.33 mm
    C. 7.5 mm
    D. 18.53 mm
    E. 24.7 mm

321. A real image formed by a thin lens in air is one-third the size of its real object. When the lens is moved 4.724 in., the image size doubles. What is the focal length of the thin lens?

    A. +4.331 in.
    B. +3.543 in.
    C. +2.657 in.
    D. +0.477 in.
    E. +3.150 in.

322. The focal length of a plano convex crown glass lens in air is 10 in. What will be the focal length of the lens in water if the refractive indices of air, glass, and water are 1, 3/2, and 4/3?

    A. 10 in.
    B. 15 in.
    C. 40 in.
    D. 7.5 in.
    E. 21 in.

323. The distance between a real object and its real image formed by a thin lens is 35 in. If the image is four times as large as the object, find the position of the object and the focal length of the lens.

    A. −7 in., $f' = 6.54$ in.
    B. −5 in., $f' = 7.27$ in.
    C. −7 in., $f' = 5.60$ in.
    D. +7 in., $f' = 5.90$ in.
    E. none of the above

324. The minimum distance possible between a virtual object and its virtual image for any negative lens is equal to
A. 2f'
B. 4f'
C. f'/2
D. f'/4
E. none of the above

325. A planoconvex round lens has a center thickness of 15.10 mm. When viewed from the flat side with a measuring microscope, the center of the lens appears to be only 10.10 mm thick. What is the index of refraction of the glass?
A. 1.5230
B. 1.3376
C. 1.4950
D. 1.6161
E. none of the above

326. A converging lens of focal length 10 cm is placed at a distance of 4 cm in front of a plane mirror that is normal to the axis of the lens. Where must an *eye* be placed in front of the lens so that it may see its own image at infinity?
A. −1.66 cm
B. −0.166 cm
C. −16.6 cm
D. −166 cm
E. −1666 cm

327. An object 35 mm tall is situated 266⅔ mm in front of a concave mirror whose curvature is 3.75 D. Determine the distance between the object and its conjugate image.
A. 0.00 mm
B. 13.33 mm
C. 26.67 mm
D. 35.55 mm
E. 37.50 mm

328. An object 3 cm high is placed 10 cm in front of a convex mirror of 60 cm radius. Find the position and size of the image.
A. +6.4 cm and −1.8 cm high
B. −6.4 cm and −1.8 cm high

C. +7.5 cm and +2.25 cm high
D. +5.6 cm and +3.6 cm high
E. none of the above

329. Compare a round plano side view mirror of 4.0 cm diameter to a convex side mirror with a curvature of 5.0 D and diameter of 4.0 cm. What is the difference in the extent of an object (a fire truck) 6.0 m from each mirror that can be seen, after reflection, by a driver whose eyes are 80 cm from each mirror?
   A. 120 cm
   B. 240 cm
   C. 360 cm
   D. 400 cm
   E. 0.00 cm

330. The power of a curved convex mirror is 8.00 D. When a lens clock calibrated for an index of 1.500 is applied to the surface, it gives a reading of
   A. −2.00 D
   B. +2.25 D
   C. +6.00 D
   D. +2.00 D
   E. −6.00 D

331. The radius of a convex cylindrical refracting surface separating air from crown glass of index 1.500 is 10 cm. What is its focal power in a normal section inclined to the axis of the cylinder at an angle of 50°?
   A. +6.57 D
   B. +2.93 D
   C. +3.47 D
   D. +5.00 D
   E. +4.00 D

332. The position of the circle of least confusion of a spherocylindrical lens, when incident light is parallel, is given by
   A. $2/(F_{max} + F_{min})$
   B. $F_{max} + F_{min}$
   C. $(F_{max} + F_{min})/2$
   D. all of the above
   E. none of the above

333. A spherocylindrical lens placed 20 in. from a point source produces a vertical line image on a screen placed 10 in. from the lens. When the source is positioned 20 in. farther away from the lens, the image screen shows a circular image having a diameter of 0.2 in. Find the power and diameter of the lens in the vertical meridian.
  A. +4.00 D and 0.8 in.
  B. +6.00 D and 0.4 in.
  C. +4.00 D and 1.0 in.
  D. +6.00 D and 1.0 in.
  E. +6.00 D and 0.8 in.

334. An achromatic doublet with a power of +6.50 D is to be made from the lenses with the following characteristics. What would be the powers of the individual components of the doublet?

	Lens A	Lens B
Mean index	1.5110	1.6890
Mean dispersion	0.00805	0.02230

  A. +13.12; −7.12
  B. +10.00; −4.00
  C. +12.66; −6.16
  D. +7.42; −1.42
  E. +13.12; −4.00

335. Longitudinal spherical aberration of a thin lens of constant form and power
  A. increases as the square of the aperture
  B. is independent of aperture size
  C. decreases as the square of the aperture
  D. decreases as the cube of the aperture
  E. none of the above

336. The top of a drafting table, inclined at an angle of 27 degrees with the horizontal, is illuminated by a single lamp suspended 4.6 ft. directly above its center. If the illuminance on the table directly beneath the lamp is 13.5 ft-C, what is the candle power of the lamp?
  A. 125 cp
  B. 222 cp

C. 321 cp
D. 148 cp
E. 175 cp

337. A neutral density filter has an optical density of 2.30. What is its transmission (T) and opacity (O)?
A. T = 0.1; O = 10
B. T = 0.01; O = 100
C. T = 2.0; O = 0.50
D. T = 0.005; O = 200
E. none of the above

338. The objective and eyepiece of a telescope are separated by a distance equal to the
A. optical tube length
B. sum of the second focal lengths of the two components
C. sum of the first focal lengths of the two components
D. least distance of distinct vision
E. none of the above

339. It is necessary to build an astronomical telescope of 5× magnification using a +2.50 D objective lens. Also, an additional plus lens (to be attached to the objective) for a working distance of 12.5 cm is required. What power eyepiece is required and what will be the magnification of the system with the additional plus lens?
A. +24 D and 12×
B. +12 D and 6×
C. +18 D and 12×
D. +36 D and 4×
E. +12.50 and 10×

340. The magnification of a telescope may be determined experimentally by
A. objective diameter/eyepiece diameter
B. exit pupil diameter/entrance pupil diameter
C. eyepiece diameter/objective diameter
D. entrance pupil diameter/exit pupil diameter
E. all of the above

341. A compound microscopic system has an ocular of −50 D and an objective of +25 D. The separation between the two optical elements is 30 mm. Utilizing 40 cm as the standard distance of distinct vision, what would be the apparent magnification produced by this system?
    A. 5.0×
    B. 8.0×
    C. 2.5×
    D. 4.0×
    E. none of the above

342. The stop or stop-image subtending the smallest angle at a given object point is the
    A. entrance port
    B. exit pupil
    C. entrance pupil
    D. exit port
    E. field of view

343. The image of the field stop formed in object space is the
    A. entrance port
    B. exit port
    C. entrance pupil
    D. exit pupil
    E. field of view

344. The field of view of any instrument is
    A. usually taken as the total field
    B. independent of the size of the entrance port
    C. equal to the field of full illumination
    D. dependent on the size of the entrance pupil
    E. usually taken as the field of one-half illumination

345. The total field of view of a system
    A. has a constant and uniform illumination
    B. gradually decreases to zero illumination at its outer portion
    C. has an illumination equal to one-half that of the object
    D. never has an illumination of less than half that of the object
    E. none of the above

346. The actual field of view of an optical instrument is equal to
  A. the apparent field of view times the magnifying power of the instrument
  B. the apparent field of view divided by the magnifying power of the instrument
  C. the apparent field of view divided by the square of the magnifying power of the instrument
  D. all of the above
  E. none of the above

347. The greatest distance an image screen may be moved away from the theoretical image position without the image appearing unsharp is called
  A. the depth of focus
  B. the hyperfocal distance
  C. the aperture ratio
  D. the depth of field
  E. 2f′

348. The lens of a camera has a diameter of 3.85 cm and a focal length of +12.5 cm. What is its f/number?
  A. 0.4
  B. 62.5
  C. 3.25
  D. 7.5
  E. none of the above

349. The correct exposure for an aperture of f/8 is 0.02 seconds. What exposure would be required with an aperture of f/12?
  A. 0.045 sec
  B. 0.015 sec
  C. 0.150 sec
  D. 2.000 sec
  E. none of the above

350. The light transmitting power of a pair of 7×35 binoculars is
  A. 5
  B. 25
  C. 15
  D. 10
  E. 40

351. An optically centered system consists of an object −20 cm from a +10.00 D lens of 2 cm diameter, a −10.00 D lens of 2 cm diameter +5 cm from the +10.00 D lens, and another +10.00 D lens of 2 cm diameter +10 cm from the first +10.00 D lens. Find the location of the entrance pupil and entrance port in relation to the −10.00 D lens and the angular total field of view.
- **A.** entrance pupil = −6 cm; entrance port = +25 cm; field = 18° 32′
- **B.** entrance pupil = −5 cm; entrance port = +25 cm; field = 23° 14′
- **C.** entrance pupil = −5 cm; entrance port = +45 cm; field = 11° 25′
- **D.** entrance pupil = −7 cm; entrance port = +40 cm; field = 10° 13′
- **E.** none of the above

352. An optical system consists of an object −50 cm from a +10 D lens of 40 mm diameter, a 10 mm diameter aperture +5 cm from the +10 D lens, and another +10 D lens (20 mm diameter) located +8.33 cm from the first lens. Find the location of the aperature stop and field stop in relation to the first +10 D lens, and also find the angular field of half illumination.
- **A.** aperture stop = 0.00 cm; field stop = +8.33 cm; field = 22° 37′
- **B.** aperture stop = +5.00 cm; field stop = +8.33 cm; field = 17° 4′
- **C.** aperture stop = 0.00 cm; field stop = +5.00 cm; field = 8° 32′
- **D.** aperture stop = +8.33 cm; field stop = 0.00 cm; field = 4° 35′
- **E.** none of the above

353. The distance between the symmetrical planes of a thin lens is equivalent to
- **A.** −xx′
- **B.** the reduced second focal length
- **C.** C F
- **D.** 4f′
- **E.** (n1′) × (n′1)

354. Relative to the principal points, the nodal points of any system
- **A.** coincide with the focal point
- **B.** are displaced toward the focal point corresponding to the medium of lower refractive index

C. are displaced toward the focal point corresponding to the medium of higher refractive index
D. coincide with the symmetrical points
E. none of the above

355. The distance between the second focal and second nodal points of any centered lens system (measured from focal to nodal) is equal to the
A. front vertex focal length
B. second focal length
C. first focal length
D. distance between principal points
E. back vertex focal length

356. An achromatic doublet is composed of two lenses, a converging crown glass lens of focal length 8 cm and a diverging flint glass lens of focal length 12 cm. Find the equivalent focal length
A. 12 cm
B. 24 cm
C. 6 cm
D. 48 cm
E. 36 cm

357. An equiconvex lens has a center thickness of 6.5 mm, an index of 1.490, and surface radii of +50 mm and −50 mm, respectively. Determine the back vertex power (a) and equivalent focal power (b) of this lens when the back surface is in contact with water (index 4/3).
A. a = 13.37 D; b = 12.80 D
B. a = 4.37 D; b = 4.87 D
C. a = 6.78 D; b = 6.67 D
D. a = b = 5.67 D
E. none of the above

358. Calculate the back and front vertex powers (a and b, respectively) of a positive meniscus spectacle lens. The lens has an index of 1.500, a center thickness of 0.5 cm, and front and back curvatures of +30 D and +6, respectively.

   A. $a = 11.79$ D; $b = 9.89$ D
   B. $a = 12.79$ D; $b = 12.03$ D
   C. $a = 7.56$ D; $b = 5.27$ D
   D. $a = b = 11.79$ D
   E. none of the above

359. Find the cardinal points of a centered system of two thin equiconvex crown glass lenses of index 1.500 that are separated by a distance of 5 cm. The curvatures of the two lenses are 8.0 D and 10.0 D, respectively.

   A. $A_1F = -12.5$cm; $A_2F' = +7.14$cm; $A_1P = +4.29$cm; $A_2P' = -3.57$cm
   B. $A_1F = -7.14$cm; $A_2F' = +10.00$cm; $A_1P = +8.00$cm; $A_2P' = +17.5$cm
   C. $A_1F = -12.5$cm; $A_2F' = +10.0$cm; $A_1P = +7.14$cm; $A_2P' = -7.14$cm
   D. $A_1F = -3.57$cm; $A_2F' = +4.29$cm; $A_1P = +3.57$cm; $A_2P' = -2.86$cm
   E. none of the above

360. The thickness of a spectacle glass is 6.00 mm and is made of glass of index 1.500. The refracting power of the first surface is +10.00 D and that of the second surface is −5.00 D. Find the equivalent focal power of the lens.

   A. +6.3 D
   B. +5.0 D
   C. +15.0 D
   D. +5.2 D
   E. +4.5 D

361. An optical system is composed of two thin convex lenses of powers +8 D and +6 2/3 D, the stronger of the two being toward the incident light. Find the back vertex focal power of the system when the distance between the lenses is 5 cm.

   A. +15 D
   B. +20 D
   C. +25 D

D. +30 D

E. +10 D

362. A thin equiconvex lens of index 1.600 has a power of +10.00 D. If one of its surfaces is silvered, what will be the power of the lens-mirror? What will be the size of the image formed if a 10 cm object is placed 6 cm in front of the lens-mirror?
   A. +46.33 D, −6.67 cm
   B. +24.56 D, −2.34 cm
   C. +36.67 D, −8.33 cm
   D. +23.45 D, −4.75 cm
   E. +24.56 D, −8.33 cm

363. If Fizeau's velocity of light experiment was performed with a distant mirror located 15 km away and a wheel having 200 teeth, how fast would the wheel have turned to allow for each pulse of light returning through the first succeeding opening to be seen?
   A. 73.9 rev/sec
   B. 126 rev/sec
   C. 50 rev/sec
   D. 36.6 rev/sec
   E. 88.2 rev/sac

364. Certain substances continue to emit light after an exciting light is removed. This phenomenon is
   A. radioactivity
   B. phosphorescence
   C. fluorescence
   D. optical activity
   E. none of the above

365. The percentage of light scattered is found to be
   A. directly proportional to the number of molecules in the optical path length
   B. directly proportional to its wavelength
   C. inversely proportional to its frequency
   D. inversely proportional to the fourth power of its wavelength
   E. none of the above

366. A narrow slit illuminated with light of an unknown wavelength is placed 150 mm from a Fresnel bi-prism (index 1.500) with angles of 1/2 degrees at its two edges. The separation between interference fringes formed on a screen located 1000 mm from the prism is 0.514 mm. Calculate the wavelength of the unknown light used.
- **A.** 585 nm
- **B.** 570 nm
- **C.** 437 nm
- **D.** 720 nm
- **E.** 380 nm

367. When a convex lens placed on an optical flat surface is illuminated with light of wavelength 420 nm (normal incidence), the diameter of the 8th black ring is found to be 1.46 cm. Calculate the curvature of the surface.
- **A.** 0.100 D
- **B.** 0.063 D
- **C.** 0.095 D
- **D.** 1.000 D
- **E.** 10.00 D

368. Calculate the reflecting power for diamond in air at normal incidence if its index of refraction is 2.450.
- **A.** 19.2%
- **B.** 17.7%
- **C.** 34.4%
- **D.** 38.4%
- **E.** 42.0%

369. What is the least size of detail visible of an object located at a distance of 1200 m when using a telescope having an objective diameter of 45 mm (assume a wavelength of 555 nm). If the eye behind the scope has a V.A. of 20/45, what magnification is required for the telescope?
- **A.** 7.77 seconds, 28.77× mag
- **B.** 6.48 seconds, 33.33× mag
- **C.** 3.10 seconds, 43.55× mag
- **D.** 1.92 seconds, 17.19× mag
- **E.** none of the above

370. Calculate the angular deviation of the 7th maxima from the central maximum produced by a diffraction grating with a grating interval of 0.05 mm. (Assume light of wavelength 589 nm.)

    A. 8° 7′

    B. 54′

    C. 4° 44′

    D. 27° 20′

    E. none of the above

371. Unpolarized light is incident on two thin polaroid filters. The second filter has a transmission axis that is rotated 35° with respect to the first filter. What percent of the incident light is transmitted? (*neglect reflection*)

    A. 33.55%

    B. 50.00%

    C. 100.00%

    D. 67.10%

    E. none of the above

372. The critical angle for a piece of glass in air is 36.5 degrees. Calculate the polarizing angle.

    A. 57.5°

    B. 59.25°

    C. 47.5°

    D. 58.9°

    E. 53.11°

Ophthalmic Optics

373. Three degrees are equivalent to how many prism diopters (Δ)?

    A. 5.24Δ

    B. 4.77Δ

    C. 3.68Δ

    D. 3.00Δ

    E. none of the above

374. What is the positional effective power of a 12Δ base-up prism situated 29.5 mm in front of the center of rotation of an eye when viewing a target located 500 mm in front of the prism?
- **A.** 14.9 prism diopters
- **B.** 13.6 prism diopters
- **C.** 14.2 prism diopters
- **D.** 11.3 prism diopters
- **E.** 12.0 prism diopters

375. In meridians oblique to the base-apex line, the power of a thin prism varies as the
- **A.** sine of the angle measurement from the base-apex line
- **B.** cosine of the angle measurement from the base-apex line
- **C.** tangent of the angle measurement from the base-apex line
- **D.** all of the above
- **E.** none of the above

376. A rotary prism device is made of two ten diopter prisms. If each prism is counter-rotated 25° from the zero position, what is the resultant effect?
- **A.** 18.13 prism diopters
- **B.** 9.06 prism diopters
- **C.** 8.45 prism diopters
- **D.** 4.23 prism diopters
- **E.** none of the above

377. Excessive base-down prism
- **A.** does not significantly alter the actual appearance of horizontal lines
- **B.** makes horizontal lines appear to be curved in a concave fashion
- **C.** makes vertical lines appear to be curved in a convex fashion
- **D.** makes vertical lines appear to be longer
- **E.** none of the above

378. The optical center of a lens is defined as
- **A.** the point on the optical axis midway between the poles of the lens
- **B.** the point on the optical axis through which light passes when the incident and emergent lights are unchanged in direction

C. the intersection of the anterior surface of the lens with the optical axis

D. all of the above

E. none of the above

379. Most ophthalmic correcting lenses are of the

  A. lenticular form

  B. meniscus form

  C. planoconvex or planoconcave form

  D. aspherical form

  E. none of the above

380. Base in prism is obtained by moving the optical center of a

  A. convex lens out

  B. concave lens in

  C. convex cylinder, axis 90, in

  D. concave cylinder, axis 180, out

  E. none of the above

381. If a lensometer reads a glass lens of index 1.523 to be +6.25 D, what must be the power of a plastic lens of index 1.490 to give the same reading?

  A. +6.25 D

  B. +5.75 D

  C. +5.37 D

  D. +5.25 D

  E. +4.12 D

382. Match the minus cylinder prescription in the left column with the appropriate plus cylinder prescription in the right column.

  A. +0.25 −0.75 × 07   1. −0.25 +0.25 × 132

  B. +1.25 −1.25 × 132   2. −0.75 +0.25 × 27

  C. −0.50 −0.25 × 107   3. −0.50 +0.75 × 97

  D. −1.00 −0.25 × 89   4. plano +1.25 × 42

  E. plano −0.25 × 42   5. −1.25 +0.25 × 179

383. By mistake a spherocylindrical lens is inserted in a lensometer backwards. If the indicated axis of the plus cylinder of this lens is 41°, what would the axis of the minus cylinder actually be?
    A. 139°
    B. 41°
    C. 49°
    D. 131°
    E. none of the above

384. What is the resultant spherocylindrical lens obtained by crossing a +4.00 D cyl. axis 20° with a +2.50 D cyl. axis 80°?
    A. +1.50 D sph. +3.50 D cyl. axis 39°
    B. +3.00 D sph. +3.50 D cyl. axis 19.5°
    C. +3.50 D sph. + 1.50 D cyl. axis 78°
    D. +1.50 D cyl. axis 61° +5.00 D cyl. axis 39°
    E. +1.50 D sph. + 3.50 D cyl. axis 78°

385. Determine the approximate decentration required to produce 1.85 prism diopter base up and 1.92 prism diopter base out with a left lens having a prescription of +4.00 sph. −2.00 cyl. × 30.
    A. 4 mm up and 6 mm out
    B. 6 mm down and 4 mm in
    C. 4 mm down and 6 mm in
    D. 6 mm up and 4 mm out
    E. none of the above

386. What is the prismatic effect produced when the optical center of the lens O.S. −5.75 +2.25 × 075 is decentered 0.7 cm down and 0.4 cm out?
    A. 4.55Δ BI and BU @ 100°
    B. 3.9Δ BI and BU @ 75°
    C. 3.845Δ BU and BI @ 106.1°
    D. 2.21Δ BU and BO @ 12°
    E. none of the above

387. A spherocylindrical round spectacle lens has meridional powers of +2.00 D and +3.00 D on its front surface, plano power on its back surface, a diameter of 4.5 cm, index of 1.523, and a center thickness of 2.92 mm. Find its minimum and maximum edge thicknesses.

A. 1.57 mm, 2.3 mm
B. 1.46 mm, 1.95 mm
C. 0.75 mm, 1.25 mm
D. 1.83 mm, 4.56 mm
E. none of the above

388. Determine the vertical prismatic imbalance at a point 8 mm below the optical centers of the following lenses: O.D. +3.00 −2.50 × 180, O.S. +3.00 −1.25 × 180?
A. 0.5 prism diopter
B. 0.0 prism diopter
C. 1.5 prism diopter
D. 1.0 prism diopter
E. none of the above

389. Slab-off prism (bicentric grind) is specified for which of the ophthalmic lenses required by the patient?
A. for the lens with the most minus power in the 90° meridian
B. for the lens with the least minus power in the 90° meridian
C. for either lens, as prescription is not a factor
D. for the lens with the most plus power in the 90° meridian
E. none of the above

390. A negative meniscus lens has surface powers of 11.50D and 1.50D, a thickness of 3.1 mm, and is made of plastic index of 1.49. The back vertex power of the lens is
A. +10.00 D
B. +11.67 D
C. −11.67 D
D. −10.00 D
E. none of the above

391. What error is induced by utilizing the approximate power equation $(F_1 + F_2 = F_T)$ for a lens of index 1.523, center thickness of 3.1 mm thick, and a front surface power of +11.75 D?
A. 0.11 D
B. 0.14 D
C. 0.29 D
D. 0.00 D
E. none of the above

392. Given a +8.75 D crown glass lens (index 1.523) worn 16 mm from the vertex of the cornea. What power is required of a plastic lens (index 1.495) worn with a vertex distance of 12 mm be to afford the same amount of correction?
  A. +10.1 D
  B. +9.07 D
  C. +6.25 D
  D. +8.75 D
  E. +9.50 D

393. Given the following RGP contact lens data: index 1.46; center thickness = 0.14 mm; r_1 = +7.05 mm and r_2 = +7.50 mm. Determine the back vertex power (Rx) of this lens.
  A. +3.92 D
  B. +4.62 D
  C. +4.12 D
  D. +4.33 D
  E. +3.87 D

394. Determine the front surface radius of an RGP contact lens of index 1.46, center thickness of 0.12 mm, back vertex power of −15.00 D, and back surface radius of +7.80 mm.
  A. +11.5 mm
  B. +7.5 mm
  C. +8.5 mm
  D. +9.5 mm
  E. +10.5 mm

395. The important aberrations considered in designing corrected curved spectacle lenses given in the following list are
  A. coma and spherical aberration
  B. marginal astigmatism and curvature of field
  C. coma and curvature of field
  D. chromatic aberration and spherical aberration
  E. all of these are equally important

396. A pantoscopic tilt of 12° induces what changes in lens power −7.25 −1.75 × 180 (assume index n = 1.5)?
  A. −0.13 D sph; −0.41 D cyl × 90
  B. −0.39 D sph; −0.41 D cyl × 90
  C. −0.39 D sph; −0.41 D cyl × 180

D. −0.13 D sph; −0.41 D cyl × 180
E. none of the above

397. The usual bifocal is placed approximately how far below the lower pupil margin?
   A. 1–2 mm
   B. 5–6 mm
   C. 3–4 mm
   D. 7–8 mm
   E. none of the above

398. Determine the amount of image jump in a flat-top 25 mm segment of power +2.50 D and segment depth of 17.5 mm.
   A. 0.50 prism diopter
   B. 0.75 prism diopter
   C. 1.00 prism diopter
   D. 1.25 prism diopters
   E. none of the above

399. Which of the following statements concerning the fitting procedure for double-segment multi-focals lenses is incorrect?
   A. The vertical dimension of the frame selected must be measured.
   B. Place the height of the lower segment at the lower lid.
   C. At least 9 mm (vertically) must be available in the upper segment.
   D. It is best to dispense a frame having adjustable-pad bridge construction.
   E. none of the above

400. Which of the following statements concerning progressive addition lenses is incorrect?
   A. Extra foveal vision is disturbed by lateral aberration zones, thereby restricting eye movements.
   B. Prism cannot be obtained by decentration and must be ground into the lens by the lab.
   C. Lens measurements must be taken on the particular frame the patient will wear.
   D. A large pantoscopic tilt to the frame allows the patient to ignore blur areas better.
   E. none of the above

401. The major reference point of a lens is
  A. the same as the geometrical center or point
  B. equal to the eye size plus the distance between the lenses
  C. a specified point where the prism power corresponds to that required in the prescription
  D. important only in complete specification of a frame using the "boxing system"
  E. the same as the optical contour

402. Which of the following factors is not a common cause for error when using a PD rule to measure the interpupillary distance?
  A. The measurer's PD differs significantly from the patient's PD.
  B. The patient is strabismic or does not fixate binocularly.
  C. Either measurer or patient moves his or her head.
  D. The measurer fails to close one eye at a time to ensure that sighting is done directly in front of the patient's eye under examination.
  E. none of the above

403. Which of the following statements concerning ophthalmic lens coatings is not correct?
  A. Polycarbonate plastic lenses require a scratch-resistant coating.
  B. Anti-reflection coatings reduce reflections and thereby reduce the transmission of lenses that are coated.
  C. Color coating can provide uniform appearance across the entire lens, even with high powers.
  D. Edge coatings are utilized to eliminate the opaqueness of bevels seen on high minus plastic lenses.
  E. none of the above

404. Which of the following statements concerning polycarbonate plastic lenses (uncoated ones) is incorrect?
  A. They are thinner than CR39 lenses.
  B. They are lighter than CR39 lenses.
  C. They are more impact resistant than CR39 lenses.
  D. They block more than 99 percent of harmful UV light.
  E. They are highly scratch and abrasion resistant.

405. If a zyl frame appears too low on the left side when placed on the patient's face, the initial adjustment should be to
A. angle the right temple out
B. angle the left temple out
C. angle the right temple down
D. angle the left temple down
E. file the bridge on the right side

Physiological Optics and Visual Optics

406. The entrance pupil of the eye is the image of the actual pupil refracted through the cornea. Utilizing Gullstrand's simplified schematic eye (No. 2 eye), determine the position and size of the entrance pupil when the actual pupil has a diameter of 4.0 mm, is in contact with aqueous of index 1.336, and is positioned 3.60 mm behind the cornea whose refracting power is +43.08 D.
A. 2.69 mm behind the corneal vertex and 4.72 mm in diameter
B. 3.60 mm behind the corneal vertex and 4.00 mm in diameter
C. 2.95 mm behind the corneal vertex and 4.72 mm in diameter
D. 3.05 mm behind the corneal vertex and 4.53 mm in diameter
E. 3.31 mm behind the corneal vertex and 4.25 mm in diameter

407. When light is reflected from the four surfaces of the eye, a series of four catoptric images is formed. These are called the Purkinje images. Which of the following statements concerning these images is correct when the eye accommodates?
A. I and II increase in size and move away from the cornea.
B. III and IV increase in size and move towards the cornea.
C. III and IV decrease in size and move away from the cornea.
D. I and II decrease in size and move toward the cornea.
E. none of the above

408. Given: Gullstrand's Simplified (No. 2) Schematic Eye—Accommodated 8.62 D. Match the numbers on the right to the appropriate lettered components on the left.

A.	corneal radius	1.	+7.8 mm
B.	lens index	2.	1.413
C.	equivalent power of eye	3.	+59.60 D
D.	anterior chamber depth	4.	3.6 mm
E.	anterior surface power of lens	5.	3.2 mm
		6.	+7.70 D
		7.	1.336
		8.	+68.22 D
		9.	+15.40 D

409. Given: Gulstrand's Simplified Schematic Eye (No. 2) for a 25-year-old aphakic eye. The cornea has a radius of +7.80 mm and separates air from eye material of index 1.336. The length of the eye is 24.17 mm. Locate the far point and the near point for this eye.

A. −82 mm, infinity
B. +7.8 mm, +207 mm
C. +242 mm, infinity
D. +82 mm, +82 mm
E. +336 mm, +182 mm

410. Astigmatism, an anomaly due to unequal refraction of light by the dioptrics of the eye, is significantly influenced by the toroidal anterior corneal surface. It is usually classified according to (1) the spherical ametropia that accompanies it and (2) whether the greatest curvature of the cornea is vertical (with the rule) or horizontal (against the rule). If an eye reveals 1.25 D of hyperopia in its vertical principal meridian and 1.25 D of myopia in its other principal meridian, the classification is

A. simple myopic astigmatism, against the rule
B. mixed astigmatism, against the rule
C. compound hyperopic astigmatism, against the rule
D. compound myopic astigmatism, with the rule
E. simple hyperopic astigmatism, with the rule

411. The ratio of the retinal image size in the corrected ametropic eye to that in the uncorrected eye (with reference to a distance object) is called
    A. spectacle magnification
    B. anisekonia
    C. relative spectacle magnification
    D. anisometropia
    E. lateral magnification

412. The effects of diffraction set the limit to the size of an image that can be formed by an optical system. This image of a point object is an Airy's disc pattern formed by a circular aperture. The size of the Airy's disc pattern formed on the retina by the eye's pupil
    A. varies directly with incident wavelength and with pupil diameter
    B. varies inversely with pupil diameter and directly with incident wavelength
    C. varies inversely with both incident wavelength and pupil diameter
    D. is independent of pupil diameter
    E. is independent of incident wavelength

413. Which of the following types of illumination will create a visible shadow of the retinal vessels or their contents?
    A. a bright light source (e.g., a candle) moving around near to the eye
    B. a bright light source that is imaged at the eye's entrance pupil and moved around
    C. a bright light source that is projected onto the sclera and moved
    D. a bright blue uniform field
    E. all of the above

414. From the following list, which anatomical structure is correctly paired with the entoptic phenomenon they create?
    A. Henle's fiber layer: Maxwell's spot
    B. macular pigment: Hadinger's brushes
    C. Henle's fiber layer: entoptically viewed FAZ
    D. retinal ganglion cell axons: Purkinje tree
    E. leukocytes: flying corpuscles

415. Lens opacities are best seen entoptically by
   A. carefully fixating a large uniformly illuminated blue field
   B. viewing a point source placed in the anterior focal plane of the eye
   C. viewing the world through a yellow filter
   D. viewing a distant point source with a plus lens
   E. none of the above

416. Phosphenes can be created by
   A. rapid eye movements
   B. local pressure applied to the eye
   C. high voltage electrical fields
   D. photochemical instability within the receptors
   E. all of the above

417. Retinal image quality in the human eye has been assessed by
   A. measuring the line spread function, using a double-pass technique
   B. measuring the effect of the eyes' optics on contrast sensitivity
   C. measuring the eyes' aberrations and calculating the MTF
   D. objectively scanning reflected retinal images
   E. all of the above

418. Which of the following contributors to "stray light" within a young eye has the least effect on vision because of the Stiles Crawford effect?
   A. scatter from the cornea
   B. scatter from the lens
   C. reflections from within the retina
   D. transmission through the iris
   E. none of the above

419. Which of the following conditions will greatly amplify foveal ocular transverse chromatic aberrations?
   A. viewing a monochromatic source with a large pupil
   B. viewing a polychromatic source with a large pupil
   C. viewing a polychromatic source with a small pupil placed on the visual axis

D. viewing a polychromatic source with a small pupil displaced 4 mm from the visual axis

E. viewing a polychromatic source with a large pupil centered on the visual axis

420. Which of the following aberrations change significantly with accommodation?
   A. axial chromatic aberrations
   B. transverse chromatic aberrations
   C. spherical aberration
   D. diffraction
   E. all of the above

421. A point source emits a total (i.e., in all directions) of 25.13 watts at a wavelength of 555 nm.
   A. It is equivalent to 2×685 candles.
   B. It has a luminous intensity of 685 lumens/steradian.
   C. It has a radiant intensity of 2 watts/steradian.
   D. It emits a total of $4 \times \pi$ joules per second.
   E. both **A** and **C**

422. A point source emits a total (i.e., in all directions) of 25.13 watts at a wavelength of 555 nm. A surface of area = 0.01 m² is placed 10 cm away from this source. It will receive
   A. 20 watts of radiant flux
   B. 4 watts of radiant flux
   C. 1370 lumens of luminous flux
   D. an illuminance of 1370 lux
   E. an illuminance of 1370 lumens/m²

423. When viewing a white sheet of paper from a distance of 1 meter, an electronic photometer gives a reading of 1000 cd/m². With your pupil diameter at 3.5 mm, the retinal image illuminance
   A. is approximately 1000 trolands
   B. decreases by a factor of 100 as you increase your viewing distance to 10 meters
   C. is approximately 10,000 trolands
   D. is unaffected by changing viewing distance
   E. both **C** and **D**

424. Retinal illuminance is determined by
   A. target luminance
   B. pupil size
   C. pupil location
   D. both **A** and **B**
   E. **A, B,** and **C**

Visual Perception

425. The trichromatic theory of human color vision
   A. states that there are three color-opponent mechanisms
   B. is consistent with the observation that normal trichromats require 3 primaries to match any color
   C. is derived from Hering's color after-image observations
   D. reflects the three cone types (L, M, and S) active at photopic light levels
   E. both **B** and **D**

426. A 2-degree patch of white light will appear
   A. pink after prolonged fixation of a 2-degree bright yellow light
   B. desaturated blue when surrounded by a large field of bright yellow
   C. yellow after prolonged viewing of saturated red
   D. desaturated green when surrounded by desaturated blue
   E. yellow after prolonged viewing of yellow

427. When mixing spectral red and green lights to hue-match a spectral yellow, which of the following requires more red than normal in order to obtain a satisfactory match?
   A. protanope
   B. protanomalous trichromat
   C. deuteranope
   D. deuteranomalous trichromat
   E. tritanomalous trichromat

428. The distance on the CIE chromaticity diagram, from the achromatic point to the sample point, divided by the distance from the achromatic point to the point on the spectrum locus that reflects the dominant wavelength of the sample, is the
  A. excitation purity
  B. colorimetric purity
  C. luminance purity
  D. saturation
  E. color contrast

429. Munsell **value,** on the Munsell color tree, has a minimum of 0 at the _____ and a maximum of 10 at the _____.
  A. center, periphery
  B. bottom, top
  C. outer edge, center
  D. top, bottom
  E. none of the above

430. Hue shifts that accompany luminosity and spectral purity changes are referred to as the _____ and _____ phenomena, respectively.
  A. Abney, Broca-Sulzer
  B. Bezold-Brücke, Abney
  C. Bezold-Brücke, Brücke-Bartley
  D. Abney, Bezold-Brücke
  E. Broca-Sulzer, Abney

431. The psychophysical correlative of purity is
  A. saturation
  B. hue
  C. brightness
  D. dominant wavelength
  E. spectral irradiance

432. The wavelength of a monochromatic stimulus is related most closely to its perceived
  A. hue
  B. saturation
  C. absolute luminosity
  D. excitation purity
  E. color constancy

433. Calculate the limiting distance at which stereopsis can be effective (distal depth interval = infinity) if the interpupillary distance is 65 mm and the stereopsis threshold is 10 sec of arc.
- **A.** 670 m
- **B.** 1110 m
- **C.** 1340 m
- **D.** 2220 m
- **E.** 2680 m

434. At the abathic distance, the Apparent Fronto Parallel Plane horopter is
- **A.** convex toward the observer
- **B.** concave toward the observer
- **C.** coincident with the Vieth-Muller circle
- **D.** irregular
- **E.** coincident with the objective frontal parallel plane

435. A circle through the two nodal points and the fixation point is known as the
- **A.** Hering-Hilderbrand horopter deviation
- **B.** Vieth Muller circle
- **C.** circle of least confusion
- **D.** the empirical horopter
- **E.** tan 2/tan 1 = R

436. What factors determine the relationship between angular horizontal disparity (θ) and linear difference in depth (ΔD)?
- **A.** viewing distance and PD
- **B.** eccentricity and PD
- **C.** viewing distance and VA
- **D.** PD and luminance
- **E.** viewing distance and eccentricity

437. Which of the following possible depth cues is probably least important to the pilot of a large jet aircraft?
- **A.** horizontal disparity
- **B.** motion parallax
- **C.** geometric perspective
- **D.** aerial perspective
- **E.** superposition

438. When viewing equidistant red and blue objects binocularly, the red ones usually (but not always) appear nearer than the blue. This phenomenon can be explained by
   A. color opponancy theory
   B. Fechner's paradox
   C. ocular chromatic aberration
   D. hue shifts
   E. none of the above

439. Size constancy
   A. maintains a constant perceived size for a fixed retinal image size irrespective of viewing distance
   B. maintains a constant perceived size for a fixed object size irrespective of viewing distance
   C. depends upon accurate perception of distance
   D. both A and C
   E. both B and C

440. Which of the following illusions can be explained by the size constancy mechanism?
   A. Muller-Lyer illusion
   B. Ponzo illusion
   C. Zollner illusion
   D. Moon illusion
   E. A, B, and D

441. Which of the following is NOT an example of luminance contrast (simultaneous contrast) determining perceived brightness?
   A. the dark patches at the intersection of a Herman grid
   B. the effect of surround luminance on the brightness of a patch of fixed luminance
   C. Mach bands
   D. Abney effect
   E. brightness constancy

442. A normal photopic foveal contrast sensitivity function (CSF), measured with extended sinusoidal gratings,
   A. typically has a peak contrast sensitivity of about 50 to 100
   B. typically has a peak contrast sensitivity between 100 and 300
   C. has a high frequency cut-off of about 20 cycles/degree
   D. exhibits lower sensitivity at 3 cycles per degree than at 0.3 cycles/degree
   E. peaks at about 15 cycles per degree

443. Experimental measurements of acuity as a function of pupil size show that, when retinal illuminance is held constant,
   A. acuity reaches its maximum values for pupil diameters of 2 to 4 mm
   B. acuities are better than those predicted by Rayleigh's criterion for pupil diameters from 5 to 8 mm
   C. acuities are worse than those predicted by Rayleigh's criterion for pupil diameters of less than 1 mm
   D. acuities are particularly sensitive to optical aberrations with small pupil sizes
   E. acuities are less sensitive to defocus with larger pupil sizes

444. Backward masking refers to
   A. covering redundant contours with screens
   B. spatial contrast effects
   C. detection threshold elevation prior to presentation of a mask stimulus
   D. the drop in detection threshold that can occur prior to the offset of a mask stimulus
   E. the failure of a positive after-image to encode

445. Which of the following phenomena can be explained by lateral inhibition in the retina?
   A. low frequency roll-off of the contrast sensitivity function
   B. gray patches in Herman's grid
   C. simultaneous contrast
   D. Mach bands
   E. all of the above

446. Hyper acuity thresholds are defined to be smaller than the angular separation of foveal cones. They have been measured with which of the following tasks?
  A. bisection acuity
  B. vernier acuity
  C. stereo acuity
  D. alignment acuity
  E. all of the above

447. Which of the following is NOT a test for visual acuity?
  A. tumbling E's
  B. Landolt C's
  C. Pelli-Robson chart
  D. Log MAR charts
  E. Snellen chart

448. The "kink" in the normal dark-adaptation curve is evidence used in support of the
  A. Ladd-Franklin theory
  B. trichromatic theory
  C. duplicity theory
  D. Hering theory
  E. Helmholtz theory

449. The "kink" in the dark-adaptation curve
  A. is absent for very small test fields centered on the fovea
  B. is absent following initial adaptation to scotopic intensity adapting lights
  C. is absent after initial adaptation to 650 nm lights
  D. both A and B
  E. A, B, and C

450. With respect to apparent brightness, Fechner's paradox suggests that binocular sensory integration is based upon
  A. right-eye, left-eye sensory independence
  B. averaging
  C. linear summation
  D. potentiation
  E. facilitation

451. At night, a dim star can disappear when fixated because
  A. at *photopic* light levels, humans exhibit a physiological central scotoma
  B. the intensity of the star may be subthreshold for the foveal *cone* system
  C. because it is too small to be resolved by the foveal cones
  D. pupil size, and hence retinal illuminance, will decrease
  E. starlight is spectrally better matched to rod sensitivity

452. The observation that the logarithm of subjective brightness is linearly related to the logarithm of stimulus luminance was shown by
  A. Weber
  B. Stevens
  C. Fechner
  D. Ricco
  E. Stiles

453. The visual effect of intraocular stray light that originates from light scattered by the neural retina may be reduced by
  A. Maxwell's spot
  B. the Stiles-Crawford effect
  C. birefringence of the fibers of Henle
  D. the Troxler phenomenon
  E. the Broca-Sulzer effect

454. Over much of the visible range of photopic light levels, just discriminable differences in luminance (ΔI or ΔL)
  A. are proportional to the background light levels
  B. exhibit the following relationship: $\Delta I/I = K$
  C. can be described by Weber's law
  D. both **B** and **C**
  E. **A, B,** and **C**

455. The effect of pupillary dilation upon perceived brightness is less than would be predicted based on the increase in incident flux on the retina that accompanies increases in pupil size. This phenomenon reflects
  A. decreased sensitivity to light entering from around the corneal margins
  B. the direction selectivity of human photoreceptors

C. the Stiles-Crawford effect
D. A, B, and C
E. neither A, B, nor C, because this effect is related to nonlinearities in the pupil response

456. With steady fixation, the minimum speed for the perception of motion is approximately
A. 1–3 sec of arc/sec
B. 10–30 sec of arc/sec
C. 1–3 min of arc/sec
D. 10–30 min of arc/sec
E. 1–3 deg of arc/sec

457. If two identical objects appear alternately at two points close to each other, subjects report that one object appears to be moving between the two positions. The apparent movement is known as
A. alpha movement
B. sigma movement
C. gamma movement
D. delta movement
E. phi movement

458. After watching a faint, small point source in an otherwise unlit room, it may appear to move about. This phenomenon is known as
A. the oculologyric illusion
B. the autokinetic illusion
C. oscillopsia
D. the anorthoscopic illusion
E. the vestibular illusion

459. Barlow and Levick's neurophysiological model of motion detection included
A. center-surround lateral inhibition
B. direction selectivity
C. orientation selectivity
D. a delayed inhibitory connection
E. both B and D

460. If a stationary dot is located in the center of a clearly visible frame and the frame is moved slowly to the right, the
   A. dot will also appear to move slowly to the right
   B. dot will appear to move slowly to the left
   C. stationary dot will appear stationary
   D. slow-moving frame will induce fast motion in the dot
   E. frame will appear to move to the left

461. If an ND filter is placed before the left eye, a swinging pendulum that is confined to the subject's fronto parallel plane will
   A. appear to swing in the opposite direction to its physical motion
   B. appear to swing in a clockwise elliptical pattern (closer to the subject when swinging right to left)
   C. appear to swing in a counterclockwise elliptical pattern (closer to the subject when swinging left to right)
   D. appear to swing in a figure eight pattern centered on the fixation point
   E. appear to swing slower than its physical motion

462. Spinning wheels can appear stationary on TV or in movies because the
   A. speed of the vehicle is too fast for the film to detect
   B. rotation rate of the wheels is very slow
   C. rotation rate of the wheels is the same as the TV or film frame rates
   D. rotation rate of the wheels is double the TV or film frame rates
   E. both C and D

463. Appearance of self motion induced by object motion is
   A. most readily observed when the object is very small
   B. most readily observed when the object fills a large proportion of the visual field
   C. called vection
   D. both A and C
   E. both B and C

464. Which of the following is an example of a motion aftereffect?
   A. optic flow patterns
   B. autokinetic movement

C. apparent motion
D. the waterfall illusion
E. the phi phenomenon

465. The perceived brightness of a light (of constant intensity) changes as a function of flash duration, increasing with increasing duration for very short durations and then decreasing with further increases in duration. This change in brightness is sometimes referred to as the
   A. Talbot-Plateau effect
   B. Brucke-Bartley effect
   C. Broco-Sulzer effect
   D. Abney effect
   E. Bezold-Brucke effect

466. When the frequency of a flickering light is above CFF, its brightness is the same as that of a continuous light of the same mean flux density. This observation is known as the
   A. Talbot-Plateau law
   B. Ferry-Porter law
   C. Bunsen-Roscoe law
   D. Bezold-Brucke effect
   E. Abney's law

467. A light flickering at 2 to 5 Hz can appear brighter than the same light flickering above CFF or not flickering (0 Hz). This phenomenon is called the
   A. Brucke-Bartley effect
   B. Granit-Harper law
   C. Broca-Sulzer effect
   D. Bezold-Brucke effect
   E. Ferry-Porter law

468. According to the Ferry-Porter law, CFF
   A. varies directly with the logarithm of stimulus luminance
   B. varies directly with stimulus luminance
   C. varies inversely with the logarithm of stimulus luminance
   D. varies inversely with stimulus luminance
   E. does not vary with stimulus luminance

469. Bloch's law, or time-intensity reciprocity, implies that
 A. flash brightness is independent of flash duration
 B. luminance increment thresholds are the same regardless of flash duration
 C. the product of flash luminance thresholds and duration is constant
 D. both B and C
 E. both A and C

470. The critical duration for temporal summation is
 A. shorter for low-luminance flashes
 B. longer for low-luminance flashes
 C. shorter for patterned stimuli than for homogeneous stimuli
 D. longer for longer wavelengths
 E. about 100 μsec for scotopic vision

Ocular Motility

471. Accommodative responses tend to be smaller than required to make the images of near objects coincident with the retina because of
 A. depth of focus of the eye
 B. accommodative lag
 C. ametropia
 D. both A and B
 E. both B and C

472. Mechanical tension within the ciliary zonules is diminished
 A. during increased accommodation
 B. when the ciliary muscle is relaxed
 C. by the instillation of a cycloplegic agent
 D. when the ciliary muscle is contracted
 E. both A and D

473. Which of the following statements about human accommodation is NOT true?
 A. Accommodation is approximately equal in the two eyes.
 B. Accommodation relaxes to zero in the absence of a stimulus.
 C. Accommodation diminishes with age to essentially zero at 55 to 65 years.

D. Over-accommodation often produces myopia at night.
E. Presbyopes lack accommodation.

474. When a young person accommodates from far to near, the
    A. anterior lens surface approaches the cornea
    B. radius of the anterior surface of the crystalline lens decreases
    C. pupil constricts
    D. lens falls slightly in the direction of gravity
    E. all of the above

475. Which of the following stimuli can induce accommodation?
    A. decreased image contrast
    B. increased target proximity
    C. convergence of the eyes
    D. image defocus
    E. all of the above

476. Accommodation from infinity to 50 cm typically follows the stimulus with a latency of about
    A. 100 msec
    B. 300 msec
    C. the same as the convergence latency
    D. the latency of a saccadic response
    E. both **A** and **D**

477. Hippus
    A. describes the pupil response to increased light level
    B. describes oscillatory pupillary constrictions and dilations
    C. describes the decrease in pupil size with age
    D. can be produced in normals by placing an intense narrow beam of light just inside the pupil margin
    E. both **B** and **D**

478. Humans have difficulty accommodating to which of the following stimuli?
    A. empty fields
    B. low spatial frequency targets
    C. medium spatial frequency targets
    D. isoluminant color-modulated targets
    E. **A, B,** and **D**

479. The sympathetic "fight or flight" response to stress and/or alarm will
  A. constrict the pupil
  B. dilate the pupil
  C. elicit a large accommodative response
  D. improve distance vision of an uncorrected myope
  E. both **B** and **D**

480. The law stating that the innervations that give rise to conjugate eye movements are themselves symmetrical is
  A. Listing's law
  B. Hering's law
  C. Donder's law
  D. Sherrington's law
  E. Horn's law

481. Which of the following extraocular muscles exhibit simple, singular actions when the eye is in the primary position?
  A. superior and inferior recti
  B. superior and inferior obliques
  C. lateral and medial recti
  D. superior rectus and inferior oblique
  E. none of the above

482. Which of the following extraocular muscles is innervated by cranial nerve IV?
  A. medial rectus
  B. inferior rectus
  C. superior oblique
  D. inferior oblique
  E. superior rectus

483. The medial rectus elevates the eye when the line of sight is
  A. in the horizontal plane
  B. oriented above the horizontal plane
  C. oriented below the horizontal plane
  D. The medial rectus never elevates the eye
  E. none of the above

484. The primary and secondary actions of the superior rectus muscle, for an eye in the primary position of gaze, are
A. elevation, abduction, and intorsion
B. elevation, adduction, and extorsion
C. elevation, adduction, and intorsion
D. elevation, abduction, and extorsion
E. elevation and abduction only

485. While in the primary position, the action of the superior oblique muscle produces
A. intorsion, depression, and slight abduction
B. intorsion, elevation, and slight adduction
C. extorsion, depression, and slight abduction
D. intorsion, depression, and slight adduction
E. extorsion, depression, and slight adduction

486. With an eye looking nasally 51 degrees from the primary position, contraction of the _____ muscle produces an _____ eye movement.
A. inferior oblique, elevation
B. superior oblique, depression
C. inferior oblique, extorsion
D. superior oblique, extorsion
E. both A and B

487. Accurate and fast eye movement control is particularly important for humans because
A. the human retina has a fovea
B. the human brain is very heavy
C. high retinal drift velocities impair vision
D. A, B, and C
E. both A and C

488. Rotation of the human eye is controlled by how many major extraocular muscles?
A. 4
B. 5
C. 6
D. 7
E. 8

489. The horizontal extent of the normal field of vision with both eyes open is approximately
- **A.** 180°
- **B.** 130°
- **C.** 100°
- **D.** 80°
- **E.** 50°

490. The direction of the fast phase of optokinetic reflex movements of the eye is
- **A.** to the subject's right if the stripes on the optokinetic drum move to his right
- **B.** to the subject's left if the stripes on the optokinetic drum move to his right
- **C.** to the subject's right if the stripes on the optokinetic drum are in the right half of his binocular field of vision
- **D.** to the subject's left if the stripes on the optokinetic drum are in the right half of his binocular field
- **E.** optokinetic nystagmus is pendular, not jerky; there is no fast phase

491. In the presence of drifting targets, the OKN reflex provides
- **A.** constant retinal image velocity for constant velocity targets
- **B.** approximate image stabilization interleaved by brief periods of very fast image motion
- **C.** retinal images that alternately drift back and forth on the retina
- **D.** a mechanism for maintaining fixation while our bodies are in motion (e.g., walking)
- **E.** both **B** and **D**

492. During attempted steady fixation of an easily visible target, eyes exhibit
- **A.** small involuntary saccades (flicks) typically less than 20 arc minutes
- **B.** slow involuntary "drifts"
- **C.** low amplitude and high frequency oscillation or "tremors"
- **D.** involuntary saccades that often correct for the uncontrolled drifts of the retinal image away from the fovea
- **E.** all of the above

493. A large nasal eye movement will
    A. expand the nasal field
    B. constrict the nasal field
    C. expand the temporal field
    D. constrict the temporal field
    E. both **B** and **C**

494. Maximum rotation of the eye in the horizontal plane is approximately
    A. 15°
    B. 30°
    C. 45°
    D. 70°
    E. 90°

495. During a normal blink,
    A. the eyes rotate upwards (Bell's phenomenon)
    B. there is a reduction in visual sensitivity
    C. there is a small, fast, inferior-nasal eye movement
    D. both **A** and **B**
    E. both **B** and **C**

496. Forced closure of the lids is achieved by
    A. contraction of the palpebral portion of the orbicularis oculi
    B. contraction of the orbital portion of the orbicularis oculi
    C. efferent activity in cranial nerve VI
    D. efferent activity in cranial nerve VII
    E. both **B** and **D**

497. The normal blink rate is approximately
    A. 5–10 per minute
    B. 20–30 per minute
    C. decreased during reading
    D. increased during reading
    E. both **B** and **C**

Answers and Discussion

Geometrical Optics

306. (B) $x/14 = (30 + x)/20$; $x = 70$ cm. The total shadow is called umbra. Surrounding the umbra is a space in the partial shadow. The partial shadow is called the penumbra.

307. (C) The image seen in the plane mirror is formed by diverging light rays and is termed a virtual image. This image is as far behind the plane mirror as the object is in front. As the mirror moves a distance (x), the image moves a distance $(2x)$.

308. (B) Use the equation for plane mirrors: the angle of incidence is equal to the angle of reflection $(i = r)$. The extent of an image seen in a plane mirror will depend on the size of the mirror and the position of the eye. The extent of the image seen is called the field of view.

309. (D) The number of whole images formed with central location $= (180/31) \times 2 = 11\,19/31 \cong 12$. Thus, 12 whole images will be formed if the object is positioned between the inclined mirrors and within the central $19°$ (overlapping) portion of object space. That is, $31° - 6° - 6° = 19°$. An application of the multiple images formed by inclined mirrors is the instrument known as the kaleidoscope.

310. (D) Use Snell's equation for refraction at a plane surface; $n \sin i = n' \sin i'$. The angle of deviation will be the difference between i (the angle of incidence) and i' (the angle of refraction). In the equation, (n) represents the object space index; (n′) represents the image space index.

311. **(B)** Use Snell's equation; $n \sin i = n' \sin i'$; solve for i, [(i′) = 90 degrees]. The critical angle (i_c) will be larger for red light than for blue light. The high brilliancy of diamond material is due to the fact that it has a small critical angle.

312. **(C)** Use the equation for lateral displacement: Disp = T[sin $(i - i')$/cos i′] and for critical angle: sin i_c = n′/n. The final direction of the exiting light ray is the same as the original direction of the incident ray; that is, the first incident and the last refracted ray are parallel.

313. **(A)** Location = 20 + 40/4/3 = 50 cm. In the equation, 4/3 represents the index of the water. 40 represents the actual thickness of the tank. Therefore, 40/4/3 represents the apparent thickness of the tank.

314. **(D)** Use the equation: apical angle (a) = 2 i_c. The greatest angle a prism can have for light to pass through it will occur when the original incident and final refracted light rays graze their respective surfaces. No light will pass through a prism when the apical angle is greater than twice the critical angle.

315. **(B)** Use the thick prism equation: deviation = $i_1 + i'_2 - a$. Note: (i_1) is the original angle of incidence, (i'_2) is the final angle of refraction, and (a) is the apical angle. Also use Snell's law: $n \sin i = n' \sin i'$. (See answer 310 for details.)

316. **(A)** Curvature at eye = 1/(0.25 + 0.25/1.5 + 0.25). Curvature (R) in diopters is equal to the reciprocal of the apparent object distance measured in meters. In the equation, [0.25/1.5] is the apparent thickness of the glass plate.

317. **(A)** Use the surface power equation: $F = (n' - n)R$, and the (fundamental) vergence equation: $L + F = L'$. Remember, (n′) is image space index, (n) is object space index, and (R) is the curvature of the surface. R is in diopters and is equal to the reciprocal of the radius of the surface, which is measured in meters.

318. (A) Use the equations: $F = (n' - n)/r$ and $L + F = L'$. Remember, L is object vergence, F is the power of the surface, and L' is image vergence. $L = n/l$ and $L' = n'/l'$ where (l) and (l') are object and image distances measured in meters.

319. (E) Use the equation: $F = (n' - n)/r$. Remember, (r) is the radius of the surface measured in meters. Note: $(n' - n)$ is the index differential between 1.490 and 1.650 when submerged.

320. (E) Use the equation: $h' = f \tan w$, for a distant object. Remember, (w) is the angular subtense of the distant object, as measured with respect to the optical axis; (h') is the size of the image; and (f) is the first focal length of the surface.

321. (E) Use the equation: magnification = image size/object size = (h'/h) = object vergence/image vergence = (L/L'). Also, use the equation: $F = L' - L = 1/f' = (1/\text{focal length})$. Remember, vergence is in diopters. Furthermore, (h') and (h) must be in the same units; also utilize (1/f') because this is a thin lens in contact with air (index = 1.000).

322. (C) First find the curvature (R) of the lens in air, utilizing the equation $F = (n' - n)R$. $R = +7.874$ D. Next, place the lens in water and utilize the same equation again. Remember, $(n' - n)$ is the index difference between glass and water. $F(H_2O) = +1.3123$ D; $f' = (1.3333/1.3123)/0.0254 = 40$ in.

323. (C) Use the equations: $F = L' - L = 1/f'$ and magnification = L/L'. Remember, $F = L' - L$ is the fundamental vergence equation. Furthermore, the thin lens is in contact with air; therefore, $F = 1/f'$. Also, the lateral magnification is found from: $h'/h = l'/l = L/L'$.

324. (B) Object and image are located in the symmetrical planes and are therefore 4f' apart. With any lens there is a position of the object and the image such that the image is the same size as the object but inverted. The magnification in this case is therefore (–1) and the object and image are said to be in symmetrical planes.

325. (C) Use the equation: n = actual thickness (l)/apparent thickness (l'). Given the equation $L + F = L'$, set $F = 0$. Therefore,

L = L′. Remember, L = n/l and L′ = n′/l′; therefore, n′/l′ = n/l and n = n′l/l′. Since n′ = 1.000, n = l/l′ or (actual thickness/apparent thickness).

326. **(A)** First, determine the equivalent mirror; change the direction of light to do this. (Use right-left optics.) Then use the curved mirror equation: F = L′ − L = −2nR, utilizing left-right optics. Remember, (R) is the curvature of the mirror and (n) is the refractive index of the substance in contact with the mirror.

327. **(A)** Use the equation for curved mirrors: F = L′ − L = −2nR. Remember, (F) is the power of the mirror, (L′) is the image vergence, (L) is the object vergence, (n) is the index of the material in contact with the mirror, and (R) is the curvature of the mirror.

328. **(C)** Use the equation for curved mirrors and the equation for lateral magnification. Lateral magnification is equal to image distance/object distance (l′/l) = object vergence/image vergence (L/L′) = image size/object size (h′/h). For curved mirrors, the dioptric power of the mirror equals: L′ − L = −2nR = (−2n)/r, where R is the curvature of the mirror.

329. **(B)** First, use the equation for curved mirrors: F = L′ − L = −2nR. Next use the relationship: object extent/(object's distance + eye's image distance) = mirror size/(eye's image distance). Note that the field of view is large for diverging mirrors (convex mirrors).

330. **(D)** First, use the equation: F(mirror) = −2n/r. Next, use F(clock) = (1.5 − 1)/r. It should be noted that (r) for the mirror is the same (r) as for the lens clock.

331. **(B)** Use the equation for curvature in oblique meridians of cylindrical refracting surfaces: RΘ = R sin²Θ. Remember, (Θ) is the angle that the oblique meridian makes with the axis of the cylinder, (R)Θ is the curvature in the oblique meridian, while (R) is the curvature in the meridian of maximum power. Next, use the surface power equation: F = (n′ − n) RΘ.

332. **(A)** The circle of least confusion lies halfway (dioptrically) between the two line foci; i.e., $L'c = (1/2)(L'_1 + L'_2)$. $L'c$ is the im-

age vergence for the circle; L'_1 and L'_2 are the image vergences for each of the principal meridians. Note: when $L = O$, $L' = F$.

333. **(A)** First, use the equations for the position and length of each line foci for the cylindrical and spherocylindrical lenses. Next, utilize the fundamental vergence equation $(L + F = L')$ for each principal meridian. Also, utilize the equation for circle of least confusion: $L'c = (1/2)(L'_1 + L'_2)$. (See answer **332**.)

334. **(C)** Use the achromatic doublet equation: $F(crown)/V(crown) = -F(flint)/V(flint)$. Also utilize the expression: $V = (n_D - 1)/n_F - n_C)$. (F) is the dioptric power of the lens and (V) is the constringence of the individual glass. Constringence is equal to the reciprocal of the dispersive power of that glass.

335. **(A)** Images formed by thin, spherical lenses suffer from the defect known as spherical aberration. Longitudinal spherical aberration occurs when a wide pencil of light is refracted by a spherical surface. Relative to the surface, the marginal rays focus at a point different than the paraxial rays. Longitudinal S.A. is measured between those two points of focus along the system's optical axis.

336. **(C)** Use the inverse square law and the cosine law. The inverse square law states that the illumination on a surface normal to the direction of the light incident from a point source is equal to the candle power of that source divided by the square of the distance between the source and the surface. The cosine law states that the illumination of a surface varies as the cosine of the angle of incidence. Therefore, $E = (I/d^2) \times (\cos i)$.

337. **(D)** Use the equation for optical density: Density $= \log_{10}$ Opacity. The reciprocal of the transparency is called opacity. The logarithm to base ten of the opacity is called optical density.

338. **(B)** When parallel light strikes such a system, parallel light leaves that system. Incident vergence is not altered by the unit system; thus, light is not brought to a focus. Such a system is called an afocal system.

339. **(E)** Optically, a compound microscope can be considered as being made up of a telescope with a simple microscope attached to

its objective. Therefore, the total magnification of the system is equal to (the apparent magnification of the telescope × the apparent magnification of the simple microscope): $Mt = (-F_2/F_1) \times F/4$. The magnification of the telescope portion is equal to the dioptric power of the telescope's eyepiece divided by the telescope's objective power. The magnification of the simple microscope portion is equal to the microscope's power divided by four.

340. (D) In image space, the exit pupil is found to be the image of the aperture stop. In object space, the entrance pupil is found to be the image of the aperture stop. The aperture stop controls the amount of light that can pass through any system.

341. (A) Use the equation for apparent magnification for a compound microscope: (mag of microscope) × (mag of telescope). Note: the objective can be divided into two parts. One is used to collimate the light from the near object (+5 D) microscope and the other part is used as part of the objective of the telescope (+20 D). Therefore, the total mag = (5/2.5) × (50/20) = 5×.

342. (C) The entrance pupil is the image of the aperture stop in object space. Its location helps govern the size of the field of view in object space. The field of view in object space is called the actual field.

343. (A) The entrance port is the image of the field stop in object space. Its size and location helps govern the size of the field of view in object space. The field stop, along with the aperture stop, controls the size of the field of view.

344. (E) The field of one-half illumination is determined by drawing lines from the edges of the entrance port to the center of the entrance pupil. It is independent of the size of the entrance pupil. The field of one-half illumination is usually taken as an instrument's field of view.

345. (B) This field is determined by drawing lines from the edge of the entrance port on one side of the optic axis to the edge of the entrance pupil on the other side of the optic axis. It is the largest of the three fields. Light incident outside this field will not pass through the optical system.

346. (B) Note: the field of view in image space is called the apparent field of view. The field of view in object space is called the actual field of view. They are related by means of the magnifying power of the system.

347. (A) This is the standard definition. The corresponding distance in object space is called the depth of field. Both distances are dependent upon the definition of the permissible diameter of blur circles.

348. (C) The f/no. is expressed as the ratio of the focal length to the diameter of the effective aperture. (The effective aperture is generally considered to be the entrance pupil.) The exposure required under any condition varies directly as the square of the f/no.

349. (A) The f/no is expressed as the ratio of the focal length to the diameter of the entrance pupil (the effective aperture) of the system. The illumination of a given image varies as the square of the diameter of the aperture. Therefore, the exposure required under any condition varies directly as the square of the f/no.

350. (B) Light transmitting power equals the square of the diameter of the exit pupil. The exit pupil must be measured in (mm). Therefore, $(35/7)^2 = 25$. This value has no significance when the diameter of the exit pupil exceeds the diameter of the apparent eye pupil behind the system.

351. (C) The entrance pupil is the image of the aperture stop in object space. The entrance port is the image of the field stop in object space. For total field, draw lines from the entrance port on one side of the optic axis to the entrance pupil on the opposite side.

352. (B) The entrance pupil is the image of the aperture stop in object space. The entrance port is the image of the field stop in object space. The field of half illumination is usually taken as the field of view.

353. (D) The object and the image are said to be in symmetrical planes of the lens when the lateral magnification is −1.000. This is the minimum distance between a real object and its real image.

Furthermore, it is the minimum distance between a virtual object and its virtual image.

354. **(C)** Utilize Gaussian optics. The principal points are the points where the principal planes intersect the optic axis. The nodal points are the points through which the chief ray passes through a system undeviated.

355. **(C)** Utilize Gaussian optics. Note: the distance between the first focal and nodal points is equal to the second focal length. In a system where the focal lengths are equal, but opposite in sign, the index in object space (n) is equal to the index in image space (n').

356. **(B)** An achromatic lens (doublet) is made of two components, two thin lenses of different glass materials. When juxtaposed, the two components have the ability to focus light (of two different colors) at the same place. The equivalent power for such a thin lens combination is equal to the sum of the power of the separate lenses. The equivalent focal length is the reciprocal of the equivalent power. Therefore, $1/[(1/.08) - (1/0.12)] = 24$.

357. **(A)** Use the back vertex power equation: $F_v' = F_1/(1 - d/n \, F_1) + F_2$. Also, utilize the equivalent power equation: $F_e = F_1 + F_2 - d/n \, F_1 \, F_2$. Note (d) is in meters, (n) is the index of refraction within the distance covered by (d), (F_1) represents the front surface power, and (F_2) represents the back surface power.

358. **(B)** Use the back vertex power equation: $F_v' = F_1/(1 - d/n \, F_1) + F_2$. Also, use the front vertex power equation: $F_v = F_e/(1 - d/n \, F_2)$. Note that (d) is in meters and (n) is the index that (d) covers.

359. **(D)** Use back vertex, front vertex, and equivalent power equations: $F_v' = F_1/(1 - d/n \, F_1) + F_2$; $F_v = F_e/(1 - d/n \, F_2)$; $F_e = F_1 + F_2 - d/n \, F_1 \, F_2$. Note that (d) is in meters and (n) is the index that (d) covers. See answer **357.**

360. **(D)** Use the equivalent power equation: $F_e = F_1 + F_2 - d/n \, F_1 \, F_2$. Note that (d) is in meters and (n) is the index that (d) covers. See answers **357** and **359.**

361. **(B)**   Use the back vertex power equation: $F_v' = F_1/(1 - d/n\, F_1) + F_2$. Note that (d) is in meters and (n) is the index that (d) covers. The back vertex power is the effective dioptric power of the front surface dioptric power at the back surface plus the dioptric power of the back surface.

362. **(C)**   Image the mirror through the other surface. Next, utilize the curved mirror equation: $F = L' - L = -2nR$. Finally, use the lateral magnification equation: $M = L/L' = h'/h$.

363. **(C)**   Use the equation for velocity: $V = d/t$. (d) is the distance traveled and (t) is the time used to travel that distance. Note that the distance traveled is (15 km) $\times$ 2 = 30 km. Furthermore, note that revolutions/seconds = 1/200(REV) $\times$ 1/time, where t(time) = 1×10^{-4} seconds.

364. **(B)**   The distinction between phosphorescence and fluorescence is based on time. A material is classified as phosphorescent if it continues to fluoresce for more than one microsecond after the exciting light is removed. Hands on clocks that glow in the dark are typical examples of this phenomenon.

365. **(D)**   This is known as the Tyndall effect. Scattered light will consist primarily of the shorter wavelengths; that is, scattered light will consist of the blue and the violet wavelengths.

366. **(A)**   Use the equation for distance between the centers of consecutive bright or dark interference bands: $Y = (DK\lambda)/b$. Also use the ophthalmic prism equation: $d = (n - 1)a$. Remember, (D) = distance to screen, (λ) is the wavelength, (K) is the phase difference, (b) = slit separation, (d) is the deviating power of the bi-prism, and (a) is the apical angle of the bi-prism at its thin edges (acute angles).

367. **(B)**   Use the equations for thin film interference: $2nt \cos i' = k\lambda$ and $r = Y_2/2t$. As seen by reflection, the patterns observed will consist of a black spot at the point of contact (called optical contact) surrounded by concentric alternate light and dark rings. The rings formed in this experiment are called Newton's rings.

368. (B)   Use the reflectance equation: $w = [(n' - n)/(n' + n)]^2 \times 100$. Note: (n) is the index of air = 1.000 and (n') is the index of diamond = 2.450.

369. (C)   Use the equation for resolving power: $w = h/l = 1.22\ \lambda/b$. The smallest value (w), for which the image of two points can be detected as double, is called the resolving power (limit of resolution). Also, use the equation for apparent magnification of a telescope (w'/w). The magnification of a telescope = w'/w = image subtense/object subtense.

370. (C)   Use the diffraction grating equation: $\sin \Theta = k\lambda/(b + c)$. Note: (b + c), the width of one slit and one opaque space, is called the grating interval and (k) is the order of the maximum from the center.

371. (A)   Use the equation: $I\Theta = I\ COS^2\Theta$. Θ is the angle between the axis of each filter. $I\Theta = .50\ COS^2\ 35° = .3355$. (I) is the intensity of incident light on the second filter. Remember, the first filter cuts out 50 percent of the original incident light.

372. (B)   Use the critical angle equation: $(\sin i_c = 1/n)$ and Brewster's law: $\tan i_p = n/n'$ (where n' = 1.000 for air). The critical angle phenomenon occurs on the dense side of the air-glass barrier. The polarizing angle occurs on the rare side of the air-glass barrier.

Ophthalmic Optics

373. (A)   One degree is equal to 1.745Δ. For ophthalmic optics, the unit adopted for deviation is the prism diopter. A prism diopter is the angle whose tangent is one divided by one hundred.

374. (D)   The image of regard is located 60 mm above its original position, which is located 529.5 mm in front of the eye's center of rotation. As the prism moves away from the eye, its effect on the eye decreases. As it moves toward the eye, its effect increases.

375. (B)   The power (d) of a prism depends upon the prism's refractive index (n) and upon its apical angle (a); that is, $d = (n - 1)a$. In

oblique meridians, the effective apical angle changes with the orientation of the prism. Therefore, as (a) increases/decreases, (d) in-
creases/decreases.

376. **(C)**   The zero position occurs when the bases of the two prisms
are opposite. As the prisms are counter-rotated, the power of the
two is equivalent to $2 \times (\Delta\sin\theta)$. Δ is the power of the component
prisms and θ is the angle of counter-rotation. Rotary prisms are
utilized in clinical optics to dissociate the two eyes, to measure
the angle of deviations (either if phoric or tropic), and to measure
the amplitude of the duction.

377. **(B)**   In oblique positions of gaze, light will pass through more
prism, thereby increasing the prism's effective apical angle. As a
result, in oblique positions of gaze, the prismatic effect of an ophthalmic prism increases. Straight lines, therefore, appear to be
curved.

378. **(B)**   The point on the lens where there are no prismatic effects is
called the optical center. A ray directed toward the optical center
of a lens is therefore undeviated. When no prismatic effect is required in an ophthalmic prescription, the optical center of the lens
is positioned directly in front of the eye's line of sight.

379. **(B)**   This lens form has surface curvatures that are both positive.
One surface of the lens is convex; the other surface is concave.
This lens design is the design of choice.

380. **(C)**   Base in prism is obtained when moving plus power in, in
the 180 meridian. As the optical center of the (+) lens is moved
away from the eye and towards the nose (moved in), the prismatic
effect of the (+) lens increases in base in power according to
Prentice's Rule. That is $d^\Delta = (C)(F)$, where (c) is the amount of
movement away from the optical center, in centimeters, and (F) is
the power of the lens.

381. **(A)**   A lensometer reading does not depend on index. A
lensometer measures either front vertex power or back vertex
power. Vertex power is the vergence of light leaving the front or
back surface of the lens when the object is at infinity on the opposite side.

382. A-3, B-4, C-2, D-5, E-1. In order to transpose a prescription from minus cylinder form to plus cylinder form, or from plus cylinder form to minus cylinder form, the following procedure is used. For the new sphere, add the power of the old sphere and cylinder algebraically. For the new cylinder, change the sign of the old cylinder, keeping the same amount. For the new axis, subtract or add 90° to the old axis (leaving the new axis 180° or less).

383. (C) The lens must be turned around to gain the appropriate reading. Remember, the ocular surface (F_2) must be placed against the aperture stop of the lensometer in order to gain the appropriate reading of back vertex power. Back vertex power is Rx.

384. (A) Use solution for the combination of crossed cylinders. See *Ophthalmic Mechanics and Dispensing,* authored by Epting; *Geometrical, Physical, and Visual Optics,* authored by Keating; and *System for Ophthalmic Dispensing,* authored by Brooks and Borish, for instructions. Note: the effects produced by decentering cylinders depend on both the power of the cylinder and on the orientation of the axes.

385. (D) Use the method for determining the prismatic effect of a decentered spherocylindrical lens. See *Geometrical, Physical and Visual Optics,* authored by Keating for instructions. Note: the prismatic effects produced by decentering cylinders depend on both the power of the cylinder and on the orientation of the axes.

386. (C) Use the method for determining the prismatic effect of a decentered spherocylindrical lens. See *Geometrical, Physical and Visual Optics,* authored by Keating for instructions. Note: the prismatic effects produced by decentering cylinders depend on both the power of the cylinder and on the orientation of the axes.

387. (B) Use the approximate sagitta equation: $r = Y^2/2S$ and the surface power equation: $F = (n' - n)/r$. Note: (Y) is the half cord, (S) is the sag, (F) is the surface power, $(n' - n)$ is the index differential, and (r) is the radius of the surface, measured in meters. Remember, this is the approximate sag equation; the exact equation is $r = Y^2/2S + S/2$.

388. (D) Vertical imbalance is the difference in prismatic effects in prism diopters between the 90° meridians of the right and left lens. First, determine the vertical power of each lens: for (OD) + 0.50 D and for (OS) + 1.75 D; the difference is, therefore, 1.25 D. Next, multiply 1.25 by 0.8 cm. $(1.25)(.8) = 1.0^\Delta$

389. (A) Slab-off or bicentric grind is ground on the back surface of the lens that has the most minus (least plus) power in the 90° meridian. Slab-off produces additional prism base toward the center of the lens. Therefore, when looking down, it results in more prism, base up.

390. (D) Use the equation for back vertex power: $F_v' = F_1/(1 - d/n\ F_1) + F_2$. The back vertex power is the effective power of the front surface power at the back surface plus the back surface power. When an object is at infinity in front of the lens, the vergence of light leaving the back surface is called back vertex power.

391. (C) Use the equation for back vertex power: $F_v' = F_1/(1 - d/n\ F_1) + F_2$. Next, compare that value to the results gained utilizing the thin lens equation: $F_T = F_1 + F_2$. As the lens gains center thickness, the two values, (F_v') and (F_T) tend to differ more.

392. (B) Use the effective power formula: $F_x = F/(1 - dF)$. As lenses move away from the eye, their effect at the eye increases in plus power and decreases in minus power. As lenses move toward the eye, their effect increases in minus power and decreases in plus power.

393. (D) First, use the surface power equation: $F = (n' - n)/r$. Next, use the back vertex power equation: $F_v' = F_1/(1 - d/n\ F_1) + F_2$. Remember that the back vertex power is the effective power of surface one at surface two plus the power of surface two.

394. (E) Use the back vertex power equation: solve for F_1: $F_v' = F_1/(1 - d/n\ F_1) + F_2$. Next, use the surface power equation: $F = (n' - n)/r$. Now solve for (r), the radius of the front surface.

395. (B) Marginal astigmatism occurs when a small bundle of light strikes a lens from an oblique angle, forming two line images of a given point source. Therefore, objects viewed at an oblique direction through the lens are blurred. In curvature of field, it is found that ophthalmic lenses do not form images of objects in a flat plane at the focal distance. The images formed are found to be curved concave toward the lens.

396. (D) Use Martin's formula for tilt: Gain in sphere = $(F \sin^2\Theta/2n)$ and Gain in cylinder = $(F \tan^2\Theta)$. (Θ) is the degree of tilt. Pantoscopic tilt is the outward inclination of the top portion of the frame front. The pantoscopic tilt allows the line of sight to pass through the optical center of the lens when the direction of gaze is pointed somewhat downward toward the ground just ahead of the patient. This is done to enhance observations during walking.

397. (C) This is the standard position for bifocal heights. A person who carries his head back would benefit from a segment placed lower. A person who carries his head down, in a stooped-over manner, would benefit from a segment placed higher.

398. (D) The amount of jump is independent of the power of the distance portion of the lens. It is calculated using Prentice's Rule: $d^\Delta = CF$: $(1.75 - 1.25)(2.50) = 1.25$. Note: (d) is the deviating power in prism diopters.

399. (E) They are all correct. A double segment has near segments in both the upper and lower portion of the lens. This design allows better vision for older individuals who require clear vision both at finite distance above and below the straight ahead position of gaze.

400. (E) They are all correct. The progressive addition lens consists of specially designed curves that produce a gradual increase in plus power in the lower portion of the lens when going from distance to near. As a result, clear vision is permitted at any given distance merely by positioning the head and eyes.

401. (C) Definition of Major Reference Point. The point on the lens where the prism equals that called for by the prescription. When no prism is required, the optical center and the major reference point coincide.

402. (E) All will cause an error in PD measurement. With higher prescriptions, use of the PD rule should be avoided. A pupillometer must be used to enhance accuracy.

403. (B) As reflection decreases, transmission increases. AR (anti-reflecting) coated lenses reduce the annoyance produced by reflected light. Furthermore, they increase the amount of light transmitted through the lens material.

404. (E) They are highly scratch resistant when appropriate coatings are applied to both surfaces. Polycarbonate lenses are considered to be the strongest lenses currently available. Their index of refraction is 1.586, making them more attractive than CR39 lenses.

405. (D) This technique moves the left portion of the frame front up. Also, note that in order to achieve the same results, the right temple can be angled up. At times, raising one temple and lowering the other is required.

Physiological Optics and Visual Optics

406. (D) Utilize Gullstrand's No. 2 unaccommodated schematic eye, the vergence equation: $L + F = L'$ and the lateral magnification equation: $m = nl'/n'l$. Note: (L) is object vergence, (F) is power, and (L') is image vergence; (n) is object space index, (n') is image space index, (l) is object distance, and (l') is image distance.

407. (E) During accommodation, Purkinje images I and II do not change since they are formed by the cornea; Purkinje images III and IV decrease in size. Purkinje image III moves toward the cornea. Purkinje image IV moves away from the cornea.

408. A-1, B-2, C-8, D-5, E-9. Gullstrand developed a simplified version of the eye's optical system. This version consists of three refracting surfaces (one corneal and two lens), and a homogeneous index for the lens material. For most optical calculations, the simplified version of the eye's optical system is sufficiently accurate.

409. (D) Use the equations: $F = (n' - n)/r$ and $L + F = L'$. Remember that an aphakic eye cannot accommodate because it has no lens.

(F) is the power of the corneal surface in contact with air, $(n' - n)$ is the index differential between adjacent media, (r) is the radius of curvature of the surface; (L) is the object vergence and (L') is the image vergence.

410. (B) This particular eye is found to have its greatest refracting power and corneal curvature in the horizontal meridian. Its circle of least confusion will be located near the the retina, because one meridian is myopic and the other meridian is hyperopic. Thus (in the uncorrected state), it will have relatively good vision.

411. (A) For any lens, the spectacle magnification depends on the shape and the power of the lens. That is, spectacle magnification = (shape factor)(power factor). The shape factor is given by $[1/(1 - t/n \, F_1)]$. The power factor is given by $[1/(1 - dF_v')]$. (t) is the thickness of the lens, (F) is the front surface power, (F_v') is the back vertex power, (d) is the distance between the back of the lens and the entrance pupil of the eye, and (n) is the index of the lens. See question **808** for a sample calculation.

412. (B) Airy disc size varies directly with the wavelength. Furthermore, it varies inversely with the pupil size. As the pupil (aperture) size decreases, diffraction increases.

413. (E) In order to visualize the shadows created on the retina by the retinal vessels, the shadows must move. This is achieved by changing the angle of incidence of the rays as they strike the retina. This can be done by 1) simply moving a bright light near the eye (e.g., a candle, as described by Purkinje) such that its image, moving on the peripheral retina, becomes a secondary source to illuminate the central retina; 2) illuminating the sclera; or 3) illuminating the retina with a narrow beam that can be moved around in the pupil plane. Alternatively, because the contents of the vessels are in motion, a bright blue field can be used, because every break in the red blood cell flow is seen as a moving bright spot (flying corpuscles).

414. (E) Maxwell's spot is the shadow cast by the macular pigment when illuminated by short wavelength light. Hadinger's brushes represent the radial polarization effects created by the alignment of macular pigment molecules with the nerve fiber layer. Purkinje tree is the shadow cast by the retinal vessels. Flying corpuscles are the gaps in the red blood cell flow that occur when individual large leukocytes pass through the capillaries.

415. **(B)**   Unlike opacities near the retina, opacities near the front of the eye generally do not cast clear shadows on the retina. In order to see them entoptically, a shadow must be cast with a very small point source. Placing a small point source near the anterior focal point of the eye will approximately collimate the light within the eye and create a shadow that has the same physical size as the opacity.

416. **(E)**   Visual phosphenes are visual events created by something other than the photo isomerization of photopigment. These events can be produced by mechanical stresses caused by eye movements. Furthermore, local pressure, high voltage, and spontaneous isomerizations of photochemical can also create these events.

417. **(E)**   Because it is not possible to place an instrument inside the eye to measure retinal images, several ingenious techniques have been developed. Objective measures of the reflected images of lines (the double-pass, lines spread measurement) have been successful, as has the measurement of contrast sensitivity with (normal view) and without (interferometric view) the eye's optics degrading the image (the ratio of the two is a measure of the eye's optical MTF). Also, from experimental measures of the eye's optical aberrations, others have calculated retinal image quality.

418. **(C)**   Stiles-Crawford effect of the first kind is the difference in brightness of two pencils of light incident on the retina at the same point. Stiles-Crawford effect of the second kind is the difference in perceived saturation and hue of two pencils of light of the same wavelength incident on the retina at the same point. Although A-D can contribute stray light to the retinal image, the reflections from the retina are thought to arrive at other photoreceptors at such an oblique angle that the directional sensitivity of the cones (which manifests itself as the Stiles-Crawford effect) significantly reduces the visual impact of these reflections.

419. (D) Transverse chromatic aberration describes the spatial separation of images of different wavelengths. This will occur whenever a polychromatic ray bundle strikes an optical surface obliquely. In the eye, this will occur for the entire ray bundle from a fixation point when a small pupil is displaced from the visual axis.

420. (C) Optical images suffer from lens defects. These are known as aberrations. The aberrations due to the form of the lens are spherical aberration, coma, astigmatism, curvature of field, and distortion. The aberration due to lens material is chromatic aberration. Diffraction is not an aberration. Spherical aberration is due to the shape of the curved surface. Because accommodation is accompanied by a change in the power and sphericity of the lens, spherical aberration can change from positive (marginal power greater than paraxial) to zero or negative with increasing accommodation.

421. (E) A point source emits in all directions; that is, throughout a sphere of 4π (or 12.56) steradians. Therefore, this source emits 2 watts per steradian. At 555 nm, 1 watt is equivalent to 685 lumens; therefore, this source emits 2×685 lumens/steradian. Because a candle emits 1 lumen per steradian, this source is equivalent to 2×685 candles.

422. (C) A 0.01 m² area placed 10 cm from a point source would subtend one steradian. Therefore, if this source emits 2 watts/steradian, then this surface will receive 2 watts of radiant flux, or 1370 lumens at 555 nm. Because the area is 1/100th of a meter, this 1370 lumens translates into 100×1370 lux (lumens per m²).

423. (E) Retinal image area and total flux within the image both decrease as the approximate square of the viewing distance. Therefore, retinal illuminance is unaffected by distance. A 3.5 mm diameter pupil has an area of approximately 10 mm². Therefore, a 1000 cd/m² target will provide 1000×10 trolands.

424. (E) Retinal illuminance is directly proportional to target luminance. It is approximately proportional to pupil size. Because of the Stiles-Crawford effect, it is also affected by the position of the pupil. Radiant energy entering the eye through the dilated pupil margin has less visual effect (i.e., as though there were less light and therefore less retinal illuminance).

Visual Perception

425. **(E)** People with normal color vision have *two* color-opponent mechanisms: R-G and Y-B, and the unique hues reflect spectral stimuli that elicit zero response from one or the other of these color-opponent mechanisms. Prior to the color-opponent mechanisms, the spectral composition of the light stimulus is coded by *three* cone-types (L, M, and S). Because the spectral information is coded into three variables (responses of L, M, and S cones), it is possible to exactly match the relative response from the three cone types elicited by any individual wavelength by a combination of three primaries. Two such stimuli matched in this way are called metamers.

426. **(B)** This question examines the complementary colors (red-green and blue-yellow) observed after color adaptation (prolonged viewing of a colored light) and induced by simultaneously viewed colored surround lights. The induced colors tend to be desaturated. Yellow will always be paired with blue, just as red and green are paired.

427. **(B)** Protanopes and deuteranopes can make matches with any ratio. Deuteranomalous trichromats need more green. Protanomalous trichromats need more red.

428. **(A)** In CIE space, the distance ratio (Achromatic Point to Sample Point)/(Achromatic Point to Spectral Locus of dominant wavelength of sample color), is the excitation purity of the sample color. The colorimetric purity and also the luminance purity of a given color represent the luminance ratio of the dominant wavelength and the achromatic white that, when added, give a particular color.

429. **(B)** In the Munsell color space (tree), "value" represents "lightness." Value has a minimum value of zero (black) at the bottom

and a maximum value of 10 (white) at the top. The other dimensions in this three-dimensional space are **croma** and **hue**.

430. **(B)** Hue changes accompanying luminance changes is the Bezold-Brücke phenomenon. Hue changes accompanying purity changes is the Abney's phenomenon (effect). Brightness increases accompanying intermediate flicker rates is the Brücke-Bartley effect. Brightness increases accompanying intermediate flash durations is the Broca-Sulzer effect.

431. **(A)** Spectral purity is zero for an achromatic stimulus and 1 for a monochromatic light. Although saturation is not equal for all spectral stimuli, it does vary monotonically with purity. Increases in purity lead to increases in saturation.

432. **(A)** Hue is the perceptual property most closely related to wavelength. However, brightness and saturation of monochromatic lights also vary with wavelength. Casual observation of a rainbow will confirm this.

433. **(C)** The distance (d) at which the distal depth interval (Δd) approaches infinity is defined by $d = a/(\tan \phi/2)$. $a = IPD/2$ and $\phi =$ the stereoscopic depth threshold in degrees (a and d are in the same units). For example, $0.0325/(\tan 10''/2) = 1341$ meters.

434. **(E)** With increasing viewing distance, the horopter tends to become less concave. It can even become slightly convex at larger distances. The distance at which it becomes planar is defined as the abathic distance.

435. **(B)** This geometrically defined circle is known as the Vieth-Müller circle. Deviations of empirically determined horopters from this circle are known as Hering-Hilderbrand deviations. Near the fixation point, the experimentally determined horopter is usually less concave than the Vieth-Müller circle.

436. **(A)** Horizontal disparity (θ) is related to differences in distance or depth (ΔD) by the following relationship: $\theta = (-2a * \Delta D)/[D^2 + (D * \Delta D)]$, where D is the viewing distance and 2a is the IPD. For a fixed ΔD, wider PD's and shorter viewing distances create larger horizontal disparities.

437. (A) Because horizontal disparity (θ) decreases with the square of the viewing distance (see answer **436**), even large differences in distance (ΔD) produce only very small angular disparities for distant objects. Because of the speed of large aircraft, only distant objects can be effectively used to control the plane visually. Beyond about 1 Km, all horizontal disparities are effectively subthreshold (see answer **433**).

438. (C) Chromostereopsis, or color stereoscopy, is observed when the foveal transverse chromatic aberration differs in the right and left eyes. Any naso-temporal (horizontal) interocular difference in foveal TCA will lead to horizontal interocular differences in the location of short and long wavelength images, and hence wavelength-dependent differences in horizontal disparities, and different colored targets will appear at different depths.

439. (E) Size constancy is either the observation of, or the mechanism responsible for, objects maintaining the same apparent size irrespective of distance. As distance increases, retinal image size decreases, yet perceived size is maintained. If distance cues are eliminated, perceived size will be dominated by retinal image size, not physical size, and hence will not exhibit size constancy.

440. (E) The Ponzo illusion (two equally long horizontal bars embedded in two converging near vertical lines) is caused by size constancy. The top line appears further away, and the brain therefore expands its perceived size. Likewise, the Muller-Lyer illusion can be explained by size constancy. The line with the standard arrowhead is perceived as the near corner of the outside of a building, whereas the arrow tails are perceived as the far corner of the inside of a building, and size constancy scales this line up. The moon appears larger near the horizon because it appears farther away. The Zollner illusion is caused by acute angle expansion.

441. (D) The white intersection points in the Herman grid appear darker because they are not surrounded by as much black ink. Likewise, the dark band of the Mach bands appears darker because it has more light adjacent to it. Both of these are examples of brightness induced by the luminance (contrast) of the surrounding area. Brightness constancy describes stability of object brightness over a wide range of illumination levels. Clearly, as illumination levels are changed, object luminance changes, but object contrast does not. Hence it is another example of how luminance contrast determines brightness. Abney's effect refers to a change in hue.

442. (B) A typical normal CSF peaks at 3–10 c/deg with a contrast sensitivity of about 100–300. It exhibits reduced sensitivity at both high and low frequencies. It has a high frequency cut-off (visual acuity) near 40 c/deg (20/15).

443. (A) Diffraction tends to limit visual acuity for small pupil sizes and this effect can be calculated using the Rayleigh criterion (2 just resolvable thin lines must be separated by at least the angular width of the diffraction line-spread function), whereas optical aberrations and defocus are the most significant factors with large pupils. These two types of optical limit produce reduced acuities for very large pupils and for very small pupils, and best image quality is achieved with intermediate sizes.

444. (C) Detection of test patterns can be interfered with by concurrently presented "masking" stimuli. Interestingly, these "masking effects" can be seen for test stimuli presented slightly before the mask is turned on. This effect is referred to as backward masking (the converse is called forward masking).

445. (E) Because of lateral inhibition, the output of retinal ganglion cells is determined primarily by the luminance contrast in the retinal image. Because of this, brightness is determined by luminance contrast, and good examples of this are the classic Mach bands, simultaneous contrast, and Herman's grid phenomena. Also, lateral inhibition enhances sensitivity to luminance modulations (contrast). The low-frequency fall-off in contrast sensitivity is because there is relatively less change in luminance over a receptive field when the image is low frequency.

446. (E) The entrance aperture of a foveal cone is approximately 2 μm, and subtends about 0.5 arc minutes (30 seconds) at the nodal point of the eye. Vernier (alignment), bisection, stereo, and displacement acuities can all be less than 10 arc seconds.

447. (C) Both tumbling E's and Landolt C's test use a range of sizes of a single letter type rotated to different positions to test acuity. The Log MAR chart uses many letters (as does the Snellen chart) of different sizes, but unlike the Snellen chart it has the same number of letters per line and the letter sizes on each line are a constant percentage of the previous line. The Pelli-Robson chart has fixed size letter of differing contrast, and therefore this is not an acuity test.

448. (C) The kink reflects the different rates of dark adaptation for rod and cone vision. When the latter has already fully dark adapted, visual sensitivity of rod vision is increasing rapidly. The kink occurs at the point in time at which the rod sensitivity surpasses that of the cones.

449. (E) A kink appears with a very bright light that produces significantly more bleaching in the rods than in the cones, yet it produces significant desensitization of the cones (a typical very bright broad spectrum white light). When the rods are unaffected by the adapting light (A), or there is no light adaptation in the cones (B), or cones and rods are equally desensitized (C), there will be no kink.

450. (B) Fechner's paradox refers to the observation that a bright stimulus viewed monocularly appears brighter than when it is viewed binocularly with an ND filter in front of one eye. The paradox is simple: by opening the filtered eye, more light enters the visual system, but the light appears darker. It appears as though the perceived brightness is determined by some average of the two monocular brightnesses.

451. (B) At night, dim stars can only be detected by the rod visual system. Clearly, if fixated under scotopic conditions, a dim star will disappear because of the central scotoma created by the absence of rods in the central fovea. This is not related to resolution (two stars vs. one), nor is it related to pupil size. If anything, starlight is better matched for photopic spectral sensitivity in that it shows a slight bias for longer wavelengths.

452. (B) Using his magnitude estimation paradigm, Stevens showed that brightness (B) was related to stimulus luminance (L) by his "power law": $B = kL^n$. The power exponent was about 0.3, and after taking the logarithm of both sides of this equation, he showed that $\log B = n\log L + k$. Fechner, using a difference limen (ΔI) technique, suggested that B (not log B) = $a\log L + k$.

453. **(B)** Unlike *unscattered* light, which strikes the retina from a narrow range of incident angles (determined by the pupil position and size), rays scattered by the neural retina can strike the photoreceptors from almost any angle. The angular selectivity of the photoreceptors, which manifests itself as the Stiles-Crawford effect (with a peak sensitivity at or near the pupil center), would reduce the effectiveness of these scattered rays.

454. **(E)** Weber's law $[(\Delta I/I) = K]$ describes the relationship between the jnd (ΔI or ΔL) for intensity or luminance as a function of the background intensity or luminance level. The linear relationship, $\Delta I = KI$, is a restatement of Weber's law and shows that ΔI is proportional to I. Weber's law is NOT a general rule for all vision; for example, it does not apply at low light levels, or for high or medium spatial frequencies.

455. **(D)** Stiles and Crawford showed that the failure to see the expected increase in brightness when the pupil dilates is due to the reduced sensitivity to light entering near the pupil margins. It is generally felt that this Stiles-Crawford effect is due to photoreceptors being more sensitive to light entering through the pupil center. Although we measure the effect at the pupil plane, it is believed that it reflects the wave-guide properties of photoreceptors.

456. **(C)** Different studies have shown that the minimum velocity that is perceived to be moving varies considerably with the stimulus conditions. However, for an easily visible target viewed foveally, results of 1–3 arc min/sec are common. Some very slowly moving objects can be identified as moving simply because they change location over time, but they do not elicit any sensation of motion.

457. **(E)** Rapid, successive alternation of lights or targets at slightly different positions or shapes creates a variety of apparent movement phenomena, which have been variously labeled by a series of Greek letters. Alpha movement refers to perceptual changes of

illusions; sigma is unrelated to this phenomenon; gamma movement is the change in perceived size caused by changing brightness; delta movement is in the opposite direction to the sequence of flashes; phi movement is perceived in the direction of the sequentially flashed stationary lights (similar to beta movement).

458. **(B)** Apparent motion of a stationary point source is known as the autokinetic effect, autokinesis, or the autokinetic illusion. It is not generally experienced under normal viewing conditions. It has been suggested that it is caused by unregistered eye movements.

459. **(E)** A key element in models of motion perception is a delayed input from a spatially adjacent point on the retina. In some models this is an excitatory (facilitatory) input, and in others it is inhibitory (such as in Barlow and Levick's classic paper on the rabbit retina). The temporal delay, combined with the spatial displacement, creates a directionally selective response. Directional selectivity is considered the key to a motion detecting system.

460. **(B)** Large objects/frames placed near to/around small objects and then moved slowly will induce the appearance of slow movement of the dot in the opposite direction. The induced motion is usually slower than the surround motion. It is most commonly observed when viewing the "small" stationary moon surrounded by "large" areas of moving clouds.

461. **(B)** The ND filter will reduce the retinal illuminance in the left eye and consequently increase the visual latency of the left eye signal. Therefore, with the left eye, the pendulum will appear to be located to the left of the apparent location observed with the right eye when moving to the right, and to the right when the pendulum is moving to the left; that is, the pendulum will have crossed disparity and appear closer when moving from right to left, and uncrossed and appear farther when moving from left to right.

462. **(E)** Whenever any cyclic motion (such as a rotating wheel) is viewed with intermittent illumination (such as TV, movies, or fluorescent lights), the motion will appear "stopped" when the cyclic

motion rate (cycles/second) equals an integer number of the illumination rate. At these rotation frequencies the wheel will always be in the same position when the light comes on or the camera shutter opens, and therefore it will appear stationary. If the wheel is circular and the spokes regularly distributed, a rotation sufficient to superimpose spokes will also create stopped motion because the wheel will appear to be in the same place on each frame (e.g., a propeller with four identical blades rotating at 1/4 the sampling rate will appear stopped).

463. **(E)** The familiar panic and rush to press the break pedal that can occur while waiting in traffic at a red light is a commonly observed illusion of self motion (vection) caused by movement of the neighboring vehicles. This effect is most pronounced when the moving stimulus fills a large area of the visual field. Vection can be linear, as in the above example, or rotational, as in the case of a subject sitting in a large rotating drum.

464. **(D)** After prolonged viewing of a waterfall (or any other steady movement), a subsequently viewed static pattern will appear to move in the opposite direction. This motion "illusion" is known as the waterfall illusion. A common laboratory example is created with a rotating spiral. Unlike the moving water in the waterfall, the "converging" or "expanding" rings in the rotating spiral cannot be tracked by eye movements (which will prevent the illusion from being created).

465. **(C)** The dependence of brightness on flash duration is referred to as the Broca-Sulzer effect. This is similar and related to the dependence of brightness on the frequency of a constant intensity flickering light (the Brücke-Bartley effect). These should be distinguished from the Bezold-Brücke effect (phenomenon), in which a small hue change accompanies a large luminance change in some spectral lights.

466. **(A)** This observation (known as the Talbot-Plateau law) shows that brightness is determined by linear summation of photons over very brief periods. Hence, the distribution of photons (modulated or stable) over very brief periods has no effect on brightness and therefore very rapid modulations will appear indistinguishable from uniform lights of the same time-average luminance.

467. (A) This observation is referred to as the Brucke-Bartley effect. As mentioned above (answer **465**), it is related to the duration dependence of the brightness of a single flash (the Broca-Sulzer effect; see answer **465**). It probably reflects the same band-pass mechanism responsible for the peaked nature of the temporal contrast sensitivity function.

468. (A) Increasing luminance produces an increase in the highest detectable temporal frequency (CFF). The quantitative relationship is best described by $CFF = k\log L + c$ (where L = luminance and k and c are constants). This relationship is known as the Ferry-Porter law.

469. (C) Bloch's law states that $L * T = K$ (where L = luminance threshold, T = flash duration, and K = a constant). It applies for very short duration flashes. Because of increased temporal summation, under scotopic conditions Bloch's law applies for longer duration flashes.

470. (B) Temporal summation is (1) longer for patterned stimuli, (2) longer at lower light levels, and (3) independent of wavelength. Typically, values of around 100 to 200 msec are obtained experimentally for spatially uniform stimuli under scotopic conditions.

Ocular Motility

471. (D) Under-accommodation to near targets, often referred to as the accommodative lag, increases in size under conditions where the depth of focus increases. There appears to be a bias to exert the minimum accommodative effort necessary to make the target "appear" in focus (i.e, be within the depth of focus).

472. (E) Accommodation is achieved by relaxing the tension on the ciliary zonules. This occurs during contraction of the ciliary muscle. Mechanical forces within the lens are no longer constrained by the forces exerted by the lens capsule during accommodation, and the lens generally becomes more spherical.

473. (B) With the exception of presbyopes (55 to 65 and older), humans accommodate synchronously in the two eyes in order to bring the images of near objects into coincidence with the retina. However, if there is no effective stimulus, e.g., a dark distant target or an empty field, many eyes will accommodate unnecessarily by, on average, about 1 diopter, creating a "myopia." These anomalous myopias are known as night myopia, empty field myopia, instrument myopia, etc.

474. **(E)** Due to decreased tension on the zonules, there is decreased tension on the lens capsule, and the anterior surface of the lens bulges forward slightly with an accompanying decrease in surface radius. Because of the decrease in zonular tension, the lens can fall in the direction of gravity. Due to a common neural response, the pupil also constricts.

475. **(E)** Decreased object distance (increased target proximity) can create (1) image defocus, (2) reduction in image contrast, and (3) binocular convergence. Studies have shown that any of these alone can initiate an accommodative response. However, recent evidence indicates that defocus is an inadequate stimulus to accommodation when presented in isolation.

476. **(B)** Accommodative response latency (300–350 msec) is greater than that of saccades (150 msec) and for vergences (200 msec). This may reflect the mechanical inertia present in the accommodative mechanism.

477. **(E)** Hippus describes oscillations of the pupil size that can occur without a light stimulus and can be induced in normals by placing a bright beam just inside the pupil margin. In this case, the pupil will constrict because of the increased light, which then occludes the beam, so, in response to the decrease in retinal illuminance, the pupil then dilates and the cycle begins again.

478. **(E)** Any stimulus lacking high frequency and medium frequency spatial modulations in luminance (luminance contrast) will prove ineffective as stimuli to control the accommodative response. Therefore, isoluminant color modulations (lacking any luminance modulation), empty fields, and low spatial frequencies all fall into this category.

479. **(B)** A large response in the sympathetic system will dilate the pupil but not elicit any accommodative response. Because of the large pupil, an uncorrected myope would have reduced distance vision rather than improved distance vision due to decreased depth of field.

480. **(B)** Hering's law states that symmetrical (conjugate) eye movements are achieved by equal innervation of the right and left eye extrinsic muscles. This law is sometimes defined as Hering's law of equal innervation. It is applied to equal and opposite (vergence) and equal and parallel (version) eye movements.

481. **(C)** Only the medial and lateral recti insertion points and contraction directions are in a single plane containing the eye's center of rotation and primary line of sight. Therefore, only these two muscles have a "simple" action, rotating the eye in only one plane. All other muscles create at least two axes of rotation.

482. **(C)** The extraocular muscles receive innovation by the III (oculomotor), IV (trochlear), and VI (abducens) cranial nerves. The superior oblique muscle is the only one innervated by the IV cranial nerve. All others, except for the lateral rectus, are innovated by cranial nerve III.

483. **(B)** When elevated, the insertion point of the medial rectus lies superior to the point of rotation of the eye. Therefore, under these circumstances, contraction of the medial rectus will lead to elevation of the direction of gaze in addition to adduction. The converse will be true during depression of gaze.

484. **(C)** The insertion point of the superior rectus muscle is anterior and nasal in addition to being superior to the point of rotation of the eye when in the primary direction of gaze. Therefore, its contraction will produce elevation, adduction, and intorsion. Elevation will be the primary action of this muscle.

485. **(A)** The insertion of the superior oblique muscle is temporal and posterior to the center of rotation. Also, it passes through the trochlea, which is anterior, nasal, and superior to the center of rotation. Therefore, it pulls the posterior/superior globe anteriorly

and nasally, producing intorsion, depression, and a slight abduction.

486. **(E)** When referenced to the primary line of sight, the effective origins of both the inferior and superior oblique muscles are both approximately 51 degrees nasal from their insertion points. Therefore, if the eye adducts by 51 degrees, these two muscles act as simple elevators and depressors.

487. **(D)** Precise and rapid saccadic eye movements are unnecessary in an animal that has no fovea because most of our saccadic eye movements are designed to fixate targets. Tracking movements maintain targets of interest relatively stabilized on the retina. Many animals (e.g., birds and reptiles), with much smaller heads (due to smaller brains) can move their heads very quickly. The large mass of the human brain prevents this option. Because high retinal drift rates tend to reduce vision, accurate tracking eye movements are necessary even without a fovea, and many birds and other small-brain animals stabilize and move retinal images via head movements.

488. **(C)** There are six extraocular muscles (4 recti and 2 obliques) that control rotation of the eye within its orbit. The large size of these muscles relative to the small weight of the globe permits very fast saccades (e.g., in excess of 200 degrees per second).

489. **(A)** The total horizontal field of a binocular person is about 180 degrees. However, because of the reduced bilateral nasal field (approximately 60–70 degrees), humans are functionally binocular only over about 120–140 degrees. Note that this varies slightly with individuals, direction of gaze, and viewing distance.

490. **(B)** OKN exhibits a slow (tracking) phase and a fast (return) phase. The tracking is in the same direction of target motion, and, of course, the fast phase is in the opposite direction. This reflex provides quite accurate retinal image stabilization during movement of the retinal image due to self-motion.

491. **(E)** Most of the time during OKN, the eye is in its slow tracking phase. Therefore, OKN creates a relatively stable (tracked) retinal image in spite of object motion. The experimental and clinical

conditions used to stimulate OKN (large moving fields) are rarely encountered in the natural environment. However, during self motion, the entire retinal image can drift across the retina. During these conditions, OKN provides reflex retinal image stabilization.

492. **(E)** During attempted steady fixation, the eye is in constant motion. In addition to a low amplitude, high frequency tremor, the eye seems to drift and lose fixation. These intermittent fixation errors are often corrected by small involuntary saccades.

493. **(B)** In the primary position of gaze, the extent of the nasal field is approximately coincident with the location of the bridge of the nose. Therefore, a nasal eye movement will image the bridge of the nose close to the fovea, thus effectively constricting the nasal field (relative to the fixation point). The converse does not happen, however, in the temporal field. Here, the visual field is not limited by the orbit, but by the retina. Therefore, a 30 degree nasal eye movement will simply translate the temporal field 30 degrees; thus, with respect to the fovea, the temporal field will still extend approximately 90 degrees.

494. **(D)** The maximum horizontal eye rotation is approximately 70 degrees. However, most eye rotations are less than 20 degrees. Eye rotations are supplemented by head rotations.

495. **(E)** Recent studies by Riggs and others have shown that the eye does not rotate upward (as it does during extended eye closures: Bell's phenomenon) during a blink. It moves very rapidly inferiorly and nasally. Visual sensitivity is reduced during the blink which may explain why we are often unaware of blinks.

496. **(E)** Normal blinking is controlled primarily by the palpebral portion of the orbicularis muscle. However, forced closure is achieved using the orbital portion. This muscle is innervated by the VII cranial nerve.

497. **(E)** The normal blink rate can vary, but approximately 20–30 is normal. However, during reading, this can drop dramatically. One clinical consequence of decreased blink rates is tear break-up during reading, which can be a problem for older patients.

References

1 Barlow HB, Mollon JD, eds. *The Senses.* Cambridge: Cambridge University Press; 1982.
2. Borish IM. *Clinical Refraction.* Vol I, 3rd ed. Chicago: Professional Press; 1970.
3. Borish IM. *Clinical Refraction.* Vol II, 3rd ed. Chicago: Professional Press; 1970.
4. Boynton RM. *Human Color Vision.* New York: Holt, Rinehart and Winston; 1979.
5. Brooks CW, Borish IM. *System for Ophthalmic Dispensing.* Chicago: Professional Press; 1979.
6. Carpenter RHS. *Movements of the Eyes.* London: Pion; 1977.
7. Cline D, Hofstetter HW, Griffin JR. *Dictionary of Visual Science,* 4th ed. Radnor, Pa: Chilton; 1989.
8. Cornsweet T. *Visual Perception.* San Diego: Harcourt, Brace & Jovanovich; 1970.
9. Davson H, ed. *The Eye, The Visual Process.* Vol 2. New York: Academic Press; 1962.
10. Davson H, ed. *The Eye, Muscular Mechanisms.* Vol 3. New York: Academic Press; 1969.
11. Davson H, ed. *The Eye.* Vol 4. New York: Academic Press; 1962.
12. Davson H. *Physiology of the Eye.* New York: Academic Press; 1980.
13. De Valois RL, De Valois KK. *Spatial Vision.* Oxford: Oxford University Press; 1988.
14. Dowaliby M. *Practical Aspects of Ophthalmic Optics,* 3rd ed. New York: Professional Press Books; 1988.
15. Duane T, Jaeger E. *Clinical Ophthalmology.* Vol 1. Philadelphia: Harper & Row; 1983.

16. Duane TD. *Clinical Ophthalmology*. Vol I, rev. ed. Philadelphia: Harper & Row; 1990.
17. Emsley HH. *Visual Optics*. Vol 1, 5th ed. London: Butterworths; 1953.
18. Epting JB, Morgret FC. *Ophthalmic Mechanics and Dispensing*. Philadelphia: Chilton; 1964.
19. Fannin TE, Grosvenor TP. *Clinical Optics*. Boston: Butterworths; 1987.
20. Fincham WHA. *Optics*, 6th ed. London: Hatton Press; 1951.
21. Freeman MH. *Optics*, 10th ed. London: Butterworths; 1990.
22. Gerstman DR. Multifocal Lens Decentration and Size as a Function of Reading Distance. *Journal of the American Optometric Association*. 55(8):575–579, 1984.
23. Gregory RL. *Concepts and Mechanisms of Perception*. London: Duckworth; 1974.
24. Grosvenor TP. *Primary Care Optometry*, 2nd ed. New York: Professional Press Books; 1989.
25. Howard IP. *Human Visual Orientation*. Chichester: John Wiley & Sons; 1982.
26. Jalie M. *The Principles of Ophthalmic Lenses*, 3rd ed. London: The Association of Dispensing Opticians; 1977.
27. Jenkins FA, White HE. *Fundamentals of Optics*, 4th ed. New York: McGraw-Hill; 1976.
28. Keating MP. *Geometrical, Physical, and Visual Optics*. Boston: Butterworths; 1988.
29. Klein MV. *Optics*. New York: Wiley; 1970.
30. Leigh RJ, Zee DS. *The Neurology of Eye Movements*. Philadelphia: FA Davis Co; 1983.
31. Leigh RJ, Zee DS. *The Neurology of Eye Movements*, 2nd ed. Philadelphia: FA Davis Co; 1991.
32. Levine MW, Shefner JM. *Fundamentals of Sensations and Perception*. Reading, Ma: Addison-Wesley; 1981.
33. Mandell RB. *Contact Lens Practice*, 4th ed. Springfield: Charles C Thomas; 1988.
34. Matlin M. *Sensation and Perception*. Boston: Allyn and Bacon, Inc; 1988.
35. Morgan M. *The Optics of Ophthalmic Lenses*. Chicago: Professional Press; 1978.
36. Moses RA, ed. *Adler's Physiology of the Eye, Clinical Applications*. 7th ed. St. Louis: Mosby; 1981.

37. Ogle KN. *Researches in Binocular Vision.* Philadelphia: WB Saunders Co; 1950.
38. Phillips AJ, Stone J, eds. *Contact Lenses,* 3rd ed. London: Butterworths; 1989.
39. Readings from Scientific American. *Perception: Mechanisms and Models.* San Francisco: Freeman; 1972.
40. Readings from Scientific American. *Recent Progress in Perception.* San Francisco: Freeman; 1976.
41. Sasieni LS. *The Principals and Practice of Optical Dispensing and Fitting,* 3rd ed. London: Butterworths; 1975.
42. Schor CM, Ciuffreda KJ. *Vergence Eye Movements: Basic and Clinical Aspects.* Boston: Butterworths; 1983.
43. Southall JPD, ed. *Helmholtz's Treatise on Physiological Optics.* New York: Dover; 1962.
44. Spillmann L, Werner J. *Visual Perception: The Neurophysiological Foundations.* San Diego: Academic Press, Inc; 1990.
45. Stein HA, Slatt BJ, Stein RM. *Fitting Guide for Rigid and Soft Contact Lenses,* 3rd ed. St. Louis: CB Mosby; 1990.
46. Von Noorden GK. *Binocular Vision and Ocular Motility.* St. Louis: Mosby; 1980.
47. Wyszecki G, Stiles WS. *Color Science Concepts and Methods, Quantitative Data and Formulas.* New York: John Wiley & Sons, Inc; 1967.

4

Psychology

DIRECTIONS (Questions 498–532): Each of the numbered items or incomplete statements in this section is followed by answers or completions of the statement. Select the ONE lettered answer or completion that is BEST in each case.

Psychophysical Methodology

498. The psychophysical method of constant stimuli is typically used to generate a psychometric function with a shape described most accurately as
   A. bell-shaped
   B. Gaussian
   C. cumulative normal
   D. hyperbolic
   E. parabolic

499. Which of the following is a measure of statistical dispersion?
   A. arithmetic mean
   B. geometric mean
   C. mode
   D. standard deviation
   E. A, B, and C

500. Adding a few extremely low scores (e.g., those from some low vision patients) to a large distribution of visual acuity data (e.g., all of the best corrected VA's from an entire class of Optometry students) will affect the value of the
   A.   mean more than the median
   B.   median more than the mean
   C.   mean and median equally
   D.   mode and mean equally
   E.   neither the mean, median or mode, because they are all measures of central tendency, not variance.

501. Which of the following are "criterion-free" psychophysical methods?
   A.   ascending method of limits
   B.   two alternatives forced choice
   C.   method of adjustment
   D.   descending method of limits
   E.   both A and D

502. Which of the following clinical procedures uses forced choice psychophysical methods?
   A.   Snellen acuity
   B.   Landolt C visual acuity
   C.   Tumbling E visual acuity
   D.   Pelli-Robson contrast sensitivity test
   E.   all of the above

503. Fechner developed which of the following psychophysical methods?
   A.   method of limits
   B.   method of constant stimuli
   C.   method of adjustment
   D.   none of the above
   E.   A, B, and C

504. A psychometric function
   A.   is the typical result obtained with a method of constant stimuli
   B.   typically has an upper asymptote near 100 percent and a lower asymptote near $1/n \times 100$ percent correct in an n-alternative forced choice experiment

C. is the relationship between percent correct or percent "see" and stimulus magnitude

D. both A and C

E. A, B, and C

505. Magnitude estimation methods

    A. were used by Stevens to develop his power law of sensation

    B. require subjects to report the apparent magnitude of a suprathreshold stimulus

    C. are used to determine threshold magnitude

    D. require subjects to report the apparent magnitude of sub-threshold stimuli

    E. both A and B

506. The theory of signal detection

    A. predicts that a high hit rate will be accompanied by a high FA rate if the signal was very difficult to detect

    B. predicts that detectability (d') is determined by the internal criterion

    C. predicts that an experimentally determined ROC function for an infinitely small signal would be a straight line from $y = o$, $x = o$ to $y = 1$, $x = 1$

    D. predicts that hit rate will be independent of false alarm rate

    E. both A and C

Human Development

507. Which of the following techniques is used to assess visual acuity in infants?

    A. optokinetic nystagmus (OKN) reflex

    B. visually evoked cortical potentials (VEP)

    C. forced choice preferential looking (PL)

    D. all of the above

    E. none of the above

508. Psychophysically determined visual acuity in newborns is approximately
  A. 20/20
  B. 20/10
  C. 20/200
  D. 20/1000
  E. none of the above, because we cannot measure VA in newborns

509. Visual acuity in the neonate (newborn) is probably limited by
  A. reduced spacing (increased density) of foveal cones
  B. increased photo efficiency of foveal cones
  C. increased outer segment length of neonate foveal cones
  D. reduced axial length of neonate eye
  E. none of the above

510. Stereopsis is
  A. absent in neonates, but appears at about 3 months
  B. present in neonates, but is inferior to that of adults
  C. present at adult levels in neonates
  D. absent in infants up to about 2 years of age
  E. none of the above

511. Visual acuity and contrast sensitivity
  A. are at adult levels at birth
  B. develop slowing during the first 6 months of age and then increase rapidly to adult levels
  C. develop rapidly during the first 6 months of age and then show a gradual improvement during the next several years
  D. approach adult levels during early adulthood
  E. none of the above

512. Infants less than 6 months of age exhibit
  A. virtually zero astigmatism
  B. a low incidence of astigmatism that increases to adult levels during the first 18 months of life
  C. a high incidence of astigmatism that decreases to adult levels during the first 18 months of life
  D. the same incidence of astigmatism as adults
  E. an absence of "against the rule" astigmatism

513. Population studies show that mean spherical refractive error in young children
   A. shows a continually increasing incidence of hyperopia with increasing age
   B. shows very little change during childhood
   C. the high incidence of infant myopia gradually declines with increasing age
   D. the high incidence of hyperopia gradually declines with increasing age
   E. does not change, but the population variance increases

514. Accommodation
   A. is absent in infants
   B. can be measured in infants using a laser optometer
   C. is present in newborns
   D. is absent in newborns but develops during the first 18 months of life
   E. both **B** and **D**

515. Monocular tests of OKN in newborns indicate that OKN is
   A. adult-like
   B. similar for nasal-to-temporal movement and temporal-to-nasal movement
   C. normal for nasal-to-temporal movement, but absent or irregular for temporal-to-nasal movement
   D. normal for temporal-to-nasal movement, but absent or irregular for nasal-to-temporal movement
   E. absent or irregular for both nasal-to-temporal movement and temporal-to-nasal movement

516. Recent animal studies of myopia development have shown that
   A. only humans have refractive errors
   B. myopia development cannot be influenced by environmental manipulation
   C. visual deprivation during early life can produce large myopias in monkeys and chicks
   D. both **A** and **B**
   E. none of the above

517. Pioneering studies by Hubel and Wiesel showed that monocular deprivation (MD)
    A. produced large changes in retinal ganglion cell densities in the deprived eye
    B. in adult cats produced large changes in cortical ocular dominance
    C. in young cats produced large increases in the size of LGN cells receiving input from the deprived eye
    D. in young cats produced a large reduction in the number of cortical cells
    E. none of the above

518. Animal studies of monocular deprivation showed that the massive cortical changes following deprivation were due primarily to
    A. loss of color input
    B. reduction in the level of retinal illumination
    C. deprivation of form information (spatial contrast)
    D. increased interocular pressure
    E. increased interocular temperature

519. Surgically or optically induced "strabismus" in young animals leads to which of the following effects in the primary visual cortex?
    A. an overall shift in ocular dominance to the ipsilateral eye
    B. a preponderance of group 4 cells in Hubel and Wiesel's ocular dominance scheme
    C. a scarcity of group 4 cells
    D. a preponderance of groups 1 and 7 cells
    E. both C and D

520. Which of the following rearing conditions will lead to the largest reduction in cell-body size within the LGN?
    A. optically induced strabismus in infant kittens
    B. surgically induced strabismus in infant monkeys
    C. binocular deprivation in adult monkeys
    D. monocular deprivation in infant monkeys
    E. monocular deprivation in adult monkeys

521. Sensitivity of the cat cortex to monocular deprivation
    A. peaks at birth and declines slowly over the first month of life
    B. peaks at about 2 weeks after birth and declines slowly over the next two months
    C. peaks at about 2 months and declines slowly over the next 2 months
    D. rises slowly during the first month and then declines rapidly
    E. remains quite stable during the first year of life

522. With advancing age, what light is absorbed most by the optical media?
    A. short wavelength
    B. 580 nm (yellow)
    C. orange
    D. long wavelength
    E. all wavelengths are attenuated equally

523. Retinal illuminance is generally reduced in old people because of
    A. reduced pupil size
    B. reduced transmission of the ocular media
    C. aphakia
    D. presbyopia
    E. both **A** and **B**

524. The effect of disability glare on visual acuity occurs because of
    A. increased retinal illumination
    B. increased retinal image contrast
    C. decreased retinal illumination
    D. decreased retinal image contrast
    E. distraction by the glare source

525. In a normal eye, age 55 to 65, with no pathology or cataract,
    A. visual acuity will be reduced significantly
    B. there will be large losses of contrast sensitivity
    C. color vision will be significantly impaired
    D. all of the above
    E. none of the above

526. The progression and level of presbyopia are generally underestimated because
A. older patients can exert additional voluntary accommodation
B. pupil sizes tend to be smaller in older patients
C. depth of focus is often mistaken for residual accommodation
D. both **B** and **C**
E. none of the above, because presbyopia is rarely underestimated

527. As part of the normal aging process, lipofuscin accumulates primarily in the
A. retinal fiber later
B. corneal stroma
C. retinal pigment epithelium
D. photoreceptor outer segments
E. lens nucleus

528. After suffering brain damage, some people find it difficult to recognize and/or orient simple objects which they can easily "see." This phenomenon is best described by the term
A. agnosia
B. aphasia
C. apraxia
D. agraphia
E. amblyopia

529. Some people find it difficult to articulate or recognize words which they "know." This phenomenon is best described by the term
A. amusia
B. apraxia
C. aphasia
D. agraphia
E. amblyopia

530. The important symptom that helps distinguish between a "neurosis" and "psychosis" is
A. anxiety
B. hallucinations
C. phobias

    D. sexual fixations

    E. depression

531. A "phobia" can be distinguished from a "paranoia" because

    A. a phobic person believes that he or she is being persecuted

    B. a paranoid person is aware, at a cognitive level, that there is no real danger

    C. a phobic individual is aware that there is no genuine reason for his or her fear

    D. a paranoid person believes that he or she is being persecuted

    E. both **C** and **D**

532. Psychopaths are characterized by

    A. deep regret for antisocial actions

    B. consuming guilt for delusions they have experienced

    C. total absence of any guilt or regret for their actions

    D. hallucinations of paranoia

    E. both **A** and **B**

Answers and Discussion

Psychophysical Methodology

498. (C) The method of constant stimuli uses multiple presentations of stimuli of different intensities to develop a "percent see" or "percent correct" vs., for example, stimulus intensity or size function. This function resembles a cumulative normal (not a bell-shaped or normal function) and is unrelated to parabolic or hyperbolic functions.

499. (D) The arithmetic mean, the geometric mean (mean of log data), and the mode (most frequently encountered case) are all measures of central tendency. Only the standard deviation is a measure of dispersion (it is the average deviation from the mean). The standard deviation is the square root of the variance.

500. (A) The mean, median, and mode are all measures of central tendency, and they can all be affected by adding new data to a distribution. Because the mode represents the most frequently observed result, it will not generally be affected by a few outliers. The median score (that score which divides the sample into two halves—50 percent scored more than this score, and 50 percent scored less) will be affected by the addition of some low outliers, but no more than if they were just slightly lower than the original median, whereas the mean is affected most because it includes the numerical value of each data point.

501. (B) Psychophysical procedures that require the patient to decide "was that sensation large enough, bright enough, loud enough, etc. for me to decide that the stimulus was present?" require the subject to compare his or her sensation level against some internal criterion and say, "Yes, I see" or "No, I don't see." Both ascending and descending methods of limits require such a comparison and decision, and so does the method of adjustment. A two alternative forced choice method requires a subject to choose between 2 alternatives irrespective of whether or not he or she thinks the stimulus was "seen." Therefore, it is referred to as a criterion-free method.

502. (E) Experimental studies and clinical experience have shown that forced choice, criterion free methods produce more meaningful patient data. Because of this, they are widespread in the clinic; e.g., Snellen acuity (26 AFC), Landolt C (4 AFC), Tumbling E (4 AFC) and Pelli-Robson contrast sensitivity (a 26 AFC letter contrast sensitivity test). Note: the number of alternatives used in a letter discrimination test is usually less than 26 (e.g., a subset of 5 or 10 letters are chosen), but the patient is rarely aware of this.

503. (E) Fechner was a 19th century psychophysicist who developed and formalized several psychophysical methods including **A, B,** and **C.** He pioneered the study of "difference limens" as a tool to investigate perception. The methods are still used widely today.

504. (E) The psychometric function can vary with the type of method and experiment, but it always reflects the probability or percentage of a certain response ("I see" or correct) as a function of stimulus strength (e.g., spot luminance or letter size). In a forced choice experiment, the *minimum* expected percent correct is determined by the number of alternatives to choose between; e.g., 50 percent ($1/2 \times 100\%$) in a 2 AFC and 25 percent ($1/4 \times 100\%$) in a 4 AFC method.

505. (E) Suprathreshold stimuli elicit sensations, and magnitude estimation methods try to measure the magnitude of such sensations by asking subjects to assign a number or some other quantitative scale (e.g., length) to the sensations elicited by a given stimulus. S. S. Stevens used this method to develop his power law ($S = kI^n$).

506. (E) For a signal that is so small that it cannot be detected ($d' = 0$), the hit rate and false alarm rate will always be the same (e.g., both high or both low); that is, when plotted in an ROC function [hit rate (Y) vs. false alarm rate (X)], the data will always fall on or near the Y = X line. A highly detectable signal can result in a *high* hit rate and a *low* false alarm rate.

507. **(D)** Infants cannot respond appropriately to most standard acuity tests. Therefore, techniques have been developed that use physiological responses (VEP) to repeated presentations of test targets. Also, reflexive sensory-motor behavior (OKN, PL) is used to monitor visual capabilities of infants.

508. **(C)** VEP techniques show responses up to 6 c/degree gratings (20/100). Preferential looking acuity estimates in newborns are approximately 3 c/deg (20/200). The reason for this discrepancy is not understood.

509. **(E)** The newborn eye has a slightly shorter axial length (17 mm) than the adult eye. The foveal cones have very short outer segments, very poor photo efficiency (1/350 of adults) and they are more widely spaced (separation is 2.3 minutes of arc as opposed to 0.6 minutes) in neonates. These "preneural" factors predict neonate VA of about 15 c/degree. The observed VA of 3 c/deg must be affected by these *and* additional poorly understood neural immaturities.

510. **(A)** Visual acuity and contrast sensitivity can both be measured at birth. However, stereopsis appears to be completely absent until about three months of age. This may reflect the inability of newborns to accurately converge at the target distance.

511. **(C)** Although some of the details of VA and CS development are still unknown, the following pattern seems certain. There is an initial period of rapid development lasting several (approximately 6) months, during which vision approaches adult levels. However, visual capabilities of young children continue to develop slowly over the next few years. The precise age at which adult performance is achieved is not known.

512. **(C)** Infants often exhibit large amounts of astigmatism. More often than not, it is "against the rule." This declines during the first 18 months.

513. (D) Young children are generally hyperopic (mean values as high as +2.5 for under 4 years old). However, this hyperopic bias gradually declines throughout childhood. Some children switch from hyperopia to myopia.

514. (C) Recent studies using a video technique (that evaluates the vergence of light leaving the eye after being reflected from the fundus) have shown that even newborns can accommodate accurately to near targets. A laser optometer requires the subject to make a judgment about the appearance of a speckle pattern, which is not possible with infants.

515. (D) Both animal and human studies indicate that temporal to nasal OKN is mediated by a subcortical pathway, whereas nasal to temporal OKN is mediated by a cortical pathway. Early monocular deprivation interferes selectively with nasal to temporal OKN, and nasal to temporal OKN in newborns is absent or irregular. Of course, binocular tests, which are always temporal to nasal in one eye, can elicit normal OKN in infants. This asymmetry in newborns disappears after about three months of age in normal children, but is found in adult amblyopes.

516. (C) Studies on monkeys, chicks, and other animals have shown that large amounts of myopia can be readily induced by visual deprivation. These experimental myopias may provide the explanation of why some people, and not others, develop myopia. However, it is important to realize that these experimental models deviate significantly from the typical conditions under which myopia develops in most humans.

517. (E) The effects of MD were almost exclusively restricted to young cats within their "sensitive period." Hubel and Wiesle observed small decreases in the LGN cell sizes in layers receiving input from the deprived eye. They found almost complete shift in ocular dominance to the nondeprived eye within the primary visual cortex, but no change in the number of cortical cells.

518. (C) Monocular deprivation of spatial contrast (form) is the key factor in creating shifts in ocular dominance and the resulting effects on visual performance. This is consistent with current models of retinal function, which emphasize that the retina's primary function is to transmit information to the cortex about spatial contrast in the retinal image. Without spatial contrast, the retinal signal to the cortex will be significantly reduced.

519. **(E)**   Hubel and Wiesel observed that cats and monkeys reared with an artificial "strabismus" lacked the normal preponderance of binocular cells (groups 2 through 6). These "strabismic" animals had almost exclusively monocular cells (groups 1 and 7) in the primary visual cortex. Since the binocular cells are thought to mediate stereopsis and normal binocular vision, their absence should preclude stereopsis.

520. **(D)**   Although strabismus has profound effects on ocular dominance within the visual cortex, it has little effect on the LGN. Monocular deprivation of infants leads to reduced cell body size in those LGN layers receiving their afferent signals from the deprived eye. In some early studies of surgically induced strabismus in cats and monkeys, LGN cell size was also reduced for the layers receiving input from the surgically manipulated eye. However, it has been suggested that this is due to deprivation created by the very radical surgeries that were used.

521. **(B)**   The sensitive, critical, or plastic period in kittens was shown to exhibit a clear sensitivity peak. Sensitivity to monocular deprivation increased during the first two weeks and then slowly declined over the first two months. Monocular deprivation and strabismus created after this period had little or no effect on cortical ocular dominance.

522. **(A)**   The yellow appearance of the aging lens is because it absorbs large amounts of the incident short wavelength light. The reduced transmission at short wavelengths may protect the aging retina from potentially damaging effects of high energy short wavelength light.

523. **(E)**   Both pupil size and optical transmission decrease with age. Retinal illuminance is virtually unaffected by presbyopia. Aphakia will tend to increase retinal illuminance. Since lens implants tend to have higher transmission than the cataractous lens that was removed, pseudophakes will also tend to have higher levels of retinal illuminance than present before surgery.

524. (D) Disability glare describes the vision problems associated with bright light sources placed within the field of view. Because of intraocular light scattered from the glare source, the optical contrast of the retinal image of a fixated target (e.g., an acuity target) will decrease. Decreases in contrast will lead to decreased visual acuity and hence disability. Note: neural factors are also thought to be involved in disability glare.

525. (E) Although reductions in contrast sensitivity, visual acuity, and color vision have been reported in healthy aging eyes (55 to 65 years), they are neither large nor universal. Assessing "normal" vision in the very old is quite difficult, since most very old people have some pathology or optical opacity.

526. (D) Separating depth of field, depth of focus, and accommodation effects is always difficult when a subjective criterion for "clear vision" is used. Because pupil sizes tend to be quite small in older people, and because depth of focus and depth of field are inversely related to pupil size, presbyopes often think they have some residual accommodation. This error is also present in much of the experimental literature documenting the progression of presbyopia.

527. (C) Lipofuscin is a ubiquitous pigment accummulated in the human body during aging. It is found in high concentrations in the retinal pigment epithelium in older humans. Interestingly, it begins to accumulate during childhood, and the short wavelength filtering properties of the lens are thought to protect against excessive accumulations.

528. (A) Agnosia refers to this condition. Amblyopia is a general loss of visual function, and apraxia describes a motor disorder. Both aphasia and agraphia describe problems articulating and writing familiar words. Agnosias typically follow traumatic damage or strokes in the parietal and/or temporal lobes of the brain.

529. (C) Expressive aphasia is the loss of the ability to articulate familiar words and language. Receptive aphasia is the loss of the ability to recognize familiar words and language. Individual patients can have either or both forms of aphasia. Aphasia can accompany traumatic brain damage or stroke.

530. (B) The term psychosis is usually applied to individuals who are suffering from hallucinations and have lost contact with the "real world." Schizophrenia is one form of psychosis.

531. (E) The distinguishing difference between a phobia and a paranoia is that with phobias, the individual is aware of the "irrational" nature of their fear; i.e., that there is no real "danger." This cognitive awareness is not characteristic of paranoias. Schizophrenics typically exhibit paranoia.

532. (C) Psychopaths experience no regret or guilt irrespective of how terrible their actions might be. Because of the absence of this restraining influence, they can be responsible for multiple episodes of very violent behavior.

References

1. Aslin RN, Alberts JR, Peterson MR, eds. *Development of Perception.* Vol 2. The Visual System. New York: Academic Press; 1981.
2. Cline D, Hofstetter H, Griffin J. *Dictionary of Visual Science.* Radnor, Pa: Chilton Trade Book Publishing; 1980, 1989.
3. Kart C, Metress E, Metress S. *Aging, Health, and Society.* Boston, Ma: Jones and Bartlett; 1988.
4. Levine MW, Shefner JM. *Fundamentals of Sensations and Perception.* Reading, Ma: Addison-Wesley; 1981.
5. Matlin M. *Sensation and Perception.* Boston: Allyn and Bacon, Inc; 1988.
6. Rosenbloom A, Morgan M. *Principles and Practice of Pediatric Optometry.* Philadelphia: JB Lippincott Co; 1990.
7. Rosner J, *Pediatric Optometry.* Boston: Butterworths; 1990.

5

Systemic Conditions

DIRECTIONS (Questions 533–592): Each of the numbered items or incomplete statements in this section is followed by answers or completions of the statement. Select the ONE lettered answer or completion that is BEST in each case.

533. All of the following are known to decrease high-density lipoprotein levels except
   A. thiazide diuretics
   B. modest consumption of alcohol
   C. beta adrenergic blockers
   D. obesity

534. A 29-year-old male, with a history of arthritis for 6 months, complains of pain, swelling, and deformation of the joints of two fingers on the left hand and the right thumb. The fingernails of the corresponding fingers are discolored and thickened. He also has a scaly, erythematous rash on his forehead and scalp. The most likely diagnosis is
   A. rheumatoid arthritis
   B. Reiter's syndrome
   C. systemic lupus erythematosus
   D. psoriatic arthritis

535. Generalized pruritic may be caused by all of the following conditions except
A. acute renal failure
B. lymphoma
C. iron deficiency without anemia
D. hyperthyroidism

536. All of the following cutaneous diseases are commonly found in patients with AIDS except
A. xerosis
B. oral candidiasis
C. vasculitis
D. seborrheic dermatitis

537. A 25-year-old male patient has complained of a dry, hacking cough and severe headaches for the past 3 days. His B.P. is 120/60 mm Hg. He relates that he works in a poultry processing plant. He also complains of a fever. Additional tests include pulse, 72 beats/min and temperature, 39°C, with splenomegaly. The likeliest diagnosis is
A. *Legionella pneumophila*
B. mycoplasma pneumonia
C. *Chlamydia psittaci*
D. *Streptococcus pneumoniae*

538. A 30-year-old male patient complained of diarrhea—4 to 5 loose stools per day, abdominal cramps, bloating, and nausea while on his vacation to Mexico. The symptoms started on the 5th day of the trip, lasted for 3 days, and was partially relieved by loperamide. The most likely cause was
A. *Escherichia coli*
B. *Salmonella* sp.
C. *Shigella* sp.
D. *Campylobacter* sp.

539. A patient complains of patches on the body. They are scaly, erythematous, reddened, raised, and serpiginous borders, with a classic annular presentation. The condition is
A. pityriasis rosea
B. erythema multiforme

C. basal cell carcinoma
D. tinea corporis *ringworm*

540. What is a common reaction associated with streptococcal infections, sarcoidosis, tuberculosis, inflammatory bowel diseases, fungal diseases, and infrequently with rheumatoid arthritis? Nodules appear on the legs, especially over the anterior tibia, and may coalesce and spread over the entire leg. The reaction is
A. erythema nodosum
B. scleroderma
C. urticaria
D. erythema multiforme

541. A lesion is produced by focal proliferation of neural tissue in the dermis with a normal epidermis. The lesion may appear as papules or nodules, and is benign. The patient may present with café au lait patches, with axillary freckling. The condition is
A. melanoma
B. lipoma
C. neurofibroma
D. Kaposi's sarcoma

542. A neoplasm is characterized by dark blue-purple macules, papules, nodules, and plaques on the legs, trunk, arms, neck, and head. The lesions appear initially as lightish papules and coalesce into larger, darker lesions. It is the most frequent neoplasm occurring in AIDS patients. The tentative diagnosis is
A. melanoma
B. Kaposi's sarcoma
C. basal cell carcinoma
D. neurofibroma

543. A patient with hyperthyroidism may exhibit all of these physical signs except
A. nervousness
B. calm
C. bulging eyes
D. sweating

544. A patient complains of being tired, and always wears a sweater. While in your office you observe that the patient is lethargic, puffy faced, obese, and has sparse hair. Your tentative diagnosis is
  A. hyperthyroidism
  B. myasthenia gravis
  C. hypoparathyroidism
  D. hypothyroidism

545. The best test for the screening of thyroid function is
  A. T4 (RIA)
  B. free T4
  C. T_3 resin uptake
  D. TRH stimulation

546. Felty's syndrome is associated with rheumatoid arthritis. What other disorders, in addition to rheumatoid arthritis, must exist? The disorders are
  A. hemolytic anemia and uremia
  B. thrombocytopenia and urethritis
  C. neutropenia and splenomegaly
  D. leukopenia and hepatomegaly

547. A young female patient complains of fatigue, low-grade fever, rashes that appear and subside, and arthralgia. She had no problems previously. What is your tentative diagnosis?
  A. systemic lupus erythematosus
  B. scleroderma
  C. polymyalgia rheumatica
  D. osteoarthrosis

548. All patients with systemic lupus erythematosus will give a positive result in which of the following tests?
  A. rapid plasma reagin
  B. erythrocyte sedimentation rate (ESR)
  C. serum glutamic-oxaloacetic transaminase (SGOT)
  D. antinuclear antibody (ANA)

549. In myocardial infarction, levels of lactic dehydrogenase activity is determined. If the ratio of 2 isoenzymes is greater than 1, it is diagnostic. Which of the 2 isoenzymes is used in the determination of this value?

   A. LDH-1/LDH-2
   B. LDH-1/LDH-5
   C. LDH-3/LDH-4
   D. LDH-2/LDH-3

550. Patients with hypertension, with normal to high renin levels, will respond best to

   A. diuretics
   B. beta blockers
   C. calcium antagonists
   D. none of the above

551. The class of drugs to which the black patient with hypertension would show the most favorable response in monotherapy would be

   A. beta blockers
   B. ACE inhibitors
   C. calcium antagonist
   D. diuretics

552. In older hypertensive patients, 60 years of age or over, peripheral resistance

   A. increases
   B. decreases
   C. shows no change

553. The most common factor responsible for hypertensive emergencies in patients with chronic essential hypertension is

   A. pheochromocytoma
   B. renovascular hypertension
   C. sudden rise in blood pressure in patients
   D. ingesting catecholamine precursors while on MAOI therapy

554. What percentage of patients with renovascular disease is due to atherosclerosis?
   A. 40
   B. 20
   C. 60
   D. 80

555. Renovascular hypertension has been associated with
   A. neurofibromatosis
   B. renal artery aneurysm
   C. atherosclerosis
   D. all of the above

556. Renovascular hypertension, due to fibromuscular dysplasia, is most likely to occur in
   A. young white males
   B. young white females
   C. young black males
   D. middle-age males

557. The most distinguishing characteristic of the case history in evaluating a severe headache is the
   A. location of the headache
   B. severity of the headache
   C. prodromal sign
   D. temporal profile of the headache

558. A patient who complains of a severe headache that lasts for several hours to several days, with no previous history of headache or with headaches that are usually less severe, should be scheduled for
   A. erythrocyte sedimentation rate (ESR)
   B. computer tomography (CT) scan
   C. magnetic resonance imaging (MRI)
   D. complete blood count (CBC)

559. In a patient presently experiencing a severe headache, the physical exam must include careful observation to
   A. structures of the head and neck
   B. generalized brain dysfunction

    C. optic fundi
    D. all of the above

560. The neurological signs of headaches due to intracranial hemor-
    rhage involving the brain parenchyma, which makes the diagnosis
    readily apparent, is/are
    A. headache
    B. vomiting
    C. atoxic gait
    D. all of the above

561. A white female patient, 80 years of age, reports having severe head-
    aches with gradual onset, but experiences sharp, boring pains lo-
    cated in the temporal regions. She also complains of scalp tender-
    ness, worsening at night and on exposure to cold. Your most
    likely diagnosis is
    A. temporal arteritis
    B. migraine
    C. Tolusa-Hunt syndrome
    D. trigeminal neuralgia

562. A visual symptom or sign not present in temporal arteritis is
    A. diplopia
    B. inferior attitudinal defect
    C. homonymous hemianopsia
    D. gradual, permanent monocular visual loss

563. A male patient, 35 years of age, complains of unilateral head-
    aches characterized by deep, severe, nonpulsating pain, localized
    around or behind the eye. The headaches frequently occur at the
    same time every day and last about 30 minutes to 2 hours. Your
    tentative diagnosis is
    A. migraine headache
    B. cluster headache
    C. sentinel headache
    D. exertional headache

564. In a patient who is suspected of having temporal arteritis, the most valuable diagnostic test is
  A. histamine provocative test
  B. erythrocyte sedimentation rate (ESR)
  C. blood urea nitrogen (BUN)
  D. creatinine clearance

565. All of the following are signs diagnostic of parkinsonism except
  A. unilateral tremor
  B. rigidity
  C. tachykinesia
  D. Myerson's sign

566. What percentage of the population over 50 years of age is affected by parkinsonism in the U.S.?
  A. 5
  B. 10
  C. 6
  D. 1

567. A pathological feature of parkinsonism is
  A. loss of neurons in substantia nigra
  B. subdural hematoma
  C. pseudotumor cerebri
  D. adenoma

568. Which of the following is/are causes of secondary parkinsonism?
  A. carbon monoxide
  B. dopamine blockers
  C. Japanese B-encephalitis
  D. all of the above

569. The distinguishing feature that indicates a multiple system atrophy, rather than parkinsonism, is
  A. unilateral tremor
  B. loss of voluntary downward and lateral gaze
  C. rigidity
  D. dementia

570. A patient complains of fatigue and lethargy. External examination reveals numerous petechiae and angular stoma. Ophthalmoscopic examination reveals retinal hemorrhages and Roth's spots. Your tentative diagnosis is
A. malignant hypertension
B. leukemia
C. anemia
D. granulocytopenia

571. Pancytopenia is characterized by a depression of
A. red blood cells
B. white blood cells
C. platelets
D. all of the above

572. All of the following agents have been implicated in the etiology of pancytopenia except
A. fluoxymesterone
B. phenylbutazone
C. hepatitis virus
D. chloramphenicol

573. The most common cause of abnormal bleeding is
A. anemia
B. sickle cell anemia
C. thrombocytopenia
D. agranulocytosis

574. The initial studies that should be performed on every patient being evaluated for anemia are listed below. Which is the most important diagnostic test and should be performed first?
A. reticulocyte count
B. peripheral blood smear
C. hemoglobin and hematocrit
D. red cell indices

575. The hemoglobin and hematocrit values in evaluating anemia provide an index as to the
    A. severity of the anemia
    B. duration of the anemia
    C. onset of the anemia
    D. classification of the anemia

576. In acute lymphocytic leukemia, a good prognostic sign is
    A. high leucocyte count
    B. age of less than 2 years
    C. age between 2 and 15 years
    D. mediastinal lymphadenopathy

577. A condition characterized by progressive osteolytic skeletal lesions, bone marrow dysfunction, renal insufficiency, and hypercalcemia is
    A. primary amyloidosis
    B. macroglobulinemia
    C. acute myelogenous leukemia
    D. multiple myeloma

578. The most common cause of meningitis in the U.S. is
    A. *Neisseria meningitidis*
    B. *Haemophilus influenzae* type b
    C. *Listeria monocytogenes*
    D. *Histoplasma capsulatum*

579. The most frequent cause of meningitis in patients over 60 years of age is
    A. *Neisseria meningitidis*
    B. *Haemophilus influenza* type a
    C. *Streptococcus pneumoniae*
    D. *Escherichia coli*

580. The most frequent cause of chorioretinitis in the immunosuppressed patient is
    A. cytomegalovirus
    B. herpes simplex virus
    C. *Histoplasma capsulatum*
    D. *Toxoplasma gondii*

581. The organism responsible for outbreaks of bacteremia in a pregnant female, after consumption of dairy products, is
A. *Escherichia coli*
B. *Clostridium botulinum*
C. *Staphylococcus aureus*
D. *Listeria monocytogenes*

582. The cause of nonseasonal encephalitis is
A. *Hemophilus influenzae* type b
B. herpes simplex virus
C. *Neisseria meningitidis*
D. *Cryptococcus neoformans*

583. Your patient presents with immunodeficiency due to HIV infection, involving multiple organ systems, which may be presented as pneumonitis, bone marrow infection, and splenomegaly; also ulcers of the palate, fever, and interstitial pneumonia. This is characteristic of
A. *Aspergillus*
B. *Blastomyces dermatitidis*
C. *Cryptococcus neoformans*
D. *Histoplasma capsulatum*

584. The most frequent cause of endocarditis in drug abusers is
A. *Staphylococcus epidermidis*
B. *Streptococcus pneumoniae*
C. *Staphylococcus aureus*
D. *Neisseria meningitidis*

585. A patient complains of a burning, pressure-like substernal discomfort that develops with exercise and is relieved with rest. What should your tentative diagnosis be?
A. gastrointestinal upset
B. angina pectoris
C. renal calculi
D. hepatitis

586. Myocardial ischemia in most patients is due to a decrease in the supply of myocardial oxygen. All of the following conditions decrease oxygen supply except
A. left ventricular dilatation
B. coronary artery vasospasm
C. microvascular atherosclerosis
D. severe anemia

587. The major noninvasive test in coronary heart disease is
A. exercise thallium test
B. radionuclide angiograph
C. Doppler test
D. exercise electrocardiographic test (ECG)

588. The diagnosis of diabetes mellitus is established when the fasting plasma glucose value on more than one occasion is greater than
A. 115 mg/dL
B. 80 mg/dL
C. 140 mg/dL
D. 100 mg/dL

589. Non-insulin dependent diabetes mellitus commonly becomes manifest in obese individuals after the age of
A. 40 years
B. 20 years
C. 60 years
D. 30 years

590. Patients with noninsulin-dependent diabetes mellitus (NIDDM) may develop all of the following conditions except
A. neovascularization
B. ketoacidosis
C. vision blurring
D. fatigue

591. The percentage of patients with untreated tertiary syphilis who may progress to symptomatic neurosyphilis is
A. 15
B. 20
C. 10
D. 30

592. The lesions of congenital syphilitic infection that closely resemble the adult stage, is the

- **A.** primary stage
- **B.** tertiary stage
- **C.** early latent stage
- **D.** secondary stage

Answers and Discussion

533. (B) Secondary causes of decreased high-density lipoprotein levels (HDL) are produced by thiazide diuretics, beta blockers, and obesity. However, excessive alcohol intake will cause hypertriglyceridemia.

534. (D) Psoriatic arthritis patients have evidence of cutaneous disease. The arthritis is not symmetrical and involves one or a few small joints in 70 percent of patients.

535. (A) Generalized pruritis generally occurs in chronic renal failure, especially in those patients receiving hemodialysis, in hyperthyroidism or hypothyroidism, myeloproliferative disorders, and iron deficiency anemia, but not in acute renal failure.

536. (C) Xerosis, oral candidiasis, and seborrheic dermatitis are commonly found in patients with AIDS. In addition, chronic, ulcerative mucocutaneous infections with the herpes simplex virus are common in the oral areas.

537. (C) In the U.S., turkeys are an important reservoir. Several large outbreaks of this disease have occurred at poultry processing plants in the U.S.

538. (A) The patient had traveler's diarrhea. It is characteristic to have 4 to 5 loose, watery bowel movement per day. *E. coli* is the most common cause.

539. (D) Tinea corporis presents with patchy, scaly, erythematous, raised, and serpiginous borders, with classic annular lesions.

540. (A) Erythema nodosum is a common reaction associated with streptococcal infection, rheumatoid arthritis, and sarcoidosis. The nodules may appear over the anterior tibia; they may coalesce and spread.

541. (C) Neurofibroma is focal proliferation of neural tissue in the dermis with a normal epidermis—the classic autosomal dominant neurocutaneous disorder in which tumors involving the sheaths of peripheral nerves are associated with cream-brown cutaneous lesions (café-au-lait spots).

542. (C) Kaposi's sarcoma is the most frequent neoplasm occurring in AIDS patients. It is characterized by dark blue-purple macules, papules, and nodules on the arms, neck, trunk, and head.

543. (B) The signs and symptoms that characterize hyperthyroidism are nervousness, sweating, restless overactivity, weight loss, tremor, palpitation, stare, lid lag, and proptosis.

544. (D) In adults, the symptoms and signs of hypothyroidism may include lethargy, cold intolerance, weight increases, and loss of appetite. The hair becomes dry and tends to fall out. Ultimately, the clinical picture of myxedema appears with sparse hair, "puffy" face, expressionless face, and pale, cool skin.

545. (B) Free T4 is the best test for screening thyroid function. The free T-4 (FT-4) concentration is not affected by changes in T-4 binding protein capacity.

546. (C) Neutropenia and splenomegaly, in association with rheumatoid arthritis, is called Felty's syndrome. Neutropenia is found in 2 percent of cases, often with splenomegaly. Mild hypergammaglobulinemia may be present.

547. (A) Unexpected fatigue, low-grade fever, evanescent rashes, and arthralgia in a previously healthy young woman should suggest systemic lupus erythematosus.

548. (D) Speckled pattern, rim, or homogeneous pattern of immunofluorescence is a positive test for serum antinuclear antibody and is suggestive of systemic lupus erythematosus.

549. (A) If the ratio of lactic dehydrogenase isoenzyme activity fraction 1:2 is greater than 1, it is diagnostic of myocardial infarction.

550. (B) Beta blockers and angiotensin converting enzyme inhibitors (ACE inhibitors) will produce the best response in patients with normal to high renin levels.

551. (D) Many studies have shown that black hypertensive patients respond less favorably to beta blocker and angiotensin converting enzyme inhibitors (ACE inhibitors) than to diuretics when these drugs are used as monotherapy.

552. (A) Peripheral resistance in patients 60 years of age or over increases because aging causes an increase in plasma norepinephrine levels, which results in a reduction in the density and sensitivity of the beta receptors.

553. (C) Sudden rise in blood pressure in patients with chronic essential hypertension is the most frequent factor in hypertensive emergencies.

554. (C) 60 percent of patients with renovascular disease is due to atherosclerosis and 40 percent of the patients with renovascular disease is due to fibromuscular dysplasia.

555. (D) Renovascular hypertension has been associated with neurofibromatosis, renal artery aneurysm, atherosclerosis, thrombosis, arteriovenous fistula, or embolism.

556. (B) Renovascular hypertension due to fibromuscular dysplasia is most likely to occur in young, white females, but is rare in blacks.

557. (D) The temporal profile of the headache is the most important factor in the case history in evaluating severe headache.

558. (B) Computer tomography (CT) scan should be scheduled for a patient who complains of a severe headache that lasts for hours to several days with no previous history of headaches.

559. (D) In evaluating a patient presenting with severe headache, careful observation of the structures of the head and neck, generalized brain dysfunction, and examination of the ocular fundi should be made.

560. (D) Cerebellar hemorrhage is a special situation in which urgent evacuation of the hematoma can be lifesaving. The patient may present with only headaches, vomiting, and gait ataxia.

561. (A) Temporal arteritis usually occurs in females 80 years of age or over. The patient experiences severe headaches of gradual onset, located in temporal regions. She also complains of scalp tenderness, worsening at night, and exposure to cold.

562. (C) Temporal arteritis produces diplopia, inferior altitudinal defect, and gradual, permanent monocular visual loss.

563. (B) Cluster headache is characterized by deep, severe nonpulsating pain around or behind the eye, occuring at the same time every day and lasting 30 minutes to 2 hours.

564. (B) The most valuable diagnostic test for a patient suspected of temporal arteritis is erythrocyte sedimentation rate (ESR).

565. (C) The characteristic clinical features of Parkinson's disease include unilateral tremor, rigidity, bradykinesia, postural instability, and Myerson's sign.

566. (D) Parkinson's disease is a disorder of middle or late life, with very gradual progresion and a long course. It affects 1 percent of the population over 50 years of age in the U.S.

567. (A) The most regularly observed changes have been in aggregates of melanin-containing nerve cells in the brain stem (substantia nigra, locus coeruleus) where there is a loss of nerve cells with reactive gliosis, most pronounced in the substantia nigra.

568. (D) Secondary parkinsonism may be caused by carbon monoxide, dopamine blockers, and Japanese B-encephalitis.

569. (B) Loss of voluntary downward and lateral gaze is the distinguishing feature indicating a multiple system atrophy.

570. (C) Retinal hemorrhages, with Roth's spots, numerous petechiae hemorrhages, and angular stomatitis is suggestive of anemia.

571. (D) Pancytopenia may occur at any age and in both sexes. It is characterized by a depression of red blood cells, white blood cells, and platelets.

572. (A) Phenylbutazone, insecticides, hepatitis virus, and chloramphenicol have all been implicated in the cause of pancytopenia.

573. (C) The most common cause of abnormal bleeding is thrombocytopenia. The signs and symptoms include petechiae, ecchymoses, and mucosal bleeding.

574. (B) The most important diagnostic test for evaluating anemia, that should be performed first, is peripheral blood smear.

575. (A) The basic evaluation of an anemic patient requires a complete blood count (CBC) including red blood cells (RBC) indices, platelet count, reticulocyte count, and a peripheral blood smear. Thus, an index to the severity of the anemia are the values of hemoglobin and hematocrit.

576. (C) In acute lymphocytic leukemia, good prognostic signs are an age between 2 and 15 years and a low leukocyte count. A poor prognosis includes a high leukocyte count, mediastinal lymphadenopathy, and being very young or an adult.

577. (D) Multiple myeloma is characterized by progressive osteolytic skeletal lesions, bone marrow dysfunction, renal insufficiency, and hypercalcemia.

578. (B) The most common cause of meningitis in the U.S. is still *Haemophilus influenzae* type b, which accounts for 48 percent, followed by *Neisseria meningitides* (19 percent).

579. (C) The most frequent cause of meningitis in patients over 50 years of age is *Streptococcus pneumoniae.*

580. (A) Cytomegalovirus infections are common in AIDS patients. The most frequent cause of chorioretinitis in the immunosuppressed patient is the cytomegalovirus.

581. (D) Bacteremia outbreaks in the pregnant female, after consumption of dairy products, have been traced to *Listeria monocytogenes.*

582. (B) Herpes simplex virus causes severe encephalitis, which comprises 10 to 20 percent of all cases. Cases are distributed throughout the year and thus are nonseasonal.

583. (D) Immunodeficiency patients with HIV infection, involving many organs, is characteristic of *H. capsulatum.* Common findings in these patients are ulcers of the palate, buccal mucosa, pneumonitis, bone marrow infection, and splenomegalies.

584. (C) *Staphylococcus aureus* causes over 50 percent of endocarditis in intravenous drug abusers, while *Streptococcus* causes about 15 percent and fungi and gram negative bacilli cause 10 to 15 percent.

585. (B) The typical symptom of angina pectoris is a burning, pressure-like discomfort in the substernal area that develops with exertion and subsides with rest.

586. (A) Left ventricular dilation is characterized by a reduced cardiac output and increased venous pressure. This increase in venous pressure leads to increased lung water and an increase in myocardial oxygen demand.

587. (D) The most widely used test in the diagnosis of ischemic coronary disease is the exercise electrocardiographic test. It is the major noninvasive test in coronary heart disease.

588. (C) A fasting plasma glucose value above 140 mg/dL on more than one occasion establishes the diagnosis of diabetes mellitus.

589. **(A)** Noninsulin-dependent diabetes mellitus (NIDDM), type 1, is a heterogenous disorder that commonly becomes manifest after age 40 in obese individuals.

590. **(B)** Patients with noninsulin-dependent diabetes mellitus (NIDDM) do not develop ketoacidosis. Diabetic ketoacidosis seems to require insulin deficiency together with a relative or absolute increase in glucagon concentration.

591. **(C)** Among untreated patients with tertiary syphilis, 10 percent progress to symptomatic neurosyphilis. The tertiary stage is characterized by progressive, destructive, mucocutaneous, musculoskeletal, or parenchymal lesions, or symptomatic central nervous system disease.

592. **(D)** The lesions of congenital syphilis most resemble the secondary stage in adults. The manifestations of congenital syphilis in the early manifestations are infectious and resemble severe secondary syphilis in the adult.

References

1. Harvey AM, Johns RJ, McKusick VA, Owens AH, Ross RS. *The Principles and Practice of Medicine.* Norwalk, Ct: Appleton & Lange; 1988.
2. Rakel RE. *Conn's Current Therapy.* Philadelphia: WB Saunders; 1991.
3. Stein JH. *Internal Medicine Diagnosis and Therapy.* 3rd ed. Norwalk, Ct: Appleton & Lange; 1993.
4. Swartz MH. *Textbook of Physical Diagnosis.* Philadelphia: WB Saunders; 1989.
5. Tierney LM, McPhee SJ, Papadakis JA, Schroeder SA. *Current Medical Diagnosis and Treatment 1993.* Norwalk, Ct: Appleton & Lange; 1993.

6

Ocular Disease/Trauma

DIRECTIONS (Questions 593–756): Each of the numbered items or incomplete statements in this section is followed by answers or completions of the statement. Select the ONE lettered answer or completion that is BEST in each case.

Ocular Adnexa

593. A congenital double row of lashes is termed
   A. distichiasis
   B. trichiasis
   C. poliosis
   D. tylosis ciliaris
   E. madarosis

594. Your 55-year-old male patient has severe unilateral neuralgia in his right forehead, brow, and upper lid area. The skin in this area appears flushed. The most likely diagnosis is
   A. impetigo
   B. early herpes zoster ophthalmicus
   C. lupus erythematosis
   D. acne rosacea
   E. herpes simplex dermatitis

595. A purulent infection of a meibomian gland of the lid is termed
 A. a chalazion
 B. an external hordeolum
 C. an internal hordeolum
 D. meibomianitis
 E. ulcerative blepharitis

596. Flat, yellow lesions of the lids, composed of lipid and often found arching in wing-shaped fashion in the region of the nasal canthi, are termed
 A. verrucae
 B. xanthelasma
 C. dermoid
 D. papilloma
 E. chloasma

597. A tumor of the lids of viral etiology is
 A. molluscum contagiosum
 B. hemangioma
 C. sebaceous cyst
 D. lymphangioma
 E. suderiferous cyst

598. Bacterial inflammation of the lids and adnexa is most commonly caused by
 A. *Staphylococcus epidermidis*
 B. *Streptococcus pneumoniae*
 C. *Pseudomonas aeruginosa*
 D. *Staphylococcus aureus*
 E. *Hemophilus influenzae*

599. Eyelid scrubs can be performed by
 A. using a baby shampoo solution and a clean face cloth
 B. using a baby shampoo solution and a cotton swab
 C. using a baby shampoo solution and a gauze pad
 D. using commercially available eyelid scrub solutions
 E. all of the above

600. A chalazion
 A. is a granulomatous inflammation of a meibomian gland
 B. may form following the resolution of an internal hordeolum

C. may resolve spontaneously
D. is a nontender, well circumscribed lid lump
E. all of the above

601. What is the most commonly encountered eyelid carcinoma?
A. sebaceous gland carcinoma
B. basal cell carcinoma
C. malignant melanoma
D. lymphosarcoma
E. squamous cell carcinoma

602. A 25-year-old female patient presents with bilateral and symmetrical dry, hyperemic, wrinkled, and irritated lids. Her main symptom is pruritis (itching). What is the most likely diagnosis?
A. immediate allergy of the lids
B. ulcerative blepharitis
C. contact dermatitis of the lids
D. seborrheic blepharitis
E. mixed seborrheic/ulcerative blepharitis

603. A 65-year-old male patient complains of ocular burning and irritation that is especially pronounced in the morning. Your examination is unremarkable except for prominent sheath-like collarettes at the base of the cilia. The most likely diagnosis is
A. *Demodex folliculorum*
B. keratitis sicca
C. ulcerative blepharitis
D. seborrheic blepharitis
E. meibomian gland dysfunction

604. Your 21-year-old male patient presents with phthiriasis palpebrarum, or pubic lice infestation of the lids. The appropriate course of therapy is
A. mechanical removal of the lice and nits from the lashes
B. general body hair hygiene with a pediculocide
C. thorough cleaning of all personal effects
D. treatment of potential transmitters, such as family members and sexual contacts
E. all of the above

605. A condition known to be caused by congenital syphilis is
    A. Hutchinson's triad
    B. Cogan's syndrome
    C. Hutchinson's sign
    D. Apert's syndrome
    E. Goldenhar's syndrome

606. Your 22-year-old white female patient complains of itching at the site of an erythematous area of her left lower lid that exhibits several opaque vesicles. She also has a fever blister on her upper lip. What is the likely diagnosis?
    A. *Demodex folliculorum* infestation
    B. seborrheic blepharitis
    C. trichiasis
    D. immediate allergy of the lids
    E. herpes simplex lid lesion

607. What do the following lid conditions have in common: *Demodex folliculorum,* meibomianitis, seborrheic blepharitis, and chalazia?
    A. The *Demodex* organism is the causative agent.
    B. Lid scrubs are an important therapeutic measure.
    C. They tend to be diagnosed in young adult patients.
    D. Burning and irritation of the eyes is noted late in the day.
    E. acute inflammation of the lid margins

Lacrimal System

608. The following statements about decreased tear secretion are true except
    A. It can be relieved by instillation of artificial tears.
    B. Contact lens discomfort may result.
    C. Punctal occlusion will usually help to relieve symptoms.
    D. Symptoms are exacerbated in warm, dry environments.
    E. Symptoms are less noticeable while reading.

609. Which of the following statements is NOT true of chronic infantile dacryocystitis?
    A. It causes epiphora.
    B. It occurs because of failure of the nasolacrimal duct to be fully canalized at birth.

C. Probing should be delayed until approximately 6 months of age.

D. As long as it is present, daily massage of the lacrimal sac is indicated.

E. It always requires surgical intervention.

610. What is the appropriate course of therapy for acute dacryocystitis?
A. topical antibiotic drops and/or ointment
B. warm compresses
C. lacrimal dilation and irrigation after resolution
D. systemic antibiotic
E. all of the above

611. Dacryoadenitis can be caused by
A. bacterial inflammation from a penetrating wound
B. systemic viral inflammation
C. degenerative enlargement
D. Mikulicz's disease
E. all of the above

612. A 32-year-old female patient complains of unilateral tearing of six months' duration. Her eyes are white and quiet except for obvious epiphora and mucous regurgitation from the lacrimal sac. The most likely diagnosis is
A. acute dacryocystitis
B. chronic dacryoadenitis
C. keratoconjunctivitis sicca
D. chronic dacryocystitis
E. canaliculitis

613. The following may be used in clinical practice to maintain globe lubrication EXCEPT
A. laser punctal oblation
B. Freeman plugs
C. collagen implants
D. Herrick plugs
E. lacrimal gland implants

Conjunctiva

614. A clinical sign that is helpful in distinguishing conjunctival from ciliary injection is the
    A. brick-red color of the vessels
    B. tortuosity of the vessels
    C. increased congestion towards the fornix
    D. movability of the vessels with the conjunctiva
    E. all of the above

615. A bright, bloody red, sharply delineated area on the bulbar conjunctiva of one eye, appearing spontaneously and surrounded by normal conjunctiva, is likely to be
    A. pink eye
    B. episcleritis
    C. erythema nodosum
    D. naevus flammeus
    E. subconjunctival hemorrhage

616. A triangular fibrovascular growth of the bulbar conjunctiva seen in the palpebral fissure with its apex attached to the cornea, particularly in persons exposed to wind and dust, is
    A. epithelioma
    B. pinguecula
    C. anterior synechia
    D. pterygium
    E. pannus

617. Viral conjunctivitis that can be transmitted by poorly cleaned ophthalmic instruments, characterized by follicles, later subepithelial corneal infiltrations, conjunctival pseudomembranes, and preauricular lymphadenopathy, is most likely
    A. pharyngoconjunctival fever
    B. trachoma
    C. herpes simplex conjunctivitis
    D. epidemic keratoconjunctivitis
    E. epidemic hemorrhagic conjunctivitis

618. During the summer, a 10-year-old boy complains of itching in both eyes. The superior palpebral conjunctivae show large, cobblestone-like papillae and a milky mucoid discharge. The most likely diagnosis is
  A. palpebral vernal conjunctivitis
  B. phlyctenular conjunctivitis
  C. trachoma
  D. swimming pool conjunctivitis
  E. limbal vernal conjunctivitis

619. During routine examination you note a small, clear, fluid-filled cyst on the bulbar conjunctiva of your patient. This finding is most likely a
  A. pinguecula
  B. hemangioma
  C. lymphangiectasia
  D. conjunctival papilloma
  E. pterygium

620. Acne rosacea is a dermatological disorder that will commonly exhibit ocular manifestations, including
  A. chronic keratoconjunctivitis
  B. scleroderma
  C. chronic open-angle glaucoma
  D. xerophthalmia
  E. chronic anterior uveitis

621. What is the best reason that trimethoprim/polymixin B solution (Polytrim®) is an appropriate drug of choice for treating bacterial conjunctivitis in a 3-year-old?
  A. It does not blur vision like Polysporin® ointment would.
  B. It is effective against *Hemophilus influenzae.*
  C. It is relatively expensive.
  D. It does not burn.
  E. It has few side effects.

622. A common complaint of a patient suffering from bacterial conjunctivitis is
    A. "My eyes itch."
    B. "My eyes are tearing."
    C. "My eyes hurt."
    D. "My eyes are matted shut in the morning."
    E. "I'm having trouble reading fine print."

623. You have been treating a 2-month-old male infant with supportive measures for unilateral chronic infantile dacryocystitis. The mother presents the infant to you because he has developed an ipsilateral bacterial conjunctivitis. Which topical ophthalmic drop would probably NOT be the antibiotic of choice?
    A. 15 percent sodium sulfacetamide
    B. 3 mg/ml gentamicin sulfate
    C. 0.5 percent chloramphenicol
    D. polymixin B/neomycin/bacitracin
    E. 10 percent sodium sulfacetamide

624. During inflammation, the lymphatic channels swell with inflammatory edema and debris. Enlargement of the superficial lymph nodes of the skin gives a clue as to the site of the infection. The lymph nodes most likely to enlarge in the presence of ocular inflammation, particularly viral conjunctivitis, are the
    A. submandibular lymph nodes
    B. submaxillary lymph nodes
    C. axillary lymph nodes
    D. preauricular lymph nodes
    E. inguinal lymph nodes

625. A 12-year-old male patient was struck in the eye by a tree branch. Within an area of conjunctival edema and hyperemia is noted a small, linear lesion that stains with sodium fluorescein but does not reveal bare sclera. The probable diagnosis is
    A. scleral perforation
    B. conjunctival abrasion
    C. conjunctival foreign body
    D. subconjunctival hemorrhage
    E. none of the above

626. A bullous disorder of the skin and mucous membranes, exhibiting conjunctival ulceration, scarring, and resultant entropion, in which sensitivity to sulfonamides seems to be an etiological factor, is

A. ocular pemphigus
B. erythema multiforme
C. dermatomyositis
D. periarteritis nodosa
E. lupus erythematosus

627. Your 29-year-old male patient has just acquired a pet cat for the first time. He presents to you complaining of itchy eyes. You observe lid edema, conjunctival injection, and chemosis, along with a mucous discharge. What is the likely diagnosis?

A. contact dermatitis
B. allergic blepharoconjunctivitis
C. marginal blepharitis
D. bilateral preseptal cellulitis
E. phlyctenular keratoconjunctivitis

628. It has been reported in the literature that herpes zoster ophthalmicus most commonly affects patients over the age of 50. Recently, however, this condition has been observed in much younger individuals who are concurrently affected with

A. leukemia
B. the HIV (AIDS) virus
C. mononucleosis
D. the herpes simplex virus
E. influenza

Cornea

629. Folds in Descemet's membrane are NOT found

A. as a result of corneal edema
B. with increased intraocular pressure (IOP)
C. early postoperatively, following cataract extraction
D. in interstitial keratitis
E. as an age-related idiopathic finding

630. Of the following, the type of corneal ulcer that is most likely to perforate if left untreated is
- **A.** dendritic
- **B.** streptococcal
- **C.** marginal
- **D.** phlyctenular
- **E.** Mooren's

631. After a healed corneal abrasion, a patient notices repeated unilateral foreign body sensation and lacrimation upon awakening. The diagnosis is most likely
- **A.** corneal laceration
- **B.** recurrent corneal erosion
- **C.** an eyelash in the fornix
- **D.** keratitis sicca
- **E.** keratomalacia

632. An endothelial corneal disorder, eventually producing stromal edema and bullae in the corneal epithelium, is
- **A.** Fuchs' dystrophy
- **B.** corneal farinata
- **C.** posterior polymorphous dystrophy
- **D.** Descemet's tears
- **E.** endothelial blebs

633. All of the following are corneal signs of aging EXCEPT
- **A.** Hassall-Henle bodies
- **B.** Descemet's folds
- **C.** limbal girdle of Vogt
- **D.** guttata
- **E.** sclerosing keratitis

634. The following statements about arcus senilis are true EXCEPT
- **A.** It may not form a complete ring.
- **B.** It expands towards the center of the cornea.
- **C.** It is separated from the limbus by a small, clear zone.
- **D.** It may appear sooner in African-American patients.
- **E.** It may or may not be associated with increased blood cholesterol levels.

635. Fleischer's ring is
A. a brownish-green ring found near the limbus in Wilson's hepatolenticular degeneration
B. a brownish ring around the base of the cone in keratoconus
C. an impression of the iris pupillary ruff on the crystalline lens
D. pigmentation at the head of an advancing pterygium
E. due to corneal siderosis from a metallic foreign body

636. Immediate first aid for chemical injuries of the eye consists of
A. patching the eye
B. instilling a drop of antibiotic into the eye and sending the patient to a physician
C. immediate and prolonged irrigation with water, continuing with normal saline solution when available
D. waiting until the doctor arrives
E. instilling a drop of topical anesthetic into the eye with the advice to repeat at home

637. A clinical procedure that uses radially placed corneal incisions to flatten the cornea, and thereby reduce myopia, is called
A. orthokeratology
B. keratophakia
C. keratomileusis
D. radial keratotomy
E. lamellar keratoplasty

638. A 23-year-old male patient complains of bilateral ocular irritation. External examination reveals symmetric sectoral conjunctival injection at 12:00 with corresponding corneal staining and papillary hypertrophy of the superior palpebral conjunctiva. The probable diagnosis is
A. episcleritis
B. chlamydial conjunctivitis
C. superior limbic keratoconjunctivitis of Theodore
D. exposure keratoconjunctivitis
E. vernal conjunctivitis

639. An anterior corneal abnormality characterized by map, dot, and fingerprint changes is known as
   A. lattice corneal dystrophy
   B. epithelial basement membrane dystrophy
   C. superficial punctate keratitis
   D. granular dystrophy
   E. epithelial mosaic

640. An example of an antigenic corneal response to inflammation is
   A. subepithelial infiltration
   B. marginal ulceration
   C. phlyctenule formation
   D. inferior superficial punctate keratitis
   E. all of the above

641. A 22-year-old male patient complains of ocular irritation and mild photophobia. Examination reveals bilateral corneal epithelial infiltrates with overlying staining but with no conjunctival injection, no follicle formation, and no preauricular lymphadenopathy. The probable diagnosis is
   A. Thygeson's superficial punctate keratitis
   B. epidemic keratoconjunctivitis
   C. pharyngoconjunctival fever
   D. herpes simplex keratitis
   E. keratoconjunctivitis sicca

642. Keratoconjunctivitis sicca may be treated with
   A. topical ocular lubricating drops
   B. punctal oblation
   C. bandage soft contact lenses
   D. silicone punctal plugs
   E. all of the above

643. Ciprofloxacin (Ciloxan®), one of the newer antiinfective agents, is especially effective for the treatment of
   A. *Acanthamoeba* keratitis
   B. preseptal cellulitis
   C. impetigo
   D. bacterial corneal ulcers
   E. internal hordeolum

644. Epithelial herpes simplex keratitis, a common form of local recurrent HSV,
   A. may result in corneal hypoesthesia
   B. is commonly treated with trifluridine drops ·
   C. appears as one or more ulcerative dendritic lesions
   D. may result in anterior stromal scarring
   E. all of the above

645. A laboratory culture of a corneal lesion
   A. helps to definitively diagnose suspected bacterial keratitis
   B. is usually taken with a sterile Kimura spatula
   C. may be directly plated onto solid agar (blood, chocolate, or Sabouraud's) or may be transferred to transport media (thioglycolate broth)
   D. is usually identified in 24–48 hours
   E. all of the above

Sclera/Episclera

646. Which of the following is NOT true of simple episcleritis?
   A. It is characterized by congestion and edema of a localized, sectoral area of the episclera and conjunctiva.
   B. It tends to recur.
   C. It usually affects visual acuity.
   D. Symptomatology is usually minimal.
   E. It usually is of unknown etiology.

647. It is NOT true that scleritis
   A. may cause scleral thinning
   B. is inconsequential, since the sclera has a poor blood supply
   C. is painful
   D. is most commonly a manifestation of a collagen disease
   E. often has intraocular involvement

648. Blue sclera may be found in
   A. Marfan's syndrome
   B. scleromalacia perforans
   C. some children, as a normal finding
   D. osteogenesis imperfecta
   E. all of the above

649. A small, discrete area of scleral thinning in an elderly patient that appears as a round, slate-gray lesion near a rectus muscle insertion is termed
    A. hyaline plaque
    B. icteric sclera
    C. scleromalacia
    D. pinguecula
    E. telangiectasia

650. Uveal bulging into an area of thinned and stretched sclera is known as
    A. scleral rigidity
    B. scleral ectasia
    C. staphyloma
    D. posterior scleritis
    E. necrotizing scleritis

651. An uncommon, localized, and unilateral inflammation of unknown etiology, involving the sclera and cornea, that produces redness, diffuse peripheral corneal infiltrates, and a moderate to severe anterior uveitis, is
    A. sclerokeratitis (sclerosing keratitis)
    B. epidemic keratoconjunctivitis
    C. scleroderma
    D. anterior scleritis
    E. Posner-Schlossman syndrome

652. Potential differential diagnoses of nodular episcleritis may include
    A. conjunctival abrasion
    B. superior limbic keratoconjunctivitis of Theodore
    C. phlytenular keratoconjunctivitis
    D. pingueculitis
    E. all of the above

Anterior Uvea (Iris and Ciliary Body)

653. Rubeosis of the iris tends NOT to develop in
    A. diabetes
    B. Eale's disease

    C. central retinal vein occlusion
    D. branch retinal vein occlusion
    E. retinal detachment

654. Adhesions of the iris to the anterior capsule of the lens are termed
    A. adherent leukoma
    B. Vossius' ring
    C. posterior synechiae
    D. epicapsular stars
    E. peripheral anterior synechiae

655. A young adult patient has a unilateral, mild anterior uveitis. The iris color is lighter in this eye. The likely diagnosis is
    A. Fuchs' heterochromic iridocyclitis
    B. sympathetic ophthalmia
    C. congenital heterochromia
    D. pigment dispersion syndrome
    E. exfoliation syndrome

656. A sign or symptom NOT typical of acute anterior uveitis is
    A. pain
    B. aqueous flare
    C. dilated immobile pupils
    D. ciliary flush
    E. lacrimation and photophobia

657. Bilateral intraocular inflammation following a unilateral globe penetrating wound, exposing uveal tissue, is termed
    A. endophthalmitis
    B. sympathetic ophthalmia
    C. traumatic uveitis
    D. iridocyclitis
    E. panophthalmitis

658. A displaced pupil is termed
    A. anisocoria
    B. corectopia
    C. polycoria
    D. coloboma
    E. leukocoria

659. The following can be found in aniridia EXCEPT
  A. glaucoma
  B. photophobia
  C. reduced visual acuity
  D. an artificial pupil painted on a contact lens will appreciably improve VA
  E. ocular nystagmus

660. Anterior uveitis can be a complication of the following systemic diseases EXCEPT
  A. myotonic dystrophy
  B. juvenile rheumatoid arthritis
  C. ankylosing spondylitis
  D. Reiter's syndrome
  E. Behcet's disease

661. The following are ocular symptoms or signs of albinism EXCEPT
  A. normal visual acuity
  B. nystagmus
  C. iris transillumination
  D. photophobia
  E. prominent choroidal vasculature

662. Iris transillumination, using the slit lamp biomicroscope,
  A. is performed by placing the illumination source co-axial with the eyepieces
  B. is important in the differential diagnosis of nystagmus
  C. detects defects in the iris pigment epithelium
  D. aids in the diagnosis of pigment dispersion syndrome
  E. all of the above

663. Chronic anterior uveitis
  A. is often bilateral
  B. tends to produce minimum symptomatology
  C. often accompanies systemic disease
  D. usually produces "muttonfat" keratic precipitates
  E. all of the above

Pupillary, Accommodative and Refractive Pathology

664. One pupil exhibits a sluggish reaction to light and to near. The affected pupil stays larger than that of the other eye in bright light; smaller in dim light. This is
A. Argyll Robertson pupil
B. Adie's tonic pupil
C. reflex iridoplegia
D. ophthalmoplegia interna
E. pupillary block

665. During pupillary reflexes testing, the penlight is swung from the left pupil to the right pupil. The right pupil then immediately dilates. This phenomenon is known as
A. hippus
B. Horner's syndrome
C. iridoplegia
D. a left afferent pupillary defect
E. a right afferent pupillary defect

666. A 65-year-old patient presents to you wearing glasses that are 5 years old with −1.50 DS in each eye. Your refraction reveals OD −3.25 DS and OS −4.00 DS with best corrected visual acuity of 20/30 in each eye. Based on these data, what type of cataractous change do you expect to observe?
A. nuclear sclerosis
B. cortical spoking
C. posterior subcapsular
D. Morgagnian
E. anterior subcapsular

667. An acquired hyperopia is NOT seen in
A. diabetes
B. central serous chorioretinopathy
C. macular cyst
D. orbital tumor
E. macular hole

668. A-scan ultrasonography of the globe is used to calculate the power of an intraocular lens (IOL) implant by
   A. measuring corneal curvature
   B. refractive index evaluation
   C. determining the depth of the posterior chamber
   D. assessing axial length
   E. determining the depth of the anterior chamber

669. In one systemic disease, there can be large fluctuations in the refractive power of the eye. This is
   A. hypercholesterolemia
   B. diabetes mellitus
   C. thyrotoxicosis
   D. multiple sclerosis
   E. acne rosacea

670. Dapiprazole (Rev-Eyes®) is now approved and available for reversing pharmacologically induced mydriasis. What is another theoretical, yet realistic, usage for this drug?
   A. treatment for accommodative esotropia
   B. nonsurgical management of reduced visual acuity resulting from posterior subcapsular cataract
   C. treatment of pigmentary glaucoma
   D. a substitution for sun glasses due to reduced pupil size
   E. correction for myopia due to a relative pinhole effect

671. Five years ago a 21-year-old patient presented to you for examination. Your refraction at that time was:

OD −4.50 −1.00 × 075, VA 20/20−
OS −4.25 −1.00 × 155, VA 20/20

Five years later your refraction is:

OD −2.50 −5.00 × 040, VA 20/30−
OS −4.00 −2.25 × 145, VA 20/25

Based on these data, what is the most likely diagnosis?
   A. bilateral pterygium
   B. corneal furrow degeneration
   C. epithelial basement membrane dystrophy
   D. keratoconjunctivitis sicca
   E. keratoconus

672. Which topically applied ophthalmic solution may be used to confirm the diagnosis of Adie's tonic pupil?
    A. 0.125 percent pilocarpine
    B. 0.5 percent tropicamide
    C. 1 percent pilocarpine
    D. 1 percent tropicamide
    E. 2 1/2 percent phenylephrine

Orbit

673. A unilateral pulsating exophthalmos is a sign of
    A. a carotid-cavernous sinus fistula
    B. Graves' disease
    C. tumor metastasis to the orbit
    D. third nerve palsy
    E. orbital cellulitis

674. It is NOT true of an injured eye that
    A. it must be enucleated immediately due to the danger of sympathetic ophthalmia
    B. a contusion of the globe may cause lens subluxation
    C. blunt trauma may cause lid ecchymosis
    D. glaucoma may develop years after ocular contusion
    E. contusion from a smaller sized object is more likely to cause hyphema

675. Following blunt trauma to the orbit, a patient exhibits unilateral enophthalmus, restricted elevation of the globe, and intraorbital nerve hypoesthesia. The probable diagnosis is
    A. Graves' ophthalmopathy
    B. blow-out fracture
    C. traumatic orbital hematoma
    D. Duane's retraction syndrome
    E. traumatic rupture of the globe

676. Bacterial orbital cellulitis
   A. can be a life-threatening condition
   B. is often caused by the spread of infection from the paranasal sinuses
   C. produces signs of unilateral inflammation with restricted globe motility
   D. requires hospitalization and aggressive systemic antibiotic therapy
   E. all of the above

677. A patient with a chief complaint of diplopia presents for examination. Your evaluation reveals unilateral painless exophthalmus, restricted extraocular muscle function, resistance of the globe to mechanical retropulsion, and induced hyperopia. The probable diagnosis is
   A. an intracranial mass
   B. cavernous sinus thrombosis
   C. a unilateral orbital mass
   D. carotid-cavernous sinus fistula
   E. orbital bacterial cellulitis

678. A twelve-year-old patient sustained a penetrating injury to the upper lid for which he sought no treatment. Three days later he presents to your office with periorbital redness, edema, and localized tenderness without ocular involvement. The most likely diagnosis is
   A. preseptal cellulitis
   B. delayed allergic dermatitis of the lids
   C. acute internal hordeolum
   D. orbital cellulitis
   E. immediate allergic dermatitis of the lids

679. Which of the following conditions may be life-threatening and is most commonly diagnosed in a child under five years of age?
   A. preseptal cellulitis caused by *Streptococcus pneumoniae*
   B. impetigo caused by *Staphylococcus aureus*
   C. acute dacryoadenitis caused by *Staphylococcus aureus*
   D. acute dacryocystitis caused by *Streptococcus pneumoniae*
   E. preseptal cellulitis caused by *Hemophilus influenzae*

Anterior Chamber, Angle Structure, and Abnormal IOP

680. A small slit lamp beam causes a Tyndall phenomenon in the aqueous. This is a sign of
A. normal aqueous
B. asteroid hyalosis
C. pseudoexfoliation
D. anterior uveitis
E. anterior cleavage syndrome

681. A finding in the anterior chamber of no serious consequence is
A. aqueous flare
B. hypopyon
C. persistent pupillary membrane
D. fibrinous exudates
E. hyphema

682. Keratic precipitates distributed in a triangular formation on the inferior portion of the corneal endothelium are a sign of
A. anterior uveitis
B. corneal dystrophy
C. corneal graft rejection
D. interstitial keratitis
E. congenital deposits

683. In primary open-angle glaucoma, the cause of the obstruction to aqueous outflow is probably in the
A. aqueous veins
B. episcleral veins
C. trabecular meshwork
D. ciliary body
E. corneal endothelium

684. Which of the following is NOT true of primary open-angle glaucoma?
A. an insidious onset
B. most common form of glaucoma
C. affected patients notice halos around lights
D. tends to be a familial disorder
E. may proceed to absolute glaucoma without pain

685. A one-year-old child shows unilateral photophobia, haziness and enlargement of the cornea, and cupping of the optic nerve head. The probable diagnosis is
  A. corneal dystrophy
  B. buphthalmos
  C. keratitis
  D. birth trauma
  E. megalocornea

686. Traumatic penetration of the globe would be expected to produce
  A. no change in the IOP
  B. elevated IOP
  C. increased diurnal fluctuation of the IOP
  D. reduced IOP
  E. none of the above

687. A 33-year-old black female patient has been treated for bilateral chronic anterior uveitis for the past three weeks. The inflammation is now resolved on a topical therapy of 1 percent prednisolone and 5 percent homatropine. Although the patient is not symptomatic, the last IOP measurement was OD 32 mm and OS 30 mm. What diagnosis should be considered?
  A. steroid-linked glaucoma
  B. chronic open-angle glaucoma
  C. acute uveitic glaucoma
  D. hemolytic glaucoma
  E. acute angle closure glaucoma

688. A 25-year-old white male patient who is a four-diopter myope has been diagnosed as having pigmentary dispersion syndrome. What clinical finding would you expect to observe?
  A. a Krukenberg's spindle
  B. grade 3–4 angle pigmentation by gonioscopy
  C. peripheral iris transillumination defects
  D. wide swings in diurnal IOP fluctuation
  E. all of the above

689. In which of the following congenital anomalies is it most likely that the accompanying glaucoma is unilateral?
  A. Rubella syndrome
  B. Sturge-Weber syndrome

C. homocystinuria
D. aniridia
E. Lowe's oculocerebrorenal syndrome

690. While playing racquetball two years ago, your patient sustained a contusion to the globe and was treated for an acute hyphema. What finding most suggests the possibility of late-onset secondary open-angle glaucoma?
A. rosette cataract
B. iris sphincter tear
C. angle recession
D. traumatic pupil mydriasis
E. choroidal rupture

691. When evaluating the need for IOP-lowering treatment in ocular hypertension, what risk factors should be taken into consideration?
A. high myopia
B. a history of glaucoma in siblings or parents
C. systemic hypertension
D. diabetes mellitus
E. all of the above

692. One of the earliest optic nerve head changes seen in primary open-angle glaucoma is
A. horizontal elongation of the optic cup
B. complete loss of the neural rim tissue
C. "bean pot" cupping
D. vertical elongation of the optic cup
E. the laminar dots sign

693. In what condition is the assessment of diurnal fluctuation of the IOP particularly important to making an accurate diagnosis?
A. low tension glaucoma
B. glaucomatocyclitic crisis
C. acute angle closure glaucoma
D. congenital glaucoma
E. neovascular glaucoma

694. When is argon laser trabeculoplasty (ALT) usually NOT considered in the treatment of primary open-angle glaucoma?
   A. when the glaucoma is not controlled on maximal medical therapy
   B. when the patient cannot tolerate the glaucoma medication
   C. when patient compliance is questionable for long-term therapy
   D. as initial treatment of choice
   E. none of the above

695. Topical carbonic anhydrase inhibitors (CAI's) are being investigated for antiglaucoma therapy and may be close to FDA approval. The following statements are true EXCEPT
   A. They will tend to induce miosis.
   B. They reduce aqueous formation.
   C. They may be used in conjunction with other topical antiglaucoma agents.
   D. They will significantly reduce intraocular pressure.
   E. They will have fewer side effects than systemic CAI's.

696. In pigment dispersion syndrome, a line of pigment is usually visible at the level of Schwalbe's line when examined during gonioscopy. This is known as
   A. Hudson-Stahli line
   B. Sampaolesi's line
   C. Ferry's line
   D. Stocker's line
   E. Turk's line

Lens/Aphakia/Pseudophakia

697. The most common congenital cataract from among the following is
   A. sutural (stellate)
   B. anterior polar or pyramidal
   C. pulvurulent
   D. anterior axial embryonal
   E. posterior polar or pyramidal

698. Which of the following is NOT true of an age-related cataract?
   A. The Morgagnian cataract is a form of mature cataract.
   B. An increase in the refractive index of nuclear cataract causes "second sight."
   C. An age-related cataract should be removed only when it has matured.
   D. Signs of incipient cataract include vacuoles, water clefts, and lamellar separation.
   E. In diabetics, age-related cataracts develop sooner than in nondiabetics.

699. Cataract formation may be found in
   A. retinitis pigmentosa
   B. long-term systemic steroid therapy
   C. chronic anterior uveitis
   D. ocular trauma
   E. all of the above

700. Vossius' ring is a
   A. pigment ring surrounding the corneal apex in keratoconus
   B. pigment ring on the anterior capsule of the lens following globe contusion
   C. ring-like after-cataract
   D. remnant of an iron foreign body on the cornea
   E. circular deposition of pigment on the posterior lens surface in pigment dispersion syndrome

701. The removal of a cataractous lens in toto is termed
   A. extracapsular extraction
   B. intracapsular extraction
   C. no stitch surgery
   D. epikeratophakia
   E. phakoemulsification

702. Blunt trauma to the eye or head may cause the eventual formation of what type of lens opacity?
   A. after-cataract
   B. reduplicated cataract
   C. zonular cataract
   D. rosette cataract
   E. lamellar clefts

703. A posterior subcapsular cataract typically produces which visual complaint?
   A. worse vision when reading
   B. improved vision with pupil mydriasis
   C. worse vision in bright light
   D. worse vision when taking 1 percent pilocarpine drops
   E. all of the above

704. Which cataract is not an age-related type?
   A. cuneiform
   B. pulvurulent
   C. cupulliform
   D. brunescent
   E. crystalline

705. Your 72-year-old patient had extracapsular cataract extraction 6 months ago. Her vision has deteriorated to 20/40 due to capsular opacification. What procedure will likely benefit this patient?
   A. YAG laser capsulotomy
   B. argon laser iridectomy
   C. xenon arc laser photocoagulation
   D. argon laser trabeculoplasty
   E. YAG laser iridotomy

Posterior Pole

706. A useful reason for utilizing red-free light in direct ophthalmoscopy is to
   A. discern areas of retinal hemorrhage more clearly
   B. distinguish drusen more easily
   C. eliminate bothersome corneal reflections
   D. perform scotopic ophthalmoscopy
   E. accentuate the red reflex in distal ophthalmoscopy

707. A method used to study the location of a leak in a retinal vessel is
   A. fluorescein angiography
   B. ophthalmodynamometry
   C. electroretinography
   D. electrooculography
   E. ultrasonography

708. B-scan ultrasonography of the globe and orbit is of diagnostic value in
   A. the presence of a dense cataract
   B. assessing intraocular tumors
   C. evaluating retinal detachments of uncertain etiology
   D. orbital tumor assessment
   E. all of the above

709. Inflammatory cells in the vitreous are usually NOT observed in
   A. toxocara canis
   B. retinoblastoma
   C. retrobulbar neuritis
   D. pars planitis
   E. active toxoplasmosis

710. The fundus shows a large boat-shaped hemorrhage delineated by an upper horizontal line. This is which type of hemorrhage?
   A. intravitreal
   B. superficial retinal
   C. preretinal (subhyaloid)
   D. deep retinal
   E. choroidal

711. Which of the following statements is NOT true of the visually evoked response (VER)?
   A. The largest response is obtained from the retinal periphery.
   B. It is an electrical response from the visual cortex to a flash of light.
   C. Attention can alter the response.
   D. The responses for the two eyes should be similar.
   E. The amplitude of the response is proportional to the stimulus intensity.

712. A retinal vessel sign which is NOT pathological is
   A. an A/V ratio of 2/4
   B. widening of the arteriolar light reflex
   C. segmental constrictions
   D. crossing phenomena beyond 2 DD from the optic nerve head
   E. sheathing of large vessels on the optic disc

713. A 20-year-old patient noticed some visual loss. The posterior fundus exhibited multiple round and linear fishtail-like yellow or yellow-white lesions. Eventually, the macular region became atrophic. The flecks on the fundus vary in size, shape, outline, and density. There is an autosomal recessive trait of inheritance. This is
   A. fundus albipunctatus
   B. fundus flavimaculatus
   C. acute multifocal posterior placoid epitheliopathy
   D. foveomacular retinitis
   E. vitelliform dystrophy

714. A 65-year-old patient reports a gradual onset of distortion of straight lines, blurring of small objects, ghost images around letters, and some disturbances of color vision. Visual acuity is nearly 20/20 in both eyes. Maculae show loss of the foveal reflex, drusen, and pigment migration. The most likely diagnosis is
   A. central serous chorioretinopathy
   B. a beginning neoplasm in the macular area
   C. age-related macular degeneration
   D. multiple sclerosis
   E. histoplasmosis

715. Flamed-shaped hemorrhages may be found in
   A. diabetic retinopathy
   B. papilledema
   C. central retinal vein occlusion
   D. hypertensive retinopathy
   E. all of the above

716. Roth's spots may be found in
   A. leukemia
   B. hypertensive retinopathy
   C. diffuse choroidal sclerosis
   D. disciform macular degeneration
   E. syphilitic chorioretinitis

717. Neovascularization of the retina is known to develop in
   A. diabetic retinopathy
   B. sickle cell retinopathy

C. retinal vein occlusion
D. Eales' disease
E. all of the above

718. What is the most common retinal finding in patients with acquired immune deficiency syndrome (AIDS)?
A. candle wax drippings
B. cotton-wool patches
C. neovascularization
D. hard exudates
E. reticular pigmentary degeneration

719. Which of the following is an age-related change that may be noted in the fundus?
A. choroidal sclerosis
B. drusen
C. macular pigment dumping
D. macular depigmentation
E. all of the above

720. A disease not transmitted transplacentally to the eyes of a newborn is
A. syphilis
B. toxoplasmosis
C. rubella
D. gonorrhea
E. acquired immune deficiency syndrome (AIDS)

721. A choroiditis caused by a fungus infection, endemic to the Ohio and Mississippi river valleys, and probably spread by avian species, is a manifestation of
A. toxoplasmosis
B. acanthamoeba
C. histoplasmosis
D. *Candida albicans*
E. blastomycosis

722. Trauma to the globe may produce which fundus finding?
    A. commotio retinae
    B. macular hole
    C. chorioretinal scar
    D. choroidal rupture
    E. all of the above

Peripheral Fundus/Vitreous

723. A 60-year-old patient exhibits small, very reflective yellow-white spherical opacities in the vitreous of one eye. The opacities move with the eye and quickly return to their original positions. Vision is not affected and the fundus examination is normal. The likely diagnosis is
    A. asteroid hyalosis
    B. vitreous syneresis
    C. tobacco dusting of the vitreous
    D. oral pearls
    E. Wagner's syndrome

724. White without pressure
    A. appears as a milky translucence to the peripheral retina
    B. is very common in patients with darkly pigmented fundi
    C. may be uniformly distributed or occur in patches
    D. is best assessed using binocular indirect ophthalmoscopy
    E. all of the above

725. A posterior vitreous detachment (PVD) is most commonly due to
    A. trauma
    B. diabetic retinopathy
    C. macular hole formation
    D. postural hypotension
    E. vitreal aging changes

726. Which symptom may be reported by a patient experiencing an acute posterior vitreous detachment (PVD)?
    A. floaters
    B. photopsia
    C. blurred vision

    D. Moore's lightning streaks
    E. all of the above

727. The clinical finding of numerous reddish brown specks in the anterior vitreous, as seen by biomicroscopy in the presence of retinal detachment, is known as
    A. Munson's sign
    B. Dalrimple's sign
    C. Krukenberg's sign
    D. Shaffer's sign
    E. Sampaolesi's sign

728. What is the most common observable clinical finding in posterior vitreous detachment (PVD)?
    A. Weiss' ring and collapsed vitreous face
    B. opaque media, more pronounced in the posterior chamber
    C. vitreous hemorrhage and fibrosis
    D. cystoid macular edema
    E. a demarcation line

729. Cloquet's canal marks the location of which embryonic structure?
    A. fetal fissure
    B. pupillary membrane
    C. hyaloid artery
    D. tunica vasculosa lentis
    E. embryonic nucleus of the lens

730. What is the appearance of the normal vitreous in a young adult patient (less than approximately 30 years of age)?
    A. individual fibrils suspended in clear fluid
    B. milky folds of gossamer veils
    C. reddish-brown cells suspended in clear fluid
    D. white cells and dots suspended in clear fluid
    E. none of the above. The vitreous is not clinically visible until the patient reaches age 65.

731. Vitreoretinal tufts
   A. tend to occur just posterior to the vitreous base
   B. often have associated retinal pigment epithelium proliferation
   C. may cause retinal tears
   D. appear as gray-white conical elevations on the retinal surface
   E. all of the above

Optic Nerve Pathology

732. A waxy, yellowish optic disc with attenuation of retinal vessels, equatorial pigmentation, and early abnormality of the electroretinogram (ERG), is typical of
   A. pernicious anemia
   B. primary optic atrophy
   C. retinitis pigmentosa
   D. secondary optic atrophy from papillitis
   E. glaucoma

733. A 22-year-old patient experiences unilateral blurred vision and pain when moving the eye. The optic disc is hyperemic and swollen, the margins are indistinct, and the veins are tortuous. A central scotoma is apparent. The most likely diagnosis is
   A. toxic ammblyopia
   B. papillitis
   C. papilledema
   D. retrobulbar neuritis
   E. temporal arteritis

734. The most common underlying etiology of retrobulbar neuritis in the 20- to 45-year-old age group is
   A. diabetic neuropathy
   B. infectious diseases
   C. Leber's optic atrophy
   D. multiple sclerosis
   E. tobacco-alcohol intoxication

735. The following statements about papilledema are true EXCEPT
   A. Papilledema can be differentiated from papillitis by the ophthalmoscope alone.
   B. Bilateral papilledema is of no value for diagnosing the laterality of a tumor.
   C. Stereoscopic optic nerve head evaluation will best detect papilledema.
   D. Papilledema is most often a sign of increased intracranial pressure.
   E. A unilateral papilledema occurs in the Foster-Kennedy syndrome.

736. Noninflammatory infarction of the prelaminar nerve head, resulting in a loss of vision in a 65-year-old patient, is known as
   A. arteritic anterior ischemic optic neuropathy
   B. papilledema
   C. papillophlebitis
   D. papillitis
   E. nonarteritic anterior ischemic optic neuropathy

737. Which of the following clinical signs is consistent with optic atrophy?
   A. optic disc pallor
   B. reduced visual acuity
   C. desaturation to red perception
   D. afferent pupillary defect
   E. all of the above

738. Bilaterally elevated, spherical hyaline bodies noted on the optic nerve heads of an otherwise normal patient are known as
   A. optic pits
   B. melanocytoma
   C. optic disc drusen
   D. retinoblastoma
   E. optic nerve gliomas

739. Larger than normal physiologic cupping of the optic nerve head may be difficult to differentiate from glaucomatous cupping. What factor typically characterizes a large but normal physiologic cup?
    A. horizontally oval cupping
    B. central placement of the cup
    C. symmetry of the cup appearance between eyes
    D. intact neuroretinal rim
    E. all of the above

740. In optic atrophy the number of fine, thread-like vessels visible on the surface of the optic nerve will decrease. This is known as
    A. Salus' sign
    B. Piltz's sign
    C. Myerson's sign
    D. Kestenbaum's sign
    E. Rochester's sign

Sensory Neuro-Visual Pathology

741. A visual field defect most annoying to the patient is
    A. bitemporal hemianopsia
    B. a Bjerrum scotoma
    C. a one-half degree central scotoma
    D. enlargement of the blind spot
    E. superior nasal depression

742. Ronne's nasal step is
    A. a horizontal step in the visual field conforming to the termination of nerve fiber bundles at the temporal raphe of the retina
    B. a vertical step produced by unequal double homonymous hemianopsias in bilateral occipital lobe injuries
    C. a vertical step produced by a large macular sparing in a hemianopic field
    D. the sharp temination of a quadranopsia at the fixation point
    E. most commonly assessed using a tangent screen

743. A binasal hemianopsia occurs from pressure on
   A. both lateral angles of the chiasm
   B. each optic nerve from the nasal aspect
   C. each occipital cortex from the lateral aspect
   D. the anterior angle of the chiasm
   E. both optic tracts from the lateral aspect

DIRECTIONS (Questions 744–748): Each set of matching questions in this section consists of a list of lettered options followed by several numbered items. For each item, select the ONE BEST lettered option that is most closely associated with it. Each lettered heading may be used once, more than once, or not at all.

   A. amaurosis fugax secondary to carotid artery disease
   B. transient visual obscurations
   C. classic migraine headache
   D. rheumatic heart valvular disease (RHVD)
   E. ocular migraine
   F. retinal detachment
   G. vertebro-basilar artery disease/TIA
   H. posterior vitreous detachment
   I. visual cortex space-occupying lesion
   J. ophthalmic migraine
   K. common migraine
   L. migraine equivalent

744. A 35-year-old male patient presents to you with the complaint of transient monocular visual loss lasting 15 minutes followed by an ipsilateral headache. He is in good general health. The dilated fundus examination and visual field analysis are normal. What is the likely diagnosis?

745. A 75-year-old male patient complains of bilateral scintillating scotomas that last for 10 minutes. He has experienced frequent visual episodes but no other systemic symptoms. He has been hypertensive for 25 years. Visual field analysis reveals left inferior homonymous quadranopsias. What is the likely diagnosis?

746. A 28-year-old female patient, who is obese, complains of momentary bilateral visual loss when she bends over to tie her shoes. She also complains of headaches and nausea. Dilated fundus examination reveals bilateral papilledema. What is the likely cause of her visual symptoms?

747. Your 45-year-old female patient has experienced migraine headaches for years. Lately, however, she has experienced 20-minute long episodes of bilateral scintillating scotomas with no associated headache. What is the likely diagnosis?

748. Your 35-year-old male patient complains of episodes of monocular visual loss. He has been under the treatment of a cardiologist for years for a "heart condition." Dilated fundus examination reveals a hard-looking, white embolus in a retinal arteriole. What is the likely diagnosis?

DIRECTIONS (Questions 749–756): Each of the numbered items or incomplete statements in this section is followed by answers or completions of the statement. Select the ONE lettered answer or completion that is BEST in each case.

Oculomotor Neuropathology

749. Bell's palsy is
  A. due to paralysis of the sympathetic nerve
  B. due to paralysis of the peripheral facial nerve (VII)
  C. always permanent
  D. upward rolling of the globes with lid closure
  E. a central nervous system disorder

750. Upon simultaneous stimulation of two symmetrical points in the field, the target may disappear in the field of the diseased side. This is termed
  A. extinction phenomenon
  B. qualitative perimetry
  C. confrontation field testing
  D. static perimetry
  E. subjective perimetry

751. Which of the following conditions may cause acquired blepharoptosis?
A. myasthenia gravis
B. Horner's syndrome
C. trauma
D. chronic contact lens wear
E. all of the above

752. Which of the following is NOT a typical ocular sign or symptom of multiple sclerosis?
A. Uhthoff's sign
B. nystagmus
C. papilledema
D. central scotoma
E. diplopia

753. Which of the following is NOT a symptom or sign of Graves' disease?
A. extraocular muscle restrictions
B. extraocular muscle infiltration on orbital CT scanning
C. diplopia
D. enophthalmus
E. exposure keratitis

754. Acquired complete third nerve palsy (total oculomotor ophthalmoplegia) results in
A. ptosis
B. exotropia
C. a dilated, nonreactive pupil
D. loss of accommodation
E. all of the above

755. Internuclear ophthalmoplegia is characterized by
A. paresis of adduction and abduction nystagmus
B. vertical gaze paresis
C. convergence insufficiency
D. divergence insufficiency
E. paresis of abduction and adduction nystagmus

756. Horner's syndrome of unilateral ptosis and miosis
- **A.** is a denervation syndrome in which the sympathetic nervous supply to the eye has been lost
- **B.** is accompanied by anhydrosis when involvement is at or below the superior cervical ganglion
- **C.** may result from carcinoma of the lung
- **D.** may produce heterochromia when congenital
- **E.** all of the above

Answers and Discussion

Ocular Adnexa

593. (A) An auxiliary row of lashes arising from the meibomian gland orifices is called distichiasis. Trichiasis refers to an inward turning of one or more lashes. Poliosis (lash whitening), tylosis ciliaris (lid thickening), and madarosis (lash loss) may result from chronic blepharitis.

594. (B) Herpes zoster ophthalmicus, also known as shingles, is the reactivation of dormant neurotrophic varicella virus. It begins with dermatomal neuralgia along the distribution of the first branch of the trigeminal nerve, followed by skin erythema and vesicle eruption. Systemic antiviral therapy (acyclovir) prescribed early in the disease course is the current treatment of choice.

595. (C) A staphylococcal abscess of a meibomian gland produces an internal hordeolum. It may "point" toward the skin or conjunctival side of the lid. An external hordeolum is a staphylococcal abscess of the glands of Zeis or Moll.

596. (B) Xanthelasma are more common in women and tend to be familial. Clinical evaluation of serum cholesterol levels may be indicated when this condition is noted; however, a direct relationship is generally not found. The lesions may be removed for cosmetic reasons.

597. (A) A low virulence virus produces molluscum contagiosum, an elevated epithelial nodule with an umbilicated center. If a molluscum lesion occurs on the lid margin, a unilateral viral conjunctivitis may result. Treatment involves mechanical or chemical removal of the lesion.

598. (D) *Staphylococcus aureus* is reported to cause approximately two-thirds of all observed ocular inflammations and infections. This organism is part of the normal ocular flora. Infection may result from an excess population of the pathogen or from reduced resistance of the host.

599. (E) Any of the described methods may be used for eyelid hygiene, often determined by practitioner preference. If a baby shampoo solution is used, it should be made daily to avoid contamination. A number of commercial lid hygiene products are now available.

600. (E) A chalazion varies from a hordeolum in that it is not a bacterial abscess. As a result, a patient with chalazion does not exhibit the four cardinal signs of inflammation. All of the listed statements apply to chalazion.

601. (B) Basal cell carcinoma comprises approximately 95 percent of eyelid malignancies. They may present as slightly elevated lesions with "pearly" margins. Associated telangiectasias and an ulcerated center are often noted.

602. (C) Contact dermatitis of the lids, a delayed hypersensitivity reaction, produces dry, wrinkled, hyperemic skin changes. This condition is not uncommon in women as a reaction to makeup or skin care products. It is typically treated with topical steroid creams or ointments.

603. (A) *Demodex folliculorum* is a skin mite that has a predilection for the sebaceous glands of individuals who are middle-age and older. Overgrowth of the mites results in irritative ocular symptoms, particularly in the morning. This condition produces a sheathing debris build-up at the base of the cilia.

604. (E) Treatment for phthiriasis palpebrarum must include local therapy for the lids as well as the other aspects cited. Since patients with phthiriasis palpebrarum may have other sexually transmitted diseases, a medical consultation is indicated. Retreatment after one week will help to eradicate organisms that hatch after the initial treatment.

605. **(A)** Congenital syphilis results in Hutchinson's triad: interstitial keratitis, deafness, and notched upper central incisors. Hutchinson's sign refers to the vesicle on the tip of the nose that may accompany herpes zoster ophthalmicus. The latter indicates involvement of the nasociliary nerve and potential involvement of the globe.

606. **(E)** Herpes simplex skin lesions present as patches of erythema with overlying opaque "dew-drop" vesicles, usually caused by Type I HSV. It is important to rule out globe involvement resulting from the lid lesion. Treatment with antiviral agents is instituted as indicated.

607. **(B)** Lid scrubs have a role in controlling or preventing all of the listed conditions. Lid scrubs are generally prescribed on a regular schedule, such as once or twice a day. Specific patient instructions regarding the lid scrub technique may enhance compliance.

Lacrimal System

608. **(E)** Dry eye symptomatology is often more pronounced while reading, due to reduced blink rates. Patients can be encouraged to blink more frequently when reading. Symptoms may also be relieved by instilling artificial tears just before they commence reading.

609. **(E)** In many infants, spontaneous canalization of the nasolacrimal duct will occur within 6 weeks of birth. If spontaneous canalization does not occur, then lacrimal probing is performed. The procedure is typically performed after the age of 6 months when the infant better tolerates general anesthesia.

610. **(E)** Acute dacryocystitis, bacterial inflammation of the lacrimal sac, requires both topical and systemic therapy. Acute dacryocystitis tends to occur when the lacrimal sac becomes blocked and the bacteria have an opportunity to incubate. Dilation and irriga-

tion may be performed after resolution of the acute infection to determine if a blockage is present.

611. **(E)** Dacryoadenitis, inflammation of the lacrimal gland, can be caused by any of the listed acute inflammatory, chronic inflammatory, or age-related causes. An S-shaped distortion of the upper lid often results. Signs of inflammation or infection will also be present based on the cause of the dacryoadenitis.

612. **(D)** Chronic dacryocystitis, an obstruction of the nasolacrimal system, is most often seen unilaterally in young adult women. It is more common in women due to the narrowness of the nasolacrimal channels and the acute angles between the nasolacrimal structures as compared to men. Dilation and irrigation of the nasolacrimal system will be diagnostic and may help to relieve the blockage.

613. **(E)** Lacrimal gland implants are not currently utilized to enhance globe lubrication. Temporary collagen implants are a helpful diagnostic technique to determine if more permanent occlusion of the puncta will help to relieve dry eye symptoms. Freeman and Herrick plugs are types of silicone plugs.

Conjunctiva

614. **(E)** In contrast to conjunctival injection, ciliary flush appears as a pink-purple circumlimbal band. It will often accompany acute anterior uveitis. Since it represents a "flush" of the ciliary body, distinct vasculature is not visible.

615. **(E)** A subconjunctival hemorrhage, a common cause of patient alarm, may occur following trauma or episodes of coughing, straining, or other Valsalva-type maneuvers. A subconjunctival hemorrhage may appear spontaneously in older patients due to the friability of the conjunctival vessels. It generally resolves within approximately two weeks.

616. **(D)** A pterygium is a proliferation of hyaline and elastic tissue that replaces Bowman's membrane of the cornea. It is thought to be an irritative phenomenon related to exposure. As a result, it is seen more commonly in patients who live in warm climates and

who have frequent exposure to sunny, dusty, and windblown environments.

617. (D) Poorly cleaned tonometers were blamed for early epidemics of epidemic keratoconjunctivitis (EKC). This condition is caused by adenovirus 8 or 19. Clinical signs and symptoms during the acute stage can be dramatic, and corneal opacities may persist.

618. (A) Palpebral vernal conjunctivitis classically occurs seasonally in young male patients who have a personal and/or family history of atopy. Limbal vernal conjunctivitis produces perilimbal injection and inflammation. Topical steroids and mast cell stabilizers are currently the common therapeutic agents used.

619. (C) Lymphangiectasias (dilated lymph channels) or lymphatic cysts commonly appear as small, clear "blisters." They may occur on the palpebral or bulbar conjunctiva. Symptoms are uncommonly associated with this finding.

620. (A) Acne rosacea is an accentuation of the normal flush reaction of the face. It is characterized by hyperemia, pustules, and sebaceous gland hypertrophy. An accompanying chronic keratoconjunctivitis is common.

621. (B) *Hemophilus influenzae* is a common pathogen in young children. Thus, an antiinfective agent that is effective against this organism is an appropriate drug of choice for treating bacterial conjunctivitis in a 3-year-old patient. Side effects of this medication are uncommon but may include superficial irritation and itching.

622. (D) Overnight, the closed lids act as an incubator for organisms causing bacterial conjunctivitis. Thus, the mucopurulent discharge increases with resultant mattering of the lashes in the morning. Treatment typically includes antibiotic drops during the day and antibiotic ointment to the conjunctival sac at bedtime.

623. (C) Due to potentially severe systemic side effects, chloramphenicol is the least preferred drug of choice among those listed for the condition described. Aplastic anemia may rarely develop as a side effect of this medication. It appears to occur as an antigenic response in certain susceptible patients.

624. **(D)** The preauricular lymph node, located directly in front of the notch of the ear, is the primary drainage site for the periocular lymphatic channels. Upon palpation, enlargement of the preauricular node will feel like a pea-sized elevation. The enlarged node may or may not be tender.

625. **(B)** Conjunctival abrasions result from traumatic loss of the superficial conjunctival epithelium. In contrast, conjunctival lacerations penetrate conjunctiva, Tenon's capsule, and episclera. Conjunctival abrasions tend to heal in a few days; topical antibiotic prophylaxis will help prevent secondary infection.

626. **(B)** Erythema multiforme (Stevens-Johnson syndrome) is an acute polymorphic skin disease. Children are most susceptible to this condition as a hypersensitivity reaction to drugs or food. Symblepharon and severe dry eye syndrome may result.

627. **(B)** Animal dander is a common cause of allergic blepharoconjunctivitis. Avoidance of the causative agent will help to minimize episodes. Treatment may include antihistamines, mast cell stabilizers, or low dose topical steroids.

628. **(B)** Patients with Acquired Immune Deficiency Syndrome (AIDS) may present with herpes zoster ophthalmicus (HZO) 20 to 30 years sooner than immunocompetent patients. The onset of HZO in a young adult patient may herald the onset of AIDS by weeks to months. AIDS-risk patients with HZO also exhibit keratitis and uveitis more commonly than the nonAIDS risk group.

Cornea

629. **(B)** Descemet folds may be present in instances of abnormally low IOP rather than elevated IOP. They tend to appear as multiple fine, short, vertical white lines in the central cornea at the level of Descemet's membrane. Descemet's folds appear similar to the striae that may be associated with soft contact lens wear.

630. **(B)** *Streptococcus pneumoniae* bacteria secrete enzymes that destroy corneal tissue and can cause perforation. This ulcer is also known as an acute serpiginous ulcer due to the "creeping" effect

of the advancing edge of ulceration and infiltration. An associated hypopyon is not uncommon.

631. (B) A corneal abrasion, even when healed, may leave a weakened epithelial basement membrane. This is especially likely when the abrasion is caused by a fingernail or paper cut. The epithelium, further weakened by edema from lid closure during sleep, will re-erode upon opening of the lids in the morning to result in recurrent corneal erosion.

632. (A) Endothelial compromise by extensive corneal guttata will produce stromal edema and epithelial bullae in Fuchs' dystrophy. This condition is most common in women in the third or fourth decade. Penetrating keratoplasty is needed in advanced cases.

633. (E) Sclerosing keratitis (sclerokeratitis) is a localized inflammation of the sclera and cornea, unrelated to aging changes. In the aging cornea, wart-like excrescences over Descemet's membrane, secreted by the endothelial cells, may occur centrally (guttata) or peripherally (Hassall-Henle bodies). Descemet's folds appear as fine "wrinkles" in the deep central cornea; limbal girdle of Vogt appears as a superficial arcuate "chalkiness" just inside the limbus at 3 and 9 o'clock.

634. (B) Arcus senilis, even when advanced, is confined to the peripheral portion of the cornea. It appears as a hazy gray ring approximately 2 mm in width and exhibits a clear zone between it and the limbus. Lipid droplets occur throughout the entire corneal thickness but are more pronounced in the superficial and deep corneal layers.

635. (B) Corneal brown lines are subtle discolorations at points of corneal stress. Fleischer's ring is the result of hemosiderin deposition at the level of Bowman's membrane associated with keratoconus. Use of a diffuse illumination beam and the cobalt filter on the slit lamp biomicroscope will enhance the appearance of Fleischer's ring, even in early keratoconus.

636. (C) Irrigation is to be started immediately to remove the chemical from the eye. Litmus paper may be utilized to determine when irrigation may be stopped to check for neutralization of severe chemical injuries. Following irrigation, additional treatment is instituted as indicated.

637. (D) Radial incisions are used in radial keratotomy to produce central corneal flattening and peripheral corneal bulging with a reduction of myopia. Careful patient selection for this procedure is important. The use of corneal laser therapy for myopia correction is also currently under intense study.

638. (C) SLK of Theodore is a bilateral inflammation of unknown etiology affecting the superior tarsus, bulbar conjunctiva, and cornea. Mild cases may be treated using topical lubrication or mild steroids. Alternative treatment includes swabbing of the superior bulbar and palpebral conjunctiva with silver nitrate, or conjunctival resection.

639. (B) EBMD is caused by thickening and reduplication of the corneal epithelial basement membrane. Patients are commonly asymptomatic but may present with symptoms of recurrent corneal erosion. Prominent EBMD lesions that are centrally located may result in corneal distortion and blurred vision.

640. (E) The cornea may respond antigenically to bacterial toxin production or to the presence of viral organisms in any of the ways listed. Treatment typically includes antibiotic therapy to control the bacterial infection. Topical steroid drop therapy is instituted as indicated.

641. (A) Thygeson's superficial punctate keratitis produces epithelial corneal infiltration in a white eye and may be of viral etiology. Treatment with mild topical steroid drops will reduce symptomatology and clear the lesions. It is very common, however, for this condition to recur.

642. (E) Any of the listed therapies may be utilized singly or in combination in the treatment of keratoconjunctivitis sicca (KCS). In the clinical setting, topical lubrication drops and/or ointment is usually the first therapy. Collagen implants are used as a diagnostic test to determine if more permanent punctal occlusion would be effective.

643. (D) Ciprofloxacin is a fluoroquinolone. It inhibits bacterial DNA synthesis and is reported to be effective against bacterial corneal ulcers when used topically. Before the availability of ciprofloxacin, a combination of topical antibiotics and fortified topical agents were needed to effectively treat bacterial corneal ulcers.

644. (E) All of the listed items describe the clinical presentation or treatment of herpes simplex keratitis. In the acute stage one or more dendritic ulcerative lesions appear which are treated with topical antiviral agents. Anterior stromal scarring may result, particularly with multiple recurrences.

645. (E) All of the listed items describe the laboratory culture of a corneal lesion. Aggressive broad spectrum antiinfective therapy is begun while waiting for the culture results. The therapy can then be adjusted more specifically when the results of the culture are known.

Sclera/Episclera

646. (C) Simple episcleritis is typically a localized, superficial inflammation that does not affect visual acuity. Treatment with topical decongestant agents or topical steroids has been described. Episcleritis is rarely associated with intraocular involvement such as anterior uveitis or underlying systemic disease.

647. (B) Recurrent scleritis can be a serious disease, causing extensive globe damage. Juvenile rheumatoid arthritis is a common cause of scleritis. The lack of a scleral blood supply means that high dosages of both local and systemic medication may be needed to reach therapeutic levels in the scleral tissue.

648. (E) Scleral thinning or increased uveal pigmentation may produce blue sclera. It is a common, normal variation in children with darkly pigmented uveal tissue. Pathological scleral thinning will allow for uveal "show through," which gives a blue appearance to the sclera.

649. (A) Hyaline plaque is an age-related degenerative change due to focal scleral thinning. It is a frequent finding in patients over the age of 60 and it produces no symptoms. This lesion appears as a small, round, translucent gray area at the point of insertion of the lateral and/or medial rectus muscles.

650. **(C)** Staphylomas appear as dark blue bulging areas in the sclera. They are usually the result of trauma or scleral inflammation. Staphylomas may be located at anterior, equatorial, or posterior points of the globe.

651. **(A)** Although rare, sclerokeratitis is the most common corneal complication of scleral disease. It represents a localized inflammation of the sclera and peripheral cornea. An accompanying anterior chamber reaction is common.

652. **(E)** Although differing in etiology and various clinical characteristics, all of the listed conditions are reasonable differential diagnoses of nodular episcleritis. The treatment of nodular episcleritis usually includes topical steroid therapy. Recurrent cases of nodular episcleritis may result in structural damage to the sclera.

Anterior Uvea (Iris and Ciliary Body)

653. **(D)** Rubeosis iridis results from generalized ischemia. The ischemic process tends not to be sufficiently widespread in a branch vein occlusion to cause iris ischemia and resultant rubeosis. If left untreated, secondary rubeotic glaucoma is common.

654. **(C)** Posterior synechiae are the result of fibrotic adherence of the iris to the anterior lens capsule. The most common cause of posterior synechiae is chronic intraocular inflammation. Peripheral anterior synechiae refers to adherence of the iris to the posterior cornea.

655. **(A)** Fuchs' heterochromic iridocyclitis is a mild, unilateral anterior uveitis with corresponding iris heterochromia and atrophy. Accompanying IOP elevation and cataract may occur. Posterior synechiae tends not to develop.

656. **(C)** In acute anterior uveitis the involved eye usually exhibits a miotic pupil due to iris congestion. Treatment typically includes

pupillary dilation and cycloplegia along with topical steroid drops. Pupil dilation and cycloplegia help to reduce iris congestion and ciliary spasm.

657. **(B)** Sympathetic ophthalmia is believed to be the result of an autoimmune reaction to uveal pigment. It is most commonly seen when uveal tissue in an injured eye is exposed to the atmosphere for at least one hour. In this condition, the uninvolved or "sympathizing" eye develops anterior uveitis in which the onset is delayed by several weeks to several years.

658. **(B)** Corectopia is a congenital eccentricity of the pupil. Anisocoria refers to a difference in pupil size between the two eyes, and polycoria refers to multiple pupil openings. Coloboma is the keyhole-shaped defect in the infero-nasal quadrant of the iris that occurs when the fetal fissure fails to close completely. Leukocoria occurs when the pupil is opacified.

659. **(D)** One of the congenital ocular anomalies accompanying aniridia is foveal hypoplasia. Thus, the visual acuity will not appreciably improve with an artificial aperture. Secondary glaucoma commonly accompanies aniridia.

660. **(A)** Myotonic dystrophy, an hereditary muscle dystrophy, is not associated with anterior uveitis. A common ocular sign of myotonic dystrophy is acquired ptosis that exacerbates during the course of the day. Cataract may also accompany this condition.

661. **(A)** One of the accompanying ocular findings of albinism is macular hypoplasia, producing abnormal visual acuity. Patients with albinism are low vision candidates for optical devices as well as filter evaluation. Patients with ocular albinism do not exhibit the diffuse cutaneous involvement of generalized albinism.

662. **(E)** All of the listed items pertain to iris transillumination using the slit lamp biomicroscope. Iris transillumination will help to determine if ocular or generalized albinism is the cause of an observed nystagmus. It is important to transilluminate the iris when a Krukenberg's spindle is noted to determine if pigment dispersion syndrome is present.

663. **(E)** All of the listed items describe chronic anterior uveitis, formerly known as granulomatous uveitis. Patients with chronic anterior uveitis tend to present with symptoms of reduced visual acuity rather than eye pain or redness. Pupil abnormalities may result if posterior synechiae develop.

Pupillary, Accommodative and Refractive Pathology

664. **(B)** Adie's tonic pupil is due to a ciliary ganglion lesion. As a result, the iris sphincter muscle contracts slowly to near stimulation and exhibits little or no direct light reaction. Adie's syndrome refers to the pupil involvement along with loss of deep tendon reflexes.

665. **(E)** Pupil dilation during the swinging flashlight test is indicative of an ipsilateral optic nerve conduction defect. This phenomenon has also been called the Marcus Gunn pupil. It is important to assess this finding when evaluating a patient with monocular visual loss.

666. **(A)** The increased index of refraction in nuclear sclerosis will often produce a myopic shift in refraction. Patients often report the acquired ability to read up close without glasses, dubbed "second sight." The other listed cataract types tend not to be associated with acquired refractive error changes.

667. **(E)** The formation of a macular hole does not shorten the axial length to produce an acquired hyperopia. Some retinal conditions result in a slight elevation of the macular tissue. In this instance, a relative shortening of the globe's axial length may manifest as a slight hyperopic shift.

668. **(D)** By assessing globe axial length, A-scan is used to determine IOL power needed for implantation. Axial length information, in conjunction with corneal curvature measurement, is integral to the determination of IOL power. The desired postoperative refractive error also impacts IOL power selection.

669. (B) Due to fluid dynamic changes in diabetes affecting the crystalline lens, fluctuations in ocular refraction are common. Significant elevation in the blood sugar level may result in a myopic shift. Lowering of the elevated blood sugar level to more normal levels will tend to reverse this myopic shift.

670. (C) Dapiprazole, an alpha-adrenergic antagonist, produces miosis without affecting accommodation. A theoretical usage of this drug is pupil constriction to reduce mechanical rubbing of the iris pigment epithelium against the lens zonules associated with pigment dispersion syndrome. Eliminating this source of pigment dispersion may reduce an associated pigmentary glaucoma.

671. (E) A common clinical sign of keratoconus is a significant change in refractive error. More specifically, an increase in astigmatism and a change in cylinder axis are noted. The best corrected spectacle visual acuity will decrease as corneal distortion develops.

672. (A) Due to denervation hypersensitivity, an Adie's tonic pupil will exhibit an accentuated miotic response to a weak cholinergic agonist agent. Thus, 0.125 percent pilocarpine solution will cause the Adie's tonic pupil to constrict, and may be used as a diagnostic test. This weak concentration of pilocarpine will not cause a normal pupil to constrict.

Orbit

673. (A) Direct communication between the carotid artery or its branches and the cavernous sinus results in a carotid-cavernous sinus fistula. A carotid-cavernous sinus fistula will allow the transmission of the vascular pulse to the orbit, causing a unilateral pulsating exophthalmus. Other ocular signs associated with this condition include dilated conjunctival vessels, dilated retinal vessels with hemorrhages and fluorescein leakage, ophthalmoplegia, and orbital bruit.

674. (A) The severity of the ocular injury will determine the need for enucleation. When the globe is perforated, systemic steroid therapy may be used as prophylaxis against sympathetic ophthalmia.

The onset of sympathetic ophthalmia following the initial injury may range from several weeks to several months.

675. **(B)** A blow-out fracture is a break in the bony orbital floor. This orbital floor fracture may entrap the inferior rectus muscle, as well as other orbital contents, to produce the described signs. Depending upon the clinical presentation, surgical repair may be delayed until tissue swelling subsides.

676. **(E)** All of the statements are true of orbital cellulitis. Two of the most common causative agents are *Hemophilus influenzae* and *Streptococcus pneumoniae*. Suspected orbital cellulitis requires prompt and aggressive medical intervention.

677. **(C)** A space-occupying lesion of the orbit may cause anterior proptosis of the globe with mechanical restriction of gaze. Relative shortening of the globe axial length due to retrobulbar pressure by the mass may induce a hyperopic shift. The mass may be primary to the orbit or may be metastatic from other lesional sites.

678. **(A)** Preseptal cellulitis is subcutaneous bacterial infection of the lids anterior to the orbital septum. It is often the result of localized injury which introduces the pathogen into the lid tissue. It is important to accurately distinguish preseptal cellulitis from orbital cellulitis, as the severity and treatment of each varies significantly.

679. **(E)** Preseptal cellulitis caused by *Hemophilus influenzae* may progress to meningitis in a young child. A child who presents with swollen lids that have a pink-purple discoloration should be viewed as having preseptal cellulitis caused by *Hemophilus influenzae*. Appropriately aggressive medical therapy must then be instituted.

Anterior Chamber, Angle Structure, and Abnormal IOP

680. **(D)** In anterior uveitis, the iris vessels become congested and dilated, resulting in escape of white blood cells and protein. The

leakage of inflammatory (white blood) cells and protein into the normally optically empty aqueous produces the Tyndall effect of cells and flare in anterior uveitis. The white blood cells appear as tiny white specks floating in the aqueous in the direction of the convection currents; flare appears as a uniform milkiness to the aqueous.

681. (C) A persistent pupillary membrane is visible as fine, cobweb-like lines bridging the iris collarette. It is an often-seen anterior chamber congenital remnant of the tunica vasculosa lentis. In many instances, clumps of pigment may be seen dangling from the membrane as a normal variation.

682. (A) In anterior uveitis, the aqueous convection currents impact the destination of anterior chamber debris. As a result, keratic precipitates (KP's) will tend to aggregate on the corneal endothelium inferiorly. In severe cases of chronic anterior uveitis, however, a more diffuse distribution of numerous KP's may be noted.

683. (C) The exact histological cause of glaucoma remains unknown and under intense study. It is believed that acceleration of the tissue-aging process at the level of the trabecular meshwork is responsible for the intraocular pressure elevation in primary open-angle glaucoma. Control of glaucoma is directed toward reducing aqueous production and/or increasing aqueous outflow.

684. (C) Acute, severe elevations ("spikes") of intraocular pressure tend to cause corneal edema. Corneal edema produces a disruption in the normally uniform corneal structure which causes light diffraction and the symptom of halos around lights. Although this symptom may be associated with acute angle closure glaucoma, it tends not to be reported by patients with primary open-angle glaucoma.

685. (B) Buphthalmos ("ox eye") is the descriptive term for congenital glaucoma, which these signs describe. In young children, the sclera is not as rigid as that in the adult. Thus, with elevations in intraocular pressure in very young children, the sclera may stretch and the eye increases in size, along with the other signs and symptoms described.

686. (D) If the globe has been penetrated, the IOP will often be reduced to low, single digit readings. A positive Seidel's sign may pinpoint the penetration point causing the loss of aqueous. A penetrating globe injury requires prompt medical intervention.

687. (A) Certain susceptible individuals will respond with an elevation in intraocular pressure when moderate- to high-potency topical steroids are used. Steroid-linked glaucoma is the probable diagnosis in a patient on topical steroid treatment for approximately two weeks or longer who then exhibits an elevated IOP and a clear anterior chamber. Steroid-linked glaucoma tends to reverse itself when the steroid is discontinued; antiglaucoma therapy is initiated as needed until the pressure returns to normal.

688. (E) The mechanical release of iris pigment epithelial particles throughout the anterior chamber in pigmentary dispersion syndrome results in all of the mentioned findings. If the pigment deposition in the angle is sufficient to block aqueous outflow, pigmentary glaucoma may result. Patients with pigment dispersion syndrome may exhibit acute IOP "spikes" following exercise or pupil dilation from a sudden increase in angle pigment.

689. (B) Sturge-Weber syndrome (encephalotrigeminal angiomatosis) produces a unilateral facial cutaneous venous angioma, also known as a nevus flammeus or port wine stain. This vascular anomaly occurs along the distribution of one or more branches of the fifth cranial nerve. Ipsilateral infantile glaucoma develops if extensive hemangioma involves the conjunctiva and episclera, and if anterior chamber angle anomalies are present.

690. (C) The presence of angle recession suggests sufficient subclinical trabecular meshwork damage that secondary open-angle glaucoma may develop 10 to 15 years after the ocular injury. This delayed onset secondary open-angle glaucoma will be unilateral. The more extensive the angle recession, the more likely it is for the glaucoma to develop.

691. (E) All of the mentioned factors place the ocular hypertensive patient at risk for possible chronic open-angle glaucoma. At a given intraocular pressure level, patients with one or more of these risk factors is more likely to develop glaucoma than if the risk factors were not present. Thus, the assessment of risk factors in a patient with slightly to moderately elevated IOP will significantly affect treatment and management plans.

692. (D) Early erosion of the optic nerve head due to glaucomatous damage will often produce vertical elongation of the optic cup. In assessing glaucomatous changes of the optic nerve head, pupillary dilation and the use of stereoscopic viewing techniques under high magnification is imperative. It is important to periodically monitor the optic nerve heads of glaucoma patients to assess therapeutic efficacy of the treatment regimen.

693. (A) Before definitively diagnosing low tension glaucoma, it is important to evaluate the diurnal fluctuation of the IOP. In doing so, one may find that the IOP is at normal levels at some time during the day but, in fact, exhibits abnormally high levels at other times of the day. Thus, patients initially determined to have low-tension glaucoma may actually be found to have primary open-angle glaucoma following diurnal evaluation of the IOP.

694. (D) Although future practice trends may dictate otherwise, ALT is currently not the initial treatment of choice for primary open-angle glaucoma. Generally speaking, ALT tends to be reserved for patients who are not controlled on maximal medical therapy, who cannot tolerate antiglaucoma medications, or who are poorly compliant. The efficacy of ALT as initial therapy for primary open-angle glaucoma has been under study.

695. (A) Topical carbonic anhydrase inhibitors will not induce miosis. Once approved by the FDA, they may prove to be a very effective means for reducing aqueous production and lowering intraocular pressure (IOP). Systemic CAI's are very effective in lowering IOP but tend to cause significant side effects.

696. (B) Lodging of pigment at the level of Schwalbe's line is known as Sampaolesi's line. Hudson-Stahli, Ferry's, and Stocker's lines are types of corneal brown lines. Keratic precipitates that distribute in a fine vertical line on the inferior corneal endothelium form Turk's line.

Lens/Aphakia/Pseudophakia

697. (D) Anterior axial embryonic cataracts occur in approximately 25 percent of the population. Routine examination of the crystalline lens following pupillary dilation will allow for identification of the common congenital cataracts. Those types listed tend not to affect visual acuity, although posterior polar cataracts may reduce VA slightly at near and in bright light.

698. (C) The timing for cataract extraction is usually based upon the visual demands of the patient rather than the appearance of the opacity. Some health care insurance programs do, however, have specific criteria for the timing of cataract extraction in order to receive reimbursement. Visual functional aspects such as glare and contrast sensitivity function tend to be adversely affected sooner by early cataract than standard visual acuity measures.

699. (E) Posterior subcapsular cataracts (PSC's) may occur in retinitis pigmentosa, systemic steroid usage, and chronic anterior uveitis. PSC's may also form from ocular contusion. Posterior subcapsular cataracts may develop at a relatively young age (late 30's/early 40's) as an early age-related cataract.

700. (B) Following ocular contusion, a pigmented, ring-like "imprint" of the pupillary ruff known as Vossius' ring may appear on the anterior lens surface. This finding will be most apparent following pupillary dilation. A traumatic anterior uveitis tends to accompany Vossius' ring.

701. (B) When the lens is removed while it is still within the capsule, the term "intracapsular cataract extraction (ICCE)" is used. Extracapsular cataract extractions (ECCE) are now the most common so that an intraocular lens implant may be placed in the capsular "bag." An ECCE is also less likely to result in cystoid macular edema than an ICCE.

702. (D) A late rosette cataract is a petal-shaped opacity that may develop years following ocular contusion. A fresh rosette cataract may occur within hours after ocular contusion due to the forcing of aqueous into the lens. While a fresh rosette cataract tends to be reversible, a late rosette cataract is permanent.

703. (E) Posterior subcapsular cataracts (PSC's), which can develop fairly rapidly, are typically positioned near the posterior pole of the lens. As a result, PSC's will cause increased visual deficits under conditions of pupil miosis. Light scattered off the opacity may also cause visual symptoms.

704. (B) A pulvurulent ("powder") cataract is a type of congenital lens opacity. It appears as a hollow sphere of punctate opacities located at the level of the fetal nucleus. A cuneiform cataract refers to the wedge-shaped opacities of age-related cortical spoking, and cupulliform cataract is another name for posterior subcapsular cataract.

705. (A) The YAG laser is useful for cutting visually disabling intraocular membranes. Capsule opacification is common after extracapsular cataract extraction. The YAG, a photodisruptor laser, has a cutting effect on the opacified capsule to result in a clear aperture along the visual axis.

Posterior Pole

706. (A) Areas of retinal hemorrhage will absorb red-free (green) light and will appear black. Thus, small dot/blot hemorrhages in early diabetic retinopathy may be more readily discernible using the red-free filter on the ophthalmoscope compared to white light. It is helpful to evaluate any vascular changes in the fundus using this technique.

707. (A) During fluorescein angiography, a small amount of fluorescein is injected into a vein in the arm. The fluorescent properties of the dye allow it to be visualized and photographed as it circulates through the choroidal and retinal vasculature. In this manner, vascular abnormalities of the eye can be precisely delineated.

708. (E) B-scan ultrasonography provides a two-dimensional assessment of globe and orbit sonolescence. When dense media opacity is present, such as a mature cataract, B-scan is utilized to help determine the state of the posterior chamber eye structures. In this manner, the potential acuity of the eye following removal/treatment of the dense media opacity can be grossly determined.

709. (C) Since the inflammatory process of retrobulbar neuritis occurs behind the globe, no seepage of inflammatory cells into the vitreous will occur. The other listed conditions do cause inflammatory reactions in the vitreous. In some instances, the presence or absence of vitreous involvement is used to distinguish an active vs inactive disease state.

710. (C) The appearance of a preretinal hemorrhage reflects its location between the retinal internal limiting membrane and the hyaloid membrane of the vitreous. It typically occurs due to damage to the superficial disc or retinal vessels. The shape of this hemorrhage reflects a gravity-dependent fluid level.

711. (A) VER measures the electrical potential in the brain that results from the introduction of a visual stimulus such as a flash of light or a flashing checkerboard pattern. The potential is measured using scalp electrodes placed over the occipital cortex. As a result, the largest VER response is obtained from the macular area.

712. (E) Embryonic remnants will often sheath the large retinal vessels on the optic disc as a normal variation. When pronounced, an epipapillary membrane may be noted. This embryonic sheathing may produce normal crossing changes within 2 DD of the optic nerve head.

713. (B) Fundus flavimaculatus is the result of an enzymatic defect in the retinal pigment epithelium of unknown etiology. Patients with this condition may have reduced visual acuity or normal visual acuity. Those with reduced visual acuity and associated macular degeneration have a small central scotoma and an abnormal ERG response.

714. (C) Age-related macular degeneration most commonly involves the disorganization and migration of the macular pigment, along with drusen formation. The presence of hemorrhagic and/or exudative involvement suggests the "wet" form of macular degeneration rather than the "dry" atrophic form. Age-related macular degeneration may evolve into predisciform changes.

715. (E) All of these conditions may produce flame-shaped hemorrhages in the superficial retinal layers. The hemorrhages take on a flame or linear shape because they conform to the array of the nerve fiber layer in the particular portion of the fundus in which they are located. Hemorrhages may be caused by any condition that alters the integrity of the vessel endothelial cells.

716. **(A)** Roth's spots are flame-shaped hemorrhages with a whitish center (white central hemorrhages). In the case of leukemia, the Roth spot is composed of a hemorrhage with a central aggregation of white blood cells. Roth's spots may also appear as the result of a cotton-wool spot with surrounding hemorrhage or a retinal flame hemorrhage with central resolution.

717. **(E)** Conditions that produce retinal hypoxia may result in neovascularization. These new vessels proliferate from surrounding, relatively normal retinal or disc vessels in an attempt to revascularize the damaged tissue. Neovascularization is comprised of very delicate vessels that have a tendency to hemorrhage and subsequently fibrose.

718. **(B)** More than 50 percent of patients with AIDS exhibit cotton-wool patches. Retinal hemorrhages are also commonly noted in AIDS patients. The cause of the retinal microvasculopathy in AIDS is unknown, but may represent immune complex deposition and increased plasma viscosity.

719. **(E)** Chorioretinal changes due to aging may produce all of the mentioned findings as a result of degenerative changes and pigment migration. In choroidal sclerosis, the choroidal vasculature appears prominent through overlying atrophic tissue. Choroidal sclerosis may be confined to the peripapillary or macular areas, or it may be diffusely distributed.

720. **(D)** Neonatal gonococcal infection occurs during the passage of the infant through the infected birth canal during delivery. If this disease is contracted by the neonate, signs of infection typically appear in 2 to 3 days. Prophylactic ocular treatment of the neonate at birth is intended to preclude the development of this condition.

721. **(C)** Histoplasmosis causes peripheral "punched-out" lesions, peripapillary atrophy, and macular lesions. Most of these presumed ocular histoplasmosis syndrome (POHS) lesions are noted

during routine examination of asymptomatic patients. Acute activation of a macular lesion or the development of a subretinal neovascular membrane in a lesion near the macula, however, may adversely affect visual acuity and result in patient symptoms.

722. (E) All of the mentioned findings may be acute or chronic sequelae of ocular trauma, particularly contusion to the globe. The potential for posterior pole involvement in an eye that has sustained a contusion injury necessitates pupillary dilation. Chorioretinal scars due to prior traumatic events are often noted during routine examination of asymptomatic patients.

Peripheral Fundus/Vitreous

723. (A) Asteroid hyalosis particles are vitreous deposits of calcium soaps. This condition is typically seen unilaterally in middle-age to elderly patients. Although asteroid hyalosis usually causes no symptoms, it has been reported as having a high association with systemic diseases such as diabetes, hypertension, and atherosclerosis.

724. (E) All of the statements listed are true of white without pressure. This finding probably represents an area of strong adhesion between the vitreous and retina. White with pressure refers to a lightening of the retinal appearance during scleral depression.

725. (E) With increasing age, approximately age 60 and older, fluid cavities (lacunae) form within the body of the vitreous. These fluid cavities break through defects in the posterior limiting membrane of the vitreous to cause a posterior vitreous detachment (PVD). Acute PVD is an important differential diagnosis when an older patient presents with the symptom of flashing lights.

726. (E) The vitreal changes that develop in acute PVD, along with the potential mechanical stimulation of the retina, can cause any of the mentioned symptoms. Since the nasal peripheral retina is seeing retina and since the vitreous base more prominently overlaps onto seeing retina in the nasal periphery, the patient will typically report vertical streaks of flashing light in the temporal periphery. A prominent floater develops when the prepapillary annulus floats in the posterior chamber and casts a shadow on the retina.

727. **(D)** Free-floating retinal pigment epithelial cells or red blood cells released from damaged retinal vessels may produce this clinical finding known as Shaffer's sign. If a positive Shaffer's sign is noted, it is likely that a retinal tear is present. An alternative name for this sign is tobacco dusting.

728. **(A)** Careful examination may reveal the presence of both of these findings in an acute or long-standing PVD. The collapsed vitreous base is often detectable with the slit lamp as it is focused into the anterior portion of the posterior chamber. The prepapillary annulus (Weiss' ring) can be detected using direct ophthalmoscopy (retroillumination) or during fundus biomicroscopy.

729. **(C)** Cloquet's canal marks the location of the absorbed embryonic hyaloid artery. Cloquet's canal terminates anteriorly as Weiger's ligament. This "ligament" appears as a subtle 9 mm diameter white-gray arc or ring on the posterior surface of the crystalline lens.

730. **(B)** The vitreous in a younger patient appears as amorphic gossamer veils. With time, the vitreous takes on a more fibrillar appearance. The change in the normal appearance of the vitreous with age is due to the separation of the solid components of the vitreous from the liquid components.

731. **(E)** All of the statements are true of vitreoretinal tufts. Vitreoretinal tufts are comprised of degenerated retinal tissue to which the vitreous is strongly adhered. The three principal types of tufts include cystic, noncystic, and zonular. The strong vitreoretinal adhesion associated with tufts is responsible for a substantial percentage of horseshoe tears that may develop in acute PVD.

Optic Nerve Pathology

732. **(C)** As a retinal degeneration involving the outer rod layers, retinitis pigmentosa (RP) results in b wave and amplitude abnormalities of the ERG. Other clinical signs associated with RP

include ascending optic atrophy, bone spicule pigmentary disturbances, and retinal vessel attenuation. Difficulties with night vision and significant visual field loss affect visual performance.

733. (B) Papillitis produces ophthalmoscopically visible signs of optic nerve inflammation. Central scotomas are the most common field defect accompanying this condition. An afferent pupillary defect will usually accompany this condition.

734. (D) Retrobulbar neuritis is a common presenting sign and/or complication of multiple sclerosis (MS). MS is a central nervous system disease of disseminated neuritis exhibiting exacerbations and remissions. The onset of MS is usually in the young adult.

735. (A) Papillitis and papilledema have a similar appearance with the ophthalmoscope. Evaluation of optic nerve function through visual acuity measurement, color vision assessment, and visual field analysis is needed to differentiate these two conditions. Although they appear ophthalmoscopically similar, papillitis will exhibit definite visual functional changes whereas papilledema generally does not.

736. (E) Ciliary vessel infarction of the optic nerve produces pale disc edema, visual field loss, and eventual optic atrophy known as nonarteritic anterior ischemic optic neuropathy. This condition most commonly affects elderly patients who are diabetic or hypertensive. An erythrocyte sedimentation rate (ESR) will help to differentiate this condition from arteritic anterior ischemic optic neuropathy (temporal arteritis).

737. (E) All of the mentioned findings are consistent with the nerve appearance and function in optic atrophy. Optic atrophy may develop from a number of causes, including vascular, degenerative, inflammatory, compressive, toxic-nutritional, metabolic, and traumatic. Glaucomatous optic atrophy will exhibit enlargement of the cup along with the atrophic signs.

738. (C) Optic disc drusen appear as glistening, irregular, and yellowish hyaline bodies. They may be superficial on the optic nerve head, or buried within the nerve, as is common in children. Optic disc drusen may be unilateral or bilateral.

739. (E) In contrast, pathologic cupping of the optic disc will generally result in vertical elongation, cup asymmetry, and irregularity of the neuroretinal rim. These characteristics are highly suggestive of glaucomatous cupping. Stereoscopic examination of the optic disc through a dilated pupil is imperative for accurate evaluation of the cup.

740. (D) Normally, 10 to 12 arterioles are visible on the optic disc. In optic atrophy the number of arterioles on the surface of the disc may drop significantly. This is known as Kestenbaum's sign.

Sensory Neuro-Visual Pathology

741. (C) Even a small central scotoma will produce reduced visual acuity and problems with fixation. This scotoma may be best detected using an Amsler grid. Magnifying devices may help the patient to function better by enlarging the image onto normal retina surrounding the scotoma.

742. (A) The retinal nerve fiber layer emanates from the optic nerve, the superior and inferior portions of which terminate at the temporal raphe. Defects in the nerve fiber bundle terminating at the temporal raphe will project into the nasal peripheral field ("nasal step"). This may be an early visual field defect in primary open-angle glaucoma.

743. (A) Interruption of the uncrossed fibers on the lateral aspects of the chiasm will produce a binasal hemianopsia. These defects are uncommon clinically and generally occur from bilateral lesions. Some of the cited causes of this field defect include fusiform aneurysms of the internal carotid artery, sclerotic plaquing of the internal carotid or anterior cerebral arteries, trauma, and severe exsanquination.

744. (E) Ocular (retinal) migraine presents as a transient monocular visual loss in a young adult patient. It is often followed by an ipsilateral headache. Ocular migraine may occur in patients with a history of other types of migraine headache.

745. (G) Transient ischemic attacks (TIA's) involving the vertebro-basilar system cause bilateral visual symptoms due to the effect on the visual cortex. A persistent bilateral visual field defect suggests that visual cortex infarction has occurred. Visual field analysis is important in a patient who has experienced a TIA.

746. (B) Momentary visual losses due to papilledema are known as transient visual obscurations. They are likely the result of postural or spontaneous changes in optic nerve head perfusion which affects the retinal blood supply. The patient described is likely suffering from essential intracranial hypertension (pseudotumor cerebri).

747. (J) Ophthalmic migraines (acephalgic migraine equivalent) exhibit the same visual symptoms as classic migraine but the headache does not occur. It is common for life-long migraine sufferers to experience a different type of migraine as they get older. Careful patient questioning will reveal the migraine history.

748. (D) Patients with rheumatic heart valve disease (RHVD) may experience amaurosis fugax due to calcific emboli that emanate from the calcified mitral valve. A calcific embolus should be distinquished from the fatty embolus known as a Hollenhorst plaque. The former is more common in younger patients with a history of RHVD; the latter may occur in older patients as a complication of ipsilateral atherosclerotic carotid artery disease.

Oculomotor Neuropathology

749. (B) Bell's palsy is an idiopathic and spontaneous paralysis of the seventh cranial nerve, causing unilateral facial paralysis. The resulting loss of facial muscular control is usually transient. In contrast, Bell's phenomenon refers to the reflex upward rolling of the globes upon lid closure.

750. (A) Parietal lobe disease may produce an inattentive hemifield (extinction phenomenon). Extensive lesions of the parietal lobe may affect vision as well as the motor pathways from the cerebrum to the spinal cord. In this event, parietal lobe syndrome symptoms may result, such as problems with simple calculations or left-right orientation.

751. (E) Acquired neurogenic, myogenic, or mechanical ptosis may result from any of the mentioned conditions. Treatment of the acquired ptosis will be determined by the etiology. In myasthenia gravis, a fatigue-dependent ptosis may be the initial presenting sign of this condition.

752. (C) Increased intracranial pressure with papilledema is generally not seen in multiple sclerosis (MS). When the optic nerve is involved in MS, papillitis or retrobulbar neuritis is generally observed. Uhthoff's sign refers to the reduction in visual acuity that may occur in patients with demyelinating disease with an increase in body temperature, such as follows exercise.

753. (D) Exophthalmus, rather than enophthalmus, is a frequent sign of Grave's disease. This finding may be unilateral or it may show asymmetric involvement between the two eyes. The exophthalmus results from an increase in orbital contents, which is largely due to thickening of the extraocular muscles.

754. (E) All of the listed findings will accompany acquired complete third nerve palsy. These clinical findings accompany this condition because the superior, medial, and inferior recti muscles are innervated by the third cranial nerve; this nerve also carries parasympathetic fibers to the pupil. Trauma, carotid aneurysm, and diabetes are the most common causes of complete third nerve palsy. In diabetic third nerve palsies, the pupil is usually spared.

755. (A) Lesions affecting the medial longitudinal fasciculus between the third and sixth nerve nuclei result in abnormalities in horizontal gaze known as internuclear ophthalmoplegia. Disconjugate horizontal eye movements result upon attempts to gaze laterally. Convergence, however, is usually preserved.

756. (E) All of the listed statements are true of Horner's syndrome. Pharmacologic testing may help to differentiate the pupil findings in Horner's syndrome from other pupillary anomalies. Other known causes of Horner's syndrome include cervical trauma and aneurysms of the carotid or subclavian artery.

References

1. Alexander L. *Primary Care of the Posterior Segment,* 2nd ed. Norwalk, Ct: Appleton & Lange; 1994.
2. Amos JF. *Diagnosis and Management in Vision Care.* Boston: Butterworths; 1987.
3. Bartlett JD, Jaanus SD, eds. *Clinical Ocular Pharmacology.* 2nd ed. Boston: Butterworths; 1989.
4. Catania LJ. *Primary Care of the Anterior Segment.* Norwalk, Ct: Appleton & Lange; 1988.
5. Fingeret M, Casser L, Woodcome HT. *Atlas of Primary Eyecare Procedures.* Norwalk, Ct: Appleton & Lange; 1990.
6. Grosvenor TP. *Primary Care Optometry,* 2nd ed. Boston: Butterworths; 1988.
7. Harrington DO, Drake MV. *The Visual Fields,* 6th ed. St. Louis: CV Mosby; 1990.
8. Jones WL, Reidy RW. *Atlas of the Peripheral Ocular Fundus.* Boston: Butterworths; 1985.
9. Miller NK. *Walsh and Hoyt's Clinical Neuro-Ophthalmology,* Vols 1–3. Baltimore: Williams & Wilkins; 1988.
10. Roy FH. *Ocular Differential Diagnosis,* 4th ed. Philadelphia: Lea & Febiger; 1989.
11. Spalton DJ, Hitchings RA, Hunter PA. *Atlas of Clinical Ophthalmology.* 2nd ed. London: Gower Medical Publishing; 1993.
12. Vaughan D, Asbury T, Tabbara KF. *General Ophthalmology,* 12th ed. Norwalk, Ct: Appleton & Lange; 1989.

7

Refractive/Oculomotor/ Sensory Integrative Conditions

DIRECTIONS (Questions 757–929): Each of the numbered items or incomplete statements in this section is followed by answers or completions of the statement. Select the ONE lettered answer or completion that is BEST in each case.

Clinical Optometry

757. Which of the following conditions produces a complaint of blurred vision?

A. under-corrected hyperopia or uncorrected astigmatism
B. night myopia or retinitis pigmentosa
C. multiple sclerosis or age-related maculopathy
D. nuclear or posterior subcapsular lens opacities
E. all of the above

758. Which of the following conditions does not produce a typical complaint of eye strain?
   A. uncorrected hyperopic astigmatism
   B. uncorrected myopia
   C. uncorrected hyperopia
   D. convergence excess
   E. divergence insufficiency

759. Which of the following conditions does not produce a patient complaint of double vision?
   A. keratoconus
   B. uncorrected astigmatism
   C. occasional exotropia
   D. occasional esotropia
   E. none of the above

760. A patient, when standing 10 feet from an acuity chart, can just read the 20/20 line. What line can be read when standing 20 feet away from the chart?
   A. 20/55
   B. 20/45
   C. 20/40
   D. 20/35
   E. 20/20

761. When calibrating a visual acuity chart (projected on a screen located 20 feet in front of the patient), the simplest procedure is to measure the overall height of the 20/200 letter. This letter should measure
   A. 5.8 mm
   B. 87 mm
   C. 58 mm
   D. 200 mm
   E. 8.7 mm

762. If static retinoscopy is done through a +1.50 D lens, the eye is neutralized in the 55° meridian at a distance of 66⅔ cm, and the eye is neutralized in the other principal meridian at a distance of 40 cm. The refractive error is
   A. $-1.50 - 1.00 \times 55$
   B. $+2.50 - 1.00 \times 145$

C. plano +2.00 × 145
D. −2.50 −1.50 × 55
E. plano −1.00 × 55°

763. According to Javal's Rule, if the keratometer readings are 42.75 at 90° and 43.50 at 180°, the expected astigmatism in the spectacle plane is
    A. −1.44 × 90
    B. −0.75 × 90
    C. −1.25 × 90
    D. −0.94 × 90
    E. none of the above

764. With proper blur, the patient reports that the 10 o'clock (4 o'clock) line is clearest on the fan dial. What is the axis of the correcting cylinder?
    A. 30°
    B. 60°
    C. 90°
    D. 120°
    E. 150°

765. Which of the following subjective tests is not used to detect and measure astigmatism?
    A. stenopak slit refraction
    B. Robinson Cohen slide
    C. paraboline test
    D. bichrome test
    E. all of the above

766. Which of the following tests cannot be used to determine the spherical portion of the distant correction?
    A. bichrome
    B. cross cylinder
    C. Thorington
    D. Maddox rod
    E. both **C** and **D**

767. When using the Mallet fixation disparity unit,
- **A.** the dominant eye is usually revealed by the fact that it is not the one that exhibits the slip
- **B.** for exophoria, the weakest base-in prism or minus lens that aligns the strips is added to the Rx
- **C.** for esophoria, the minimum base-out prism that aligns the strips is added to the Rx
- **D.** by pushing the device up, the near points of both accommodation and convergence can be measured
- **E.** all of the above

768. A disadvantage encountered when utilizing the autorefractor as a substitute for retinoscopy is that the practitioner may miss such subtle clues as
- **A.** the presence of early cortical changes in the crystalline lens
- **B.** the scissors motion of the reflex that occurs when the patient has large pupils
- **C.** the rapidly changing reflex due to spasm of accommodation in latent hyperopia
- **D.** the act of squinting
- **E.** all of the above

769. Which of the following clinical instruments is utilized to accurately perform corneal thickness measurements?
- **A.** direct ophthalmoscope
- **B.** photokeratoscope
- **B.** VER with stenopak slit
- **D.** optical pachymeter
- **E.** ophthalmodynamometer

770. Which of the following clinical instruments is utilized to perform corneal curvature measurements?
- **A.** gonioscope
- **B.** slit-lamp biomicroscope
- **C.** video (photo) keratoscope
- **D.** ophthalmodynamometer
- **E.** exophthalmometer

771. Given a patient with a far PD of 65 mm: What would be his near PD for a viewing distance of 25 cm?
  A. 59 mm
  B. 62 mm
  C. 58 mm
  D. 60 mm
  E. 61 mm

772. Which of the following statements concerning cycloplegic refraction is correct?
  A. Cycloplegic refraction is useful with children who display a convergent strabismus.
  B. Cycloplegic refraction is typically not useful in patients over the age of 40 years.
  C. Cycloplegic refraction is often useful in young adults, ages 16 to 40, who complain of headaches associated with near work but who display little or no hyperopia and no other visual anomaly.
  D. all the above
  E. none of the above

773. The purpose of binocular balancing is to
  A. balance the visual acuity of the two eyes
  B. balance the state of accommodation of the two eyes
  C. balance the heterophoria between the two eyes
  D. all of the above
  E. none of the above

774. Which of the following clinical techniques is NOT useful in obtaining binocular balance?
  A. prism dissociation
  B. alternate occlusion
  C. bichrome test
  D. all of the above
  E. none of the above

775. A distometer is used to measure the
  A. center thickness of a myodisc
  B. diameter of a spectacle lens
  C. edge thickness of a cataract lens
  D. vertex distance
  E. field of view of a telescope

776. Lenses alone will correct about
  A. 60 percent of all exotropes
  B. 50 percent of all alternating exotropes
  C. 78 percent of all accommodative esotropes
  D. 65 percent of all esotropes
  E. none of the above

777. Which of the following statements concerning the correction of latency in hyperopia is not correct?
  A. A full distance correction should be given for intermittent esotropia.
  B. A partial distance correction should be given for divergent strabismus.
  C. A full distance correction should be given (over time) for severe eye strain.
  D. A partial distance correction should be given for very young patients.
  E. none of the above

778. In compound hyperopic astigmatism with accommodation relaxed,
  A. one principal meridian focuses on the retina while the other focuses behind the retina
  B. one principal meridian focuses in front of the retina while the other focuses behind the retina
  C. one principal meridian focuses in front of the retina while the other focuses on the retina
  D. both principal meridians focus behind the retina
  E. both principal meridians focus in front of the retina

779. If the refractive correction is O.S. +0.25 −1.25 × 41, the refractive diagnosis would be
  A. mixed astigmatism
  B. compound myopic astigmatism

    C. simple hyperopic astigmatism
    D. compound hyperopic astigmatism
    E. simple myopic astigmatism

780. Given a patient with the following spectacle Rx: O.D. −8.50 sph, VA 20/40; O.S. −7.50 sph, VA 20/35 (vertex distance 14 mm); determine his contact lens Rx (to the nearest 1/8 diopter) and the VA (to the nearest line).
    A. O.D. −7.62 VA 20/35; O.S. −6.75 VA 20/30
    B. O.D. −8.00 VA 20/40; O.S. −6.50 VA 20/25
    C. O.D. −8.25 VA 20/45; O.S. −7.25 VA 20/35
    D. O.D. −7.87 VA 20/30; O.S. −7.50 VA 20/40
    E. none of the above

781. Accurate measurement of multifocal adds using the lensometer requires that the
    A. surface containing the bifocal or trifocal addition be placed against the lens stop
    B. concave surface is placed against the lens stop
    C. segment and major portion split the field of view
    D. readings are corrected for curvature
    E. readings are corrected for differences in index

782. What can be done to reduce specular reflections from ophthalmic prescriptions?
    A. change the base curve of the lens
    B. change the tilt of the frame front
    C. reduce the distance between eyes and lenses
    D. prescribe an antireflective coating
    E. all of the above

783. Tinted lenses are useful for all but one of the following conditions.
    A. reduction of the intensity of ultraviolet radiation entering the eye
    B. reduction of the total amount of light entering the eye
    C. cosmetic improvement
    D. elimination of reflected glare
    E. reduction of the intensity of infrared radiation entering the eye

784. CR 39 plastic lenses have a distinct advantage compared to glass lenses in what ways?
   A. can be tinted (dyed)
   B. lighter weight
   C. fog resistance
   D. increased light transmission
   E. all of the above

785. What combination frame adjustment is recommended if the bifocal segments are too low?
   A. decrease the distance between the pads
   B. decrease the face form tilt
   C. increase the pantoscopic tilt
   D. increase the distance between the pads
   E. none of the above

786. Which of the following plastic frame adjustments is recommended if one lens is farther from the face than the other?
   A. decrease the temple angle on the side where the lens is farther from the face
   B. increase the temple angle on the side where the lens is farther from the face
   C. increase the temple angle on the side where the lens is closer to the face
   D. all of the above
   E. none of the above

787. Which of the following ocular disorders is not considered a leading cause of blindness in the elderly?
   A. diabetic retinopathy
   B. age-related maculopathy
   C. glaucoma
   D. traumatic injury
   E. none of the above

788. Which of the following statements concerning the subjective examination of the aged patient is not correct?
   A. A trial frame examination is better than a refractor examination.
   B. Because the aged fatigue quickly, the exam should be brief.

C. The morning hours are better for testing than the afternoon hours.

D. It is advisable to begin with the patient's old Rx and check by modification rather than start at the beginning.

E. none of the above

789. Halberg trial clips are

A. spring-loaded clips that have two lens cells which, when fitted over existing spectacle lenses, are useful for overrefraction, especially in the elderly

B. trial frames having short temples and small P.D. capabilities useful for testing children

C. clip-on occluders that are useful for home testing and training

D. all of the above

E. none of the above

790. What minimum amplitude of accommodation is expected for a 50-year-old individual?

A. 2.50 D

B. 3.50 D

C. 4.50 D

D. 5.50 D

E. 6.50 D

791. Given the following 48-year-old patient:

Rx   OD −10.00   Vertex   15 mm   PD 64
     OS −10.25

(A) How much must the patient accommodate to clearly view an object (a book) situated 25 cm in front of her spectacles?

(B) Can the patient clearly view the same object located at the exact same place if she were fitted with contact lenses?

A. 3.50 D; Yes

B. 4.00 D; No

C. 2.12 D; Yes

D. 2.87 D; No

E. none of the above

792–794. Utilize the data given in question **792** to work problems in questions **792–794.**

792. A 67-year-old presbyopic patient with a PD of 64 mm is found to have a corrected distance visual acuity of 20/65 O.U. and wishes to be able to read book print demanding a minimum of 20/50 acuity. The distance prescription is: O.D. +10.00 +1.00 × 180; O.S. +10.00 +1.50 × 180 and vertex 14 mm. If the patient desires reading glasses, what prescription is required to meet the patient's near complaint?

   A. O.D. +12.50 +1.25 × 180; O.S. +12.50 +1.50 × 180; NPD 62 mm
   B. O.D. +12.75 +1.00 × 180; O.S. +12.50 +1.25 × 180; NPD 61 mm
   C. O.D. +13.75 +1.00 × 180; O.S. +12.75 +1.50 × 180; NPD 60 mm
   D. O.D. +13.25 +1.00 × 180; O.S. +13.25 +1.50 × 180; NPD 59 mm
   E. O.D. +13.50 +1.25 × 180; O.S. +13.50 +1.00 × 180; NPD 58 mm

793. If the patient desires multifocals instead of reading spectacles, what bifocal additions and reading distance are required to meet the patient's near complaint?

   A. +3.25 D adds; 30.77 cm
   B. +4.00 D adds; 25.00 cm
   C. +4.50 D adds; 22.22 cm
   D. +5.00 D adds; 20.00 cm
   E. +5.50 D adds; 18.18 cm

794. What bifocal segment decentrations and widths are required to produce zero prismatic effects in near viewing and to maintain a minimum effective segment diameter of 20 mm?

   A. inset = 8.5 mm; 25 mm round segment
   B. decenter out = 8.2 mm; 30 mm round segment
   C. inset = 10.0 mm; 35 mm round segment
   D. decenter out = 12.8 mm; 28 mm round segment
   E. inset = 4.0 mm; 28 mm flat-top segment

795. Which of the following techniques is utilized to handle the near vision needs of the presbyope who wants (needs) contact lenses for distant vision?
A. contact lenses and reading glasses
B. monovision fitting system
C. bifocal contact lenses
D. all of the above
E. none of the above

796. Which of the following methods is/are utilized to determine the tentative reading addition required by the presbyopic patient?
A. plus build-up technique
B. binocular crossed cylinder test
C. leaving one-half of the measured amplitude of accommodation in reserve
D. estimate the patient's accommodation based on age, then leave one-half of the amplitude in reserve
E. all of the above

797. If an older patient wears bifocals, it is probably inadvisable to prescribe trifocals unless the near addition is between
A. +0.50 to +0.75
B. +0.75 to +1.00
C. +1.75 to +2.00
D. +1.50 to +1.75
E. +1.00 to +1.25

798–799. Use the data from **798** to work both **798** and **799.**

798. Given an aphakic patient wearing the following contact lenses: O.D. +12.75 sph and O.S. +11.75 sph. You determine that you must switch the patient to spectacles. What spectacle correction is required for this patient if a vertex distance of 15 mm is needed?
A. O.D. +12.75 sph; O.S. +11.75 sph
B. O.D. +10.75 sph; O.S. +10.00 sph
C. O.D. +12.25 sph; O.S. +11.25 sph
D. O.D. +11.75 sph; O.S. +10.75 sph
E. O.D. +11.25 sph; O.S. +10.25 sph

799. If the aphakic patient has visual acuities of 20/30 utilizing contact lenses, what visual acuities will he have with spectacles?
   A. O.D. 20/20; O.S. 20/20
   B. O.D. 20/25; O.S. 20/25
   C. O.D. 20/30; O.S. 20/30
   D. O.D. 20/35; O.S. 20/35
   E. O.D. 20/40; O.S. 20/40

800. Dominancy is an important consideration in the correction of aphakia. Which of the following statements concerning dominancy in aphakia is not correct?
   A. If the aphakic eye is the dominant one, a contact lens correction is usually well accepted.
   B. If the nondominant eye is the aphakic one, occlusion of this eye is readily accepted.
   C. If the phakic eye is the nondominant one, occlusion of the fellow aphakic eye is readily accepted.
   D. all of the above
   E. none of the above

801. Aphakic patients with which of the following conditions usually benefit from extended-wear contact lenses?
   A. arthritis
   B. senility
   C. unsteady hands
   D. unable to handle daily-wear contact lenses
   E. all of the above

802–803. The data given in question **802** also apply to question **803.**

802. Given a patient whose right eye has been implanted with a posterior chamber intraocular lens: If the left eye has poor visual acuity due to a dense cataract or amblyopia, the optimal postoperative monocular correction for the pseudophakic right eye is
   A. +1.00
   B. −1.50
   C. −1.00
   D. +0.75
   E. plano

803. If the left eye has good visual acuity, the postoperative refraction in the operated right eye ideally should be within what dioptric value of the prescription required in the unoperated left eye (a binocular correction is indicated here)?
    A. 2.00 to 3.00 D
    B. this is not an important consideration
    C. 1.00 to 2.00 D
    D. 3.00 to 4.00 D
    E. none of the above

804. In which of the following patient/conditions are intraocular lenses (IOLs) usually contraindicated?
    A. patients with anterior uveitis
    B. high myopes
    C. children
    D. patients with proliferative diabetic retinopathy
    E. all of the above

805. The condition in which the two ocular images are different in size and/or in shape is referred to as
    A. anisometropia
    B. metamorphopsia
    C. aniseikonia
    D. anomalous retinal correspondence
    E. none of the above

806. Aniseikonia is usually the result of magnification differences brought about by corrective lenses; it tends to cause which of the following ocular symptoms?
    A. eye strain/headaches
    B. tilting or curving of vertical objects
    C. light flashes/spots before eyes
    D. unequal pupil size/excessive tearing
    E. both A and B

807. Which of the following statements concerning aniseikonia and its correction is true?
   A. If the more ametropic of the two eyes has axial ametropia, the amount of induced aniseikonia is expected to be at a minimum if contact lenses are fitted.
   B. If the more ametropic of the two eyes has refractive ametropia, the amount of induced aniseikonia is expected to be at a minimum when ophthalmic lenses are fitted.
   C. If the more ametropic of the two eyes has axial ametropia, the amount of induced aniseikonia is expected to be at a minimum if ophthalmic lenses are fitted.
   D. all of the above
   E. none of the above

808. Given a unilateral aphakic patient:

Rx: O.D. +12.75 D
      O.S. +1.25 D   Vertex distance   14 mm   PD   65 mm

The patient is fitted with plastic (CR-39) ophthalmic lenses of index 1.495. The center thickness of the right lens is 7.1 mm and of the left lens is 2.4 mm. The curvature for the front surface of the right lens is R = +30.30 D and for the left lens is R = +14.14 D. Determine the spectacle magnification produced by the right lens, the left lens, and the difference in retinal image size for the two eyes.
   A. 27.7%; 2.7% and 25.0%
   B. 29.8%; 4.1% and 25.7%
   C. 33.4%; 1.6% and 31.8%
   D. 37.5%; 3.3% and 34.2%
   E. 39.1%; 4.4% and 34.7%

Low Vision

809. Legal blindness is defined as vision of
   A. 20/70 or less in the better corrected eye or a monocular visual field limited to 20° or less in the greatest diameter in the better eye
   B. 20/200 or less in the better corrected eye or a monocular visual field limited to 20° or less in the greatest diameter in the better eye

C. 20/40 or less in the better corrected eye or a monocular visual field limited to 50° or less in the greatest diameter in the better eye

D. all of the above

E. none of the above

810. Low vision, or partial sight, refers to

A. vision loss that is severe enough to impede the performance of daily tasks but that still allows useful visual discrimination

B. vision loss that cannot be corrected to normal performance levels with conventional spectacles, contact lenses or intraocular lenses

C. corrected vision that is inferior to the normal as represented by such standards as acuity, field of vision, or motility

D. all of the above

E. none of the above

811. Which of the following statements concerning the VCTS (Vision Contrast Test System used to evaluate contrast sensitivity) and the partially sighted patient is correct?

A. Visual acuity measurements are better predictors of the ability to read continuous text than are VCTS measurements.

B. Visual acuity measurements are better predictors of the preferred eye than are VCTS measurements.

C. The VCTS adds little or no useful information about the visual capabilities of the partially sighted.

D. All of the above

E. None of the above

812. Which of the following ocular conditions is (are) not effectively treated with optical aids?

A. aphakia

B. glaucoma

C. keratoconus

D. proliferating diabetic retinopathy

E. both B and D

813. Patients with which of the following eye diseases function best in minimum illumination?
A. albinism
B. aniridia
C. achromatopsia
D. central corneal opacities
E. all of the above

814. Patients with which of the following eye diseases function best in high illumination?
A. pathological myopia
B. glaucoma
C. retinitis pigmentosa
D. optic atrophy
E. all of the above

815. Relative distance magnification (approach magnification) is defined as that magnification
A. which results when an enlarged image of an opaque object is produced on a screen
B. brought about by increasing the actual size of the true object
C. brought about by reducing the distance between the object and the eye
D. given by the equation: nl'/n'l
E. none of the above

816. The chief disadvantage of large-type print material is that
A. large print restricts the field of view
B. large print reduces the normal working distance
C. large print material is expensive and the variety is limited
D. all of the above
E. none of the above

817. Braille may be indicated for people who
A. cannot read smaller than 8 point type
B. have distance vision of 2/200 or less
C. do not have the intelligence to read
D. are able to read type at a very slow speed
E. lack sufficient finger sensitivity

818. Given a 67-year-old partially sighted patient wearing the following distance prescription: O.D. +7.25 −2.75 × 41 V.A. O.D. 20/60, O.S. +7.00 −2.25 × 11 V.A. O.S. nil. What dioptric power used in conjunction with his spectacles correction is required in the form of a round magnifier in order for the patient to read print demanding a visual acuity of approximately 20/50?
   A. +4.80 D
   B. +6.00 D
   C. +3.00 D
   D. +5.00 D
   E. none of the above

819. Which of the following is not a disadvantage of hand-held magnifiers?
   A. reduces reading speed
   B. difficult to use if the patient has a tremor
   C. occupies both hands, one for the magnifier and the other for the reading material
   D. reduces field of view compared with a spectacle correction
   E. none of the above

820. The size of the field of view of a simple microscope lens system is dependent on the
   A. diameter of the lens system
   B. power of the lens system
   C. vertex distance
   D. diameter of the pupil of the eye
   E. all of the above

821. Which of the following statements concerning the procedure of prescribing/fitting high bifocal additions (simple magnifiers) for the older, partially sighted patient is not correct?
   A. The distance between lens and eye does not alter the field of view.
   B. The distance between lens and eye does alter, to a small degree, the induced magnification.
   C. The reading materials should be held in the focal plane of the add.
   D. The lowest power add (magnifier) that provides satisfactory results should be prescribed.
   E. none of the above

822. Which of the following is an advantage of spectacle microscopic lenses (as compared to hand-held scopes)?
   A. useful for prolonged reading tasks
   B. most acceptable visual aid, psychologically
   C. frees up both of the patient's hands to hold material
   D. can be used monocularly or binocularly (for lower powers)
   E. all of the above

823. Which of the following is an advantage of a fixed-focus stand magnifier?
   A. limited number of aids exist over +20 diopters
   B. the patient's posture may be tiring and awkward
   C. restricted field of view
   D. not practical unless placed on a flat surface
   E. none of the above

824–826. The following patient data given in question **824** apply to the next three problems.

824. A 67-year-old partially sighted patient can read book print (demanding a visual acuity of approximately 20/50 held at 40 cm) when held at a distance of 20 cm in front of her reading correction of O.D.: balance lens, O.S.: −7.50 sph and vertex distance of 14 mm. What will be the patient's distance correction (vertex 14 mm) and distance visual acuity for the left eye?
   A. −7.50 D; V.A. 20/50
   B. −12.50 D; V.A. 20/100
   C. −11.25 D; V.A. 20/80
   D. −10.50 D; V.A. 20/50
   E. −10.50 D; V.A. 20/80

825. If the patient desires a contact lens correction for distance, what will be the power of the contact lens (to the nearest 1/8 diopter) for the left eye and what visual acuity can be achieved?
   A. −6.62 D; 20/80
   B. −8.62 D; 20/50
   C. −8.75 D; 20/75
   D. −10.62 D; 20/85
   E. none of the above

826. If the contact-lens-corrected patient desires to read book print (demanding a visual acuity of 20/50 when held at 40 cm), what near spectacle correction, vertex 14, will be required for the left eye to be used in conjunction with the contact lens? What will be the new reading distance?
  A. +4.01 D sph.; reading distance = 25.00 cm
  B. +4.25 D sph.; reading distance = 23.53 cm
  C. +2.75 D sph.; reading distance = 36.36 cm
  D. +3.25 D sph., reading distance = 30.77 cm
  E. none of the above

827. A +11.25 aphakic patient measured in the spectacle plane, vertex distance 17 mm, needs a contact spectacle lens telescope of 1.29× magnifying power. What will be the power required in the contact lens portion of the system? What power will be required in the spectacle portion (vertex 17 mm)?
  A. −2.62 D, +17.12 D
  B. −4.78 D, +13.87 D
  C. −3.15 D, +13.22 D
  D. −12.87 D, +11.25 D
  E. none of the above

828. Which of the following statements concerning the utilization of telescopes in low vision care is not correct?
  A. Ophthalmic telescopes are of either the Galilean design (convex objective and concave ocular) or of the Keplerian design (convex objective, convex ocular, and erecting prism).
  B. Keplerian telescopes are bulky and are used mainly as hand-held telescopes.
  C. When the ophthalmic telescope is adapted for near usage, a convex lens (reading cap) must be mounted in front of the objective.
  D. If the low vision patient's best corrected acuity is less than 20/100, prognosis is poor for the use of telescopes.
  E. One of the more useful bioptic telescopes is the 2.2×.

829. Which of the following ocular disorders can be treated with pinhole contact lenses?
A. cataracts
B. aniridia
C. glaucoma
D. albinism
E. both **B** and **D**

830. Which of the following ocular conditions is best treated with contact lenses?
A. achromatopsia
B. retinal detachment
C. degenerative myopia
D. diabetes mellitus
E. none of the above

831. The principle of hemianopsia spectacles is to
A. place images of objects on the blind side to the seeing portion of the retina
B. magnify the image of the seeing portion
C. increase the luminance of the retinal image
D. magnify the retinal image in order to image a larger part of the environment on the seeing side
E. both **C** and **D**

832. Partially sighted patients often complain of light sensitivity, glare, and photophobia, especially when outdoors. The NoIR filters have been found to be useful in addressing these problems. Which filter is found to be the most utilized by individuals who display age-related maculopathy, glaucoma, or retinitis pigmentosa?
A. #107 NoIR—2% dark amber
B. #102 NoIR—18% gray-green
C. #101 NoIR—10% medium amber
D. #108 NoIR—1% dark gray-green
E. none of the above

833. Absorptive lenses for partially sighted patients should have which of the following properties?
A. cover a wide range of optical transmission (between 80 percent and 2 percent)

B. reduce visual acuity minimally

C. distort color minimally

D. absorb ultraviolet light below 400 nanometers

E. all of the above

834. Traveling often presents special problems for the visually impaired. Orientation and mobility training offers help (techniques/skills) that assist the partially sighted individual in walking safely. This help takes the form of

A. sighted guide or dog guide/training

B. electronic travel aids (ETAs)/training

C. mobility lamp or long cane/training

D. telescopic low vision aids/training

E. all of the above

835. Which of the following statements concerning driving motor vehicles while wearing bioptic telescopic spectacles (BTS) is correct?

A. Only a few states permit driving with bioptic telescopes.

B. The vision requirements among states for a BTS license are fairly standardized.

C. Individuals who qualify for a BTS license must typically have 20/40 VA through the telescope and must pass both a written and driving road test.

D. The use of bioptic telescopes for driving is not a controversial issue.

E. none of the above

836. The major advantage of electronic magnifiers as compared with spectacle or hand-held optical aids is

A. increase in reading speed

B. contrast enhancement

C. reduction of aberration and distortion

D. increased duration of reading time

E. all of the above

837. Which of the following statements is/are not true concerning a closed-circuit television (CCTV) reading system?
    A. Writing and typing are done less easily under a television camera than with optical aids.
    B. Television systems cover a greater range of magnification than spectacle aids.
    C. Television systems may be used binocularly with normal convergence.
    D. all of the above
    E. none of the above

Sensory Anomalies of Binocular Vision/Strabismus

838. The interocular difference in retinal image size induced by correction of **refractive** anisometropia is
    A. zero if the lens is placed at the anterior focal point of the eye
    B. approximately zero with a contact lense correction
    C. approximately 0.25 percent per diopter for spectacle lenses
    D. approximately 1.5 percent per diopter for spectacle lenses
    E. both **B** and **D**

839. Knapp's Law states that
    A. only aniseikonia greater than 5 percent is significant
    B. aniseikonia can be minimized in refractive anisometropes with spectacle lens correction
    C. aniseikonia can be minimized in axial anisometropes with spectacle correction
    D. aniseikonia can be minimized in refractive and axial anisometropes with contact lens correction
    E. none of the above

840. Sorsby reported that the
    A. majority of anisometropias of less than 2 D were axial
    B. majority of anisometropias of more than 2 D were axial
    C. majority of anisometropias of more than 2 D were refractive
    D. refractive and axial anisometropias of more than 2 D were about equally common
    E. the relative incidence of axial anisometropia was unrelated to its amount in diopters

841. Amblyopia is often found in association with which of the following?
   A. anisometropia
   B. antimetropia
   C. esotropia
   D. unilateral congenital cataracts
   E. all of the above

842. When tested in the clinic, human strabismic amblyopes tend to exhibit which of the following visual anomalies with their amblyopic eye?
   A. poor letter acuity
   B. increased "crowding" effects
   C. poor color vision
   D. both A and B
   E. both A and C

843. Strabismic amblyopes, forced to fixate with the amblyopic eye while the better eye is occluded, will
   A. suffer severe diplopia
   B. see normally
   C. accurately fixate the target
   D. often exhibit eccentric fixation
   E. A, B, and D

844. Functional stereopsis (depth sensation from differences in horizontal disparities)
   A. is poor in normals when targets are outside Panum's fusional area
   B. is generally absent or severely degraded in strabismic subjects
   C. is superior for targets presented at or near the horopter
   D. both A and B
   E. A, B and C

845. The space eikonometer **cannot** be used to measure aniseikonia in patients with which of the following conditions?
   A. visual acuity of 20/30
   B. vertical phoria
   C. fixation disparity
   D. no measurable stereopsis
   E. lateral prism corrections

846. Using the linear filament after-image test, which of the following patients (none having eccentric fixation) will see the same after-image pattern seen by normal patients?
   A. esotropes with NRC
   B. esotropes with harmonious ARC
   C. esotropes with unharmonious ARC
   D. all of the above, because the test is monocular
   E. none of the above, because the test is independent of ARC

847. What would a patient with mirror symmetric oblique astigmatism, corrected with spectacle lenses, be expected to observe when viewing a Space Eikonometer?
   A. the two front vertical rods at different distances
   B. the cross tilting about a horizontal axis
   C. the cross tilting about a vertical axis
   D. the back two vertical lines tilting forwards
   E. none of the above

848. When visual acuity is assessed for an amblyopic eye,
   A. amblyopes are typically found to be normal
   B. amblyopes will behave like a normal subject who has a defocused retinal image
   C. amblyopes will produce letter identification errors over a wide range of letter sizes
   D. amblyopes will score perfectly for larger letters and then suddenly fail every letter in a line
   E. both **B** and **D**

849. Which of the following statements regarding strabismus is true?
   A. Paresis will probably create a concomitant strabismus.
   B. Nonconcomitancy indicates that there is a central neurological problem.

   C. Nonconcomitancy indicates that there is either palsy, paresis, or paralysis.
   D. all of the above
   E. neither **A, B,** nor **C** is correct, because concomitancy is unaffected by paresis

850. A patient has a paresis of the *superior rectus of the left eye.* In order for the patient to try and maintain orthotropia, his/her head posture would best be
   A. face down and to the right, with head tilt to the right
   B. face up and to the right, with head tilt to the right
   C. face down and to the left, with head tilt to the left
   D. face up and to the left, with head tilt to the left
   E. face down and to the right, with head tilt to the left

851. A patient has an amblyopic left eye exhibiting a +0.5 mm angle kappa and a right eye exhibiting a +1 mm angle kappa. This patient has
   A. eccentric fixation of both eyes, but more central in the left eye
   B. exotropia of the left eye
   C. nasal eccentric fixation of the left eye
   D. orthotropia
   E. esotropia of the right eye

852. A patient has 10^Δ nasal eccentric fixation of the left eye and esotropia of the left eye of 10^Δ and harmonious anomalous retinal correspondence (HARC). In response to the Hering-Bielschowsky after-image test, he would report that
   A. the right eye image displaced 10^Δ to the right
   B. the left eye image displaced 10^Δ to the left
   C. both images centered on each other, creating a perfect cross
   D. both **A** and **B**
   E. none of the above

853. A test for detecting eccentric fixation by comparing angles kappa of the right and left eyes is known as the
   A. Hess screen test
   B. Von Noorden test
   C. Helmholtz test
   D. Hirschberg test
   E. Worth test

854. A patient exhibits 4 degrees nasal eccentric fixation of the right eye. When a Haidinger's brush test is performed at a distance of 40 cm on the right eye, the patient would be expected to report seeing the brushes approximately spinning concentric about a point
   A. 2.8 cm to the right of the fixation spot
   B. 2.8 cm to the left of the spot
   C. superimposed on the spot
   D. 5.6 cm to the right of the spot
   E. 5.6 cm to the left of the spot

855. When viewing a point source through Bagolini striated lenses, a normal appearance can occur in which of the following patient types?
   A. esotropes with harmonious anomalous retinal correspondence
   B. esotropes with normal retinal correspondence
   C. exotropes with normal retinal correspondence
   D. esotropes with ARC and a central scotoma
   E. none of the above

856. Which of the following tests can diagnose eccentric monocular fixation?
   A. visuoscope
   B. scanning laser ophthalmoscope
   C. Maxwell's spot
   D. Haidinger's brushes
   E. all of the above

857. When objects appear to the patient to have different sizes and/or have distorted shapes, the patient has
   A. anisometropia
   B. metamorphopsia
   C. aniseikonia
   D. anomalous retinal correspondence
   E. both B and C

858. Orthoptic treatment is given to patients exhibiting
   A. eccentric fixation
   B. amblyopia
   C. suppression

D. diplopia
E. all of the above

859. When using conventional patching as a treatment for amblyopia in very young patients,
   A. the patching should be complete, continuous, and prolonged in order to take full advantage of the sensitive period
   B. visual acuity must be frequently checked in the amblyopic eye
   C. visual acuity should be frequently checked in the patched eye
   D. both **A** and **B**
   E. none of the above, because patching is never used on young children

860. Which of the following **has not been** suggested as a treatment for amblyopia?
   A. patching the amblyopic eye
   B. patching the nonamblyopic eye
   C. intermittent patching of the nonamblyopic eye
   D. forcing the amblyope to stare at rotating stripes with the amblyopic eye
   E. forcing the amblyope to stare at rotating stripes with the nonamblyopic eye

861. In Pleoptic training for amblyopia,
   A. the nonamblyopic fovea is desensitized by a bright light
   B. the amblyopic fovea is desensitized by a bright light
   C. the area surrounding the amblyopic fovea is desensitized by a bright light
   D. the area surrounding the nonamblyopic fovea is desensitized by a bright light
   E. the entire retina of the nonamblyopic eye is desensitized by a bright light

862. When tested with the distant Worth Dot Test, which of the pairs of numbers listed below reflect the number of dots seen by a normal (first number) and a 20-prism diopter esotrope who is not suppressing (second number)?
    A. 3 and 5
    B. 4 and 3
    C. 4 and 5
    D. 3 and 4
    E. 5 and 4

Anomalies of Eye Movements

863. Esofixation disparities are often found in which of the following patients?
    A. patients with esophorias
    B. patients with exophorias
    C. patients forced to converge with base-out prism
    D. patients forced to diverge with base-in prism
    E. both A and D

864. A prominent epicanthal fold can lead to the false diagnosis of
    A. exotropia
    B. hypermetropia
    C. esotropia
    D. hypotropia
    E. esophoria

865. Orthophoria is defined as
    A. eye alignment deviations that occur only when the fusion reflex is interrupted
    B. present in all cases of orthotropia
    C. either esophorias or exophorias
    D. perfect eye alignment even when the fusion reflex is interrupted
    E. none of the above

866. An esotropic patient exhibits 20^Δ of eso-tropia with upward gaze and 10^Δ eso with downward gaze. This patient exhibits
    A. "V pattern" esotropia
    B. "A pattern" esotropia

C. comitant esotropia
D. both **B** and **C**
E. both **A** and **C**

867. A person exhibiting 2^Δ exophoria at a fixation distance of 4 m and 13^Δ exophoria at a fixation distance of 40 cm is said to have
   A. convergence excess
   B. convergence insufficiency
   C. divergence excess
   D. divergence insufficiency
   E. simple exophoria

868. The alternate or alternating cover test alternately covers the patient's right and left eyes
   A. at a very high frequency; e.g., 8 Hz
   B. to test for monocular fixation errors
   C. to test for tropias
   D. to test for phorias
   E. both **A** and **D**

869. Using the Hirschberg test to diagnose heterotropia
   A. requires assumptions about angle Kappa
   B. does not allow for diagnosis of cyclodeviations
   C. is only a crude technique for making an approximate diagnosis
   D. requires the patient to fixate
   E. all of the above

870. Which of the following must a patient with a right eye lateral rectus palsy do in order to binocularly fixate an object directly in front of him or her?
   A. turn his or her head to the right, and gaze left
   B. turn his or her head to the left, and gaze right
   C. turn his or her head to the right, and gaze right
   D. turn his or her head to the left, and gaze left
   E. it is impossible to be orthotropic with a palsied lateral rectus muscle

871. Base-in prisms placed in front of both eyes of an animal have been used as an experimental model of what human condition?
   A. bilateral deprivation
   B. esophoria
   C. convergence myopia
   D. exotropia
   E. esotropia

872. When the angle of squint remains fairly constant in all fields of gaze, the squint is said to be
   A. nonconcomitant
   B. paralytic
   C. concomitant
   D. anomalous
   E. none of the above

873. A nystagmic patient only manifests nystagmus when looking in the direction of the fast (saccadic) component. This condition is known as
   A. first-degree nystagmus
   B. second-degree nystagmus
   C. third-degree nystagmus
   D. optokinetic nystagmus
   E. pendular nystagmus

874. If the horopter, determined by the nonius method, lies closer to the observer than the fixation point, this indicates that the subject demonstrates
   A. anomalous "retinal" correspondence
   B. paradoxical correspondence
   C. ESO fixation disparity
   D. EXO fixation disparity
   E. physiological disparity

875. Wearing a 5 percent axis 90° **magnifying** lens before her **right** eye, a subject might be expected to observe which of the following distortions while looking binocularly at the far wall of a room?
   A. The far wall will appear rotated away from the subject on her right side.
   B. The far wall will appear to lie in the fronto parallel plane.

C. The far wall will appear to lie in the apparent fronto parallel plane.

D. The far wall will appear rotated away from the subject on her left side.

E. The far wall will appear slanted away at the top.

876. With a 4 percent meridional **magnifying** lens placed in front of the **left** eye, **axis 180,** the apparent fronto parallel plane (AFPP) will lie

A. closer to the left-hand side

B. closer to the right-hand side

C. unaffected, due to cancellation of induced and geometrical effects

D. in the same location as observed with an axis 90, 4 percent minifying lens in front of the right eye

E. both **B** and **D**

877. Flat prisms with their bases out are placed before both the right and left eyes. If normal fusion is maintained by vergence eye movements, how will the objective front-parallel plane appear?

A. titled, with the right side closer

B. displaced, closer to the subject than the fixation point

C. rotated around a vertical axis through the binocular center of projection

D. distorted, appearing as a concave surface, with reference to the subject

E. distorted, appearing as a convex surface, with reference to the subject

878. An overall ocular image size difference between the right and left eyes of a binocularly normal individual

A. is **more** spatially disorienting than an equal magnitude axis 90° meridional image size difference

B. is **less** spatially disorienting than an equal magnitude axis 90° meridional image size difference

C. is **less** spatially disorienting than an equal magnitude axis 180° meridional image size difference

D. both **A** and **C**

E. both **B** and **C**

879. Poor performance on a clinical stereopsis test may reflect
 A. suppression of one eye
 B. unequal retinal image quality in the two eyes
 C. misconvergence of the two eyes
 D. amblyopia
 E. all of the above

Anomalies of Accommodation and Accommodative Convergence

880. The CA/C ratio
 A. describes the amount of convergence elicited by accommodation
 B. describes the amount of accommodation elicited by convergence
 C. tends to be high in presbyopes
 D. tends to be high in myopes
 E. B, C, and D

881. The AC/A ratio
 A. describes the ratio of accommodation in diopters driven by convergence to the convergence in prism diopters
 B. describes the ratio of convergence in prism diopters driven by accommodation to the accommodation in diopters
 C. tends to be high in uncorrected myopes
 D. tends to be low in uncorrected myopes
 E. both B and C

882. What is the calculated stimulus-based AC/A ratio for a patient with a 60 mm interpupillary distance if he manifests 1 prism diopter of exophoria at six meters and 3 prism diopters of esophoria at fifty centimeters?
 A. 16/1
 B. 2.5/1
 C. 5/1
 D. 8.2/1
 E. 15/1

883. Which of the following influences the characteristics of the zone of clear, single, binocular vision?
  A. the AC/A ratio
  B. the accommodative amplitude
  C. the amplitudes of positive and negative fusional vergence
  D. Panum's fusional areas
  E. all of the above

884. Clinically, the calculated AC/A ratio is determined by measuring
  A. the phorias at two target distances
  B. accommodative amplitude and the associated tropias at two distances
  C. accommodative amplitude and the associated phorias at two distances
  D. accommodative amplitude at two different vergences
  E. none of the above

885. A patient views a near target (40 cm) through their distance Rx and then through the distance Rx + a 1D add. Phorias without the add are 1Δ exo and 3Δ exo with the +1D add. What is this patient's AC/A ratio?
  A. 0.8
  B. 2.5
  C. 2
  D. 5
  E. −4

886. In a normal subject, what would be the expected relative magnitudes of the "true" (response) and the clinical (stimulus) measures of the AC/A ratios?
  A. exactly the same
  B. the same, or the response measure slightly lower
  C. the response measure significantly lower
  D. the response measure slightly higher
  E. the response measure much higher

887. The following five examples list the distance (6 meters) and near (0.33 meter) phorias. Which of the following patients would be considered to have the highest AC/A ratio?
  A. orthophoria at distance, 15Δ exophoria at near
  B. 15Δ esophoria at distance, orthophoria at near
  C. orthophoria at distance, 15Δ esophoria at near
  D. 15Δ exophoria at distance, 15Δ exophoria at near
  E. 15Δ esophoria at distance, 15Δ esophoria at near

888. A patient who is slightly esophoric at distance and has a large esophoria at near is described as having
  A. a high CA/C ratio
  B. a low AC/A ratio
  C. divergence excess
  D. convergence excess
  E. convergence insufficiency

889. Accommodative **facility** can be assessed clinically using
  A. a prism-rock test
  B. a lens-rock test
  C. an alternating cover test
  D. a push-up test
  E. all of the above

890. What is the relationship between the Mallett test and the magnitude of fixation disparity?
  A. The Mallett test measures the amount of fixation disparity in prism diopters.
  B. The magnitude of fixation disparity is not measured with the Mallett test.
  C. The Mallett test measures the amount of prism-induced disparity vergence necessary to eliminate the fixation disparity.
  D. both A and C
  E. both B and C

891. On a plot of fixation disparity as a function of the power of base-in (left side of graph) or base-out (right side of graph) prisms, most subjects exhibit
  A. a sigmoidal function with increasing eso-fixation disparity with base-in prisms and increasing exo-fixation disparity with base-out prisms

B. a sigmoidal function with increasing eso-fixation disparity with base-out prisms and exo-fixation disparity with base-in prisms

C. increasing eso-fixation disparity with base-in prisms, but a constant amount of exo-fixation disparity with base-out prisms

D. increasing eso-fixation disparity with base-out prisms, but a constant amount of exo-fixation disparity with base-in prisms

E. fixation disparity is linearly related to prism power

892. Prolonged forced convergence through base-out prisms can
    A. lead to adaptation of the tonic convergence response
    B. lead to adaptation of the tonic accommodation response
    C. lead to a reduction in the near exophoria when viewing through the prisms
    D. lead to an increase in distance esophoria when viewing without prisms
    E. all of the above

893. Adaptation of the tonic accommodation system can
    A. occur because of prolonged accommodation
    B. occur because of prolonged forced vergence
    C. can result in pseudomyopia
    D. can result in hypertonic myopia
    E. all of the above

894. Pseudoaccommodation describes
    A. voluntary control of accommodation
    B. reflexive accommodation
    C. depth of focus
    D. a purely optical effect
    E. an opto-motor effect

Contact Lenses

895. The greatest contraindication for a contact lens wearer is
  A. lack of motivation
  B. steep cornea (47.00 D)
  C. conjunctivitis
  D. astigmatism greater than 2.50 D

896. Fluorescein in solution can be effectively kept free of *Pseudomonas* by
  A. benzalkonium chloride as a preservative
  B. autoclaving
  C. chlorobutanol
  D. thimerosal

897. To decrease the fitting characteristics of a "tight" lens, one should
  A. decrease the optical zone diameter
  B. decrease the optical zone radius
  C. decrease lens thickness
  D. decrease the peripheral curve

898. The amount of oxygen flow beneath a contact lens with each blink is dependent on all of the following factors except
  A. amount of tears exchanged with each blink
  B. frequency of blink
  C. lens position
  D. volume of tear reservoir behind the lens

899. The silicone monomer combined with methacrylate provides some of the most desirable qualities in rigid gas permeable lenses. What is the most desirable property of the silicon monomer?
  A. negative charge on the surface
  B. flexibility
  C. oxygen permeability
  D. hydrophobicity

900. The methacrylate monomer in the silicone acrylate type of rigid gas permeable lenses provides
  A. oxygen permeability
  B. lens flexure

C. hydrophilic characteristics
D. good wetting surface characteristics

901. The addition of a fluorine monomer to silicone acrylate provides desirable properties except
A. deposit resistance
B. good flexibility
C. high oxygen permeability
D. good wetting

902. The beneficial effect of T-butylstyrene rigid oxygen permeable material in fitting a keratoconus patient is that
A. it can be fitted steep over the cone to minimize touch
B. it is flexible so that it follows the contour of the cone
C. it provides a high amount of oxygen to the cornea
D. it can be made in thin lens designs

903. On blinking, the percentage of tears exchanged with a hydrogel lens is
A. 4
B. 10
C. 14
D. 1

904. The percentage of tears exchanged with a rigid lens on a blink is
A. 5–10
B. 16–19
C. 1–4
D. 20–25

905. The soft perm lens is a hybrid lens; that is, it combines a rigid center with a hydrogel periphery. The polymers are
A. N-butylstyrene with hydroxyethyl methacrylate
B. silicone acrylate with hefilicon
C. fluoro-silicon acrylate with etafilicon
D. fluoroacylate with hydroxyethyl methacrylate

906. In the hydrogen peroxide soft lens care system, the percentage of hydrogen peroxide used for disinfection is
A. 1
B. 5
C. 10
D. 3

907. The neutralizer in the hydrogen peroxide system (Concept) is
A. catalase
B. cyclase
C. sodium thiosulfate
D. sodium transferase

908. Which of the following is not used as a preservative in soft contact lens chemical care systems?
A. Polyquad
B. benzalkonium chloride
C. Dymed
D. chlorhexidine

909. Which one of the following disinfection techniques was found to cause destruction to soft lens polymers too rapidly to be used directly?
A. ultraviolet
B. heat
C. chemical
D. hydrogen peroxide

910. In the patient with a marginally dry eye, the water content of the hydrogel lens best suited is
A. < 45 percent
B. > 45 percent < 70 percent
C. > 55 percent < 70 percent
D. > 70 percent

911. Protein deposits on soft lenses is a major cause of lens spoilage. All of the following factors favor protein deposits build up except
A. thermal disinfection
B. incomplete blinking
C. altered tear composition
D. chemical disinfection

912. An aphakic patient is to be prescribed contact lenses. The power of the contact lenses, with respect to the spectacle prescription, should be
   A. more plus power
   B. same as the spectacle prescription
   C. decrease the plus by 1.00 D
   D. less plus power

913. Poor "wetting" characteristics of a rigid gas permeable lens can produce all of the following except
   A. bulbar conjunctival injection
   B. palpebral conjunctival hypertrophy
   C. marginal corneal dystrophy
   D. gradual decrease in wearing time

914. Oxygen transmission through a contact lens is inversely related to
   A. water content of the lens
   B. diameter of the lens
   C. equivalent oxygen percentage
   D. lens thickness

915. The diffractive bifocal contact lenses perform satisfactorily but are a poor choice when
   A. pupil size is greater than 4 mm
   B. ambient lighting is good for visual tasks
   C. ambient lighting is poor for visual tasks
   D. pupil size lens is less than 4 mm

916. The bifocal contact lens available, which provides the sharpest vision for both distance and near, is
   A. diffrax bifocal
   B. concentric bifocal
   C. prism ballasted bifocal
   D. central addition bifocal

917. The most effective method of stabilizing the rotation of a front toxic hydrogel lens is
   A. truncation
   B. slab-off lenticular design
   C. thinning the superior and inferior margins
   D. prism ballast

918. Given a patient with the following spectacle prescription and keratometer findings: What would be your simplest contact lens selection for this patient?

Refraction: −3.00 D −3.00 × 180
Keratometry: 44.50 D at 180; 43.00 D at 90

    A. spherical soft lens
    B. spherical rigid lens
    C. rigid back toric lens
    D. rigid front toric lens

919. All of the following are true of disposable lenses except that they are
    A. extremely comfortable and convenient
    B. the simplest way of providing extended wear
    C. available for high astigmatic correction
    D. available in a wide range for myopic and hyperopic correction

920. Acanthamoeba infection is most commonly associated with
    A. extended wear soft lenses
    B. disposable lenses
    C. rigid gas permeable lenses
    D. daily wear soft lenses

921. Acanthamoeba keratitis associated with contact lens wear has been traced to
    A. aerosol saline solution
    B. saline solution made with salt tablets and nonsterile distilled water
    C. disinfecting and storage solutions
    D. nonpreserved sterile saline solution

922. The major disadvantage of monovision fitting of the presbyope over other types of bifocal contact lenses is
    A. the peripheral field of vision is worse
    B. the adaption period, during which patients may experience headaches and fatigue
    C. more difficult to fit
    D. more expensive than bifocal contact lenses

923. Corneal infiltrates in contact lens wear have been associated with all except
- **A.** degradation of the lens polymer
- **B.** hypoxia
- **C.** toxicity and hypersensitivity to solution preservatives
- **D.** debris entrapment between lens and cornea

924. Which of the following statements is not true of the acanthamoeba organism?
- **A.** It cannot penetrate the intact corneal epithelium.
- **B.** It can adhere to contact lenses.
- **C.** It can contaminate lens care systems.
- **D.** Bacterial organisms may provide a food source that supports persistent contamination by acanthamoeba.

925. Which of the following preservatives in disinfection systems is effective against both the cyst and trophozoite forms of acanthamoeba?
- **A.** polyamino propylbiguanide (Dymed)
- **B.** benzalkonium chloride plus EDTA
- **C.** polyquaternium-1 (Polyquad.)
- **D.** thimerosal

926. A patient with the following findings wishes to be fit with contact lenses. What should be the lens of choice for the simplest, best fit, assuming that you have both soft and rigid lenses at your disposal?

Keratometry: 44.00 D at 180; 45.75 D at 90
Refraction: −2.25 D sph.

- **A.** spherical rigid gas permeable lens
- **B.** toric soft lens
- **C.** back surface toric rigid lens
- **D.** spherical soft contact lens

927. The simplest, best fit contact lens for the following patient:

Keratometry: 43.00 D at 180; 44.75 D at 90
Refraction: −3.00 −1.75 D × 180

   A. spherical soft contact lens
   B. front toric rigid contact lens
   C. spherical rigid contact lens
   D. back toric rigid contact lens

928. A patient with superior limbic keratitis may experience
   A. itching
   B. photophobia
   C. foreign body sensation
   D. all of the above

929. A contact lens patient has 3 and 9 o'clock staining. The cause could be
   A. edge lift of the lens is excessive
   B. the lens is too tight
   C. too much movement of the lens
   D. the optic zone is too large

Answers and Discussion

Clinical Optometry

757. (E) In order to understand a complaint of blurred vision, the optometrist must consider the possible conditions that could be responsible. All of the items listed produce a complaint of blurred vision. A chief complaint of blurred vision associated with a reduction in visual acuity (with no significant refractive change) demands additional testing.

758. (B) The typical complaint of an uncorrected or under-corrected myope is blurred vision. Eye strain (asthenopia) typically involves feelings of discomfort, fatigue, or pain. Eye strain is usually localized in or about the eyes and is thought to be associated with use of the eyes.

759. (E) All may produce a complaint of double vision. A patient who complains of double vision (diplopia) should be asked if the perceived images are seen with one eye or with both eyes. Furthermore, he or she should be asked if the two images are somewhat blended or if they are actually separated, either horizontally or vertically.

760. (C) As an object moves closer to the eye, it subtends a larger visual angle. The detail of a 20/20 letter located at 10 feet subtends a visual angle of 2 minutes of arc. The detail of a 20/40 letter situated at 20 feet subtends 2 minutes of arc at the eye.

761. (B) An 87 mm target located 20 feet (6000 mm) away subtends an overall visual angle of 50 minutes of arc. The tangent of 50′ is $(0.8333°)$ = .0145 = 87/6000. A 20/20 letter that is (1/10) the size of a 20/200 letter would therefore subtend the desired overall angle of 5′ (50′/10) of arc.

762. (E) Neutralizing power in 55° meridian = (+1.50) +(−1.50) = plano. Neutralizing power in 145° meridian = (+1.50) + (−2.50) = −1.00 D. Therefore, plano at 55° combined with −1.00 D at 145° converts to plano −1.00 × 55° (in minus cylinder form).

763. (A) Spectacle astigmatism = (42.75 −43.50) × 1.25 + (−0.50) = −1.44 × 90°. Total ocular astigmatism is made up of two parts, internal astigmatism and corneal astigmatism. Javal's Rule is an attempt to predict the total astigmatism by measuring only the corneal astigmatism portion, multiplying this by a vertex distance correcting factor and adding the internal component.

764. (D) In order to determine the axis of the required correcting cylinder, the smaller of the two numbers is multiplied by 30°. Given the (10–4) o'clock meridian as the clearest: (4) is therefore utilized and is multiplied by 30°. 30° × 4 = 120°.

765. (D) The Bichrome test (red-green test) is used as a subjective test for the spherical component of the prescription. It can be used either as a monocular end-point test or as a binocular balancing test. This test should always begin with excess plus power over and above the estimated Rx.

766. (E) The Thorington and Maddox Rod tests are used to determine the degree of phoria present. The Maddox Rod test is utilized for distance testing (both vertical and horizontal). The Thorington test is utilized for distance and near testing (both vertical and horizontal).

767. (E) All are correct. The purpose of the Mallett test is to detect and eliminate fixation disparity by utilizing either prisms or spherical lenses. Two test units are available, one for distance and one hand-held for near.

768. (E) All are correct. There are, however, some definite advantages to the use of an autorefractor. It saves time for the busy practitioner; patients tend to be impressed with the use of the latest automated equipment.

769. (D) An optical pachymeter is an optical beam splitter used in conjunction with the optics of a slit lamp biomicroscope. It measures corneal thickness. Changes in corneal thickness are utilized by the eyecare practitioner to aid in the fitting of contact lenses.

770. (C) A video (photo) keratoscope is useful in measuring the curvature of large portions of the human cornea. It is based on the optical principals developed by Gullstrand (1896). A placido disc target reflected from the entire cornea is photographed and converted to radius of curvature.

771. (A) Near PD equals far PD minus 2(I). Utilize the 3/4 rule to determine (I). For every diopter of dioptric demand (1/viewing distance in meters), the I value equals 0.75 (3/4) mm. Therefore, far PD − 2I = 65 − 2(.75 × 4) = 59 mm.

772. (D) All are correct. Cycloplegic agents paralyze the constrictor pupillae as well as the ciliary muscle. Therefore, these agents produce mydriasis as well as cyclopegia.

773. (B) The purpose is not to balance corrected visual acuity. The purpose is to balance the state of accommodation.

774. (E) All are useful. Remember, the purpose of these tests is to balance the state of accommodation. The purpose is not to balance visual acuity.

775. (D) This instrument is used to measure the distance between the eye and the correcting lens. Vertex distance is measured in (mm). It is of significance, especially when the required prescription is of high power.

776. (C) According to Hirsch and Wick (1963), accommodative esotropia occurs as a result of uncorrected (or under-corrected) hyperopia. The application of plus lens power will correct the hyperopia and eliminate (reduce) the need to accommodate. As accommodation is reduced, convergence (of the lines of sight) is reduced (AC/A ratio). As convergence is reduced, esotropia is reduced.

777. **(E)** All are correct. Latent hyperopia is known as the condition in which the patient's hyperopia is compensated for by the tonicity of the ciliary muscle. The patient may suffer severe eye strain until the hyperopia is found and corrected.

778. **(D)** The uncorrected eye does not have enough plus power in either of its two principal meridians to bring light to focus on the retina. Therefore, light is focused behind the retina. The ophthalmic correction for this condition would be an astigmatic lens varying in plus power along its principal meridians.

779. **(A)** In the uncorrected state, the 41° meridian will focus light (from a distant point) behind the retina. The 131° meridian will focus light in front of the retina. In one principal meridian the eye is myopic and in the other meridian it is hyperopic.

780. **(A)** Use the effectivity equation: $Fx = F/1 - d\,F$. Note, as a correction is moved closer to the eye, its power must increase in plus (or decrease in minus) in order to maintain a constant vergence at the eye. With contacts, the myope's acuity is enhanced. Utilize the apparent magnification equation $M = -F_2/F_1$ for this part.

781. **(A)** The bifocal add power is the difference between the vertex power of the add and the vertex power of the distance lens measured on the side of the bifocal add. Do not attempt to read the difference on the side opposite to the add. Otherwise, you must take into account the thickness and curvature of the lens.

782. **(E)** All are correct. Both **B** and **C** are in-office procedures that may be attempted first. Anti-reflecting (AR) coatings provide the most effective control of specular reflections.

783. **(D)** Tinted lenses do not eliminate glare. In order to effectively eliminate glare from objects of regard, polaroid lenses must be utilized. With their axis positioned at 90°, polaroid filters reduce most glare from shining horizontal surfaces such as highways, rain, or snow.

784. **(E)** All are correct. Because of these factors, the popularity of plastic lenses has increased during the course of the last decade. The majority of all lenses fitted are now made of some form of plastic material.

785. **(A)** This technique raises the entire frame front. If this procedure is not sufficient, then bend the guard arms down. If both of these do not provide the appropriate results, then you may reduce the pantoscopic angle (tilt).

786. **(B)** If the patient complains of the frame hurting one side of the nose, unequal spread of the temple angles might be suspected. The answer is **B**; this technique allows the frame front to move closer to the head on the side where the lens is farther out. If additional adjustment is needed, you may decrease the temple angle on the side of the face where the frame front is closer to the face.

787. **(D)** Age-related maculopathy, diabetic retinopathy, and glaucoma account for a large majority of new cases of blindness. Age-related maculopathy (macular degeneration) affects the macular region impairing central vision. Diabetic retinopathy reduces acuity and changes color vision. Glaucoma results in damage to the optic nerve, resulting in visual field loss, impaired night vision, reduction in color vision, and contrast sensitivity.

788. **(E)** All of these statements are correct. In addition, taking the case history from an aged patient may be difficult, because the older patient tends to be forgetful. Therefore, in order to help establish the chief complaint, confer (when possible) with a member of the patient's family.

789. **(A)** Halberg clips are useful when working with the patient's habitual prescription. The patient has the opportunity to directly evaluate the V.A. change resulting from a change in either the sphere or cylinder in his existing spectacles. Furthermore, he can evaluate the change in the bifocal addition.

790. **(A)** 15-1/4 (50) = 2.50 D. The amplitude of accommodation is the dioptric difference between the far point and the near point. The far point is the point conjugate to the retina when the eye is unaccommodated. The near point is the point conjugate to the retina when the eye is fully accommodated.

791. (D) The contact lens corrected patient requires 3.75 D of accommodation to view the object. Utilizing minimum amplitude equations, the patient has only 3.00 D of available accommodation. A myope fitted with contact lenses is required to provide more accommodation to observe an object at a given finite distance than is the same myope who is fitted with ophthalmic spectacles.

792. (D) The bifocal add equals (65/50) (2.5) = 3.25. Next, add this amount (3.25) to the spherical portion of the distance Rx. The NPD is found by utilizing the 3/4 rule. FPD − 2I = NPD. I = (0.75)(3.25) = 2.5 mm.

793. (A) The patient is 67 years old and cannot accommodate. Therefore, the reading distance equals the reciprocal of the bifocal add (1/3.25 = 30.77 cm). The bifocal add (+3.25) was calculated in answer **792.**

794. (C) Use Prentice's rule and the 3/4 rule. Prentice's rule is given by the equation $d^A = CF$. The 3/4 rule states that for every diopter of dioptric demand, the lines of sight move in 0.75 mm.

795. (D) All are utilized. In as much as the presbyope cannot accommodate, there is a need to provide some form of plus refracting power at near. All of these methods provide plus power.

796. (E) All can be utilized. If one technique is not effective, then try another. After the tentative add has been determined, place it in a trial frame (along with the distance Rx). Now you can modify it based on the patient's near complaint.

797. (C) In the other cases the patient still has enough accommodation left to see at intermediate distances. However, when a +2.00 bifocal addition is required, not enough accommodation is left to allow a large enough range of clear vision through the bifocal add. Therefore, a trifocal add must be considered.

798. (B) Use the effectivity equation: $Fx = F/1-dF$. For the right eye, the calculation is $12.75 = 10.75/[1-.015(10.75)]$. For the left eye, the calculation is $11.75 = 10.00/[1-.015(10.00)]$.

799. (B) Use the magnification equation: $M = -F_2/F_1$. In this equation, F_2 = the contact lens Rx; F_1 represents the spectacle Rx. Therefore, for OD, apparent magnification $= 12.75/10.75 = +1.186x$. For OS, apparent magnification $= 11.75/10.00 = +1.175x$. Visual acuity for $OD = 30/1.186$ and for $OS = 30/1.175$.

800. (C) The patient does not readily accept occlusion of the dominant aphakic eye. In prescribing, the dominant eye should be given the better vision when possible. Furthermore, if a prism is prescribed, it should be placed before the nondominant eye.

801. (E) All of the statements are correct. Even though most new cataract cases result in the implantation of intraocular lenses (IOLs), there still exists a significant number of older patients who were fitted with contact lenses. Remember that a family member or friend should assume responsibility for periodic lens removal, cleaning, disinfection, and reinsertion.

802. (C) 1.00 of uncorrected myopia allows the patient to focus on objects located 100 cm in front of his or her eyes; that is, the patient's far point is located 1 m away. Therefore, when viewing objects located at distance (6 m) or at near (40 cm), the patient, although somewhat out of focus, can see well enough to travel about in his or her home without the use of a spectacle correction.

803. (C) To maintain binocularity, no more than 1.00 to 2.00 D difference is generally recommended. If the dioptric difference is greater than this value, the corresponding retinal images will be too different. As a result, diplopia may occur.

804. (E) In all of these conditions, IOLs are not indicated. In uveitis, the IOL may cause exacerbation of the inflammation. In high myopia, aphakia may be preferred, because the required spectacle correction will be weak and more optically acceptable. In children, not enough information is available about the long-term effects of IOLs. In diabetic retinopathy, treatment by photocoagulation may be limited.

805. (C) This is the standard definition. It is usually produced by a magnification difference between the two eyes brought about by correcting lenses. It tends to cause symptoms of eye strain and headaches.

806. (E) Different retinal image sizes/shapes often produce these symptoms. The headaches and eye strain produced here are usually localized near and around the eyes. The curving of straight/ vertical objects is called distortion.

807. (C) Axial ametropia is defined as ametropia due primarily to the axial length of the globe. Refractive ametropia is defined as ametropia due to refractive power (dioptric power of the eye). If the more ametropic of the two eyes has refractive ametropia, the induced aniseikonia will be at a minimum utilizing contact lenses.

808. (D) Use the equation for spectacle magnification. The description of this equation is found in question **411.** Spectacle magnification = $\{1/[1-(.0071/1.495)(15)]\} \times \{1/[1-(.017)(12.75)]\}$ = 37.5% for the right lens; do the same operation for the left lens and calculate the difference.

Low Vision

809. (B) This is taken as the standard definition. Even though patients in this category are considered blind, a large portion can be treated clinically, utilizing various optical aids. Such aids include telescopes, microscopes, and compound microscopes.

810. (D) All of these are correct. The population of low-vision patients is made up primarily of those having congenital eye diseases and those having degenerative diseases occurring later in life. Older patients account for a majority of the low-vision population.

811. (E) In contrast sensitivity testing, the patient is presented with stimuli in the form of gratings (not letters) at different contrast and spatial frequency levels. When compared to visual acuity measurements, VCTS measurements are better predictors of the preferred eye. Furthermore, VCTS measurements are better predictors of the ability to read continuous text.

812. (E) Advanced glaucoma and diabetic retinopathy lead to a poor prognosis. Aphakia can be treated with contact lenses, ophthalmic spectacle lenses, or even intraocular lenses. Keratoconus can be treated, often successfully, utilizing contact lenses.

813. (E) Patients with either **A, B,** or **C** are disturbed by bright light. Patients with **D,** central corneal opacities, function better in dim light. A larger pupil (in dim light) allows some light rays to circumvent the opacified area of the lens.

814. (E) All of these patients need bright light in order to function as well as possible. Indoors, high illumination levels can be achieved by reducing the distance between the target and the light source. Small high intensity gooseneck lamps are useful for reading or sewing while seated in a chair.

815. (C) Moving closer to an object increases the object's angular subtense at the eye. A larger angular subtense produces a larger retinal image. For example, an object at 20 feet produces a retinal image that is two times the size of the retinal image produced when the object is located at 40 feet.

816. (C) Large type print books are bulky and hard to handle. Few books are available in large type print. Furthermore, the ones that are available are very expensive.

817. (B) Utilize the relationship: $2/200 = 20/x$; $x = 2000$. Therefore, a VA of 2/200 is equivalent to 20/2000. When the corrected visual acuity is 20/2000 or less, the chances of providing ophthalmic help are poor.

818. (C) The magnification required by the round magnifier is equal to the visual acuity demanded by the print divided by the patient's corrected visual acuity; that is, apparent magnification $= (20/50)/(20/60) = +1.20x$. Therefore, $F = +2.5 \times 1.2 = +3.00$ D.

819. (E) Hand-held magnifiers are usually round or rectangular in shape. Some have internal illumination systems built in to enhance image quality. Still, all present disadvantages for the reasons listed.

820. (E) All influence the size of the field of view. As the required magnification (power of system) increases, the field of view decreases. Therefore, it is important that all the factors are manipulated to some degree in order to maintain as large a field as possible.

821. (A) Vertex distance (the distance between eye and lens) is most critical. As the vertex distance is decreased, the field of view is increased. As the vertex distance is increased, the field of view is decreased.

822. (E) All are correct. Note: a spectacle microscope can be transported about with relative ease. Therefore, it can be employed by the partially sighted patient when he or she is in almost any setting.

823. (E) All are disadvantages. Note: they cannot be transported about easily. They are usually bulky and do not fit easily into pockets of clothing.

824. (B) Remember, the bifocal add is equal to the reciprocal of the reading distance. Furthermore, the apparent magnification produced is given by the equation $M = ADD/2.5$. Therefore, the distance Rx $= (-7.50) + (-5.00) = -12.50$; VA $= 20/(5/2.5 \times 50) = 20/100$.

825. (D) Use the effectivity equation to determine the contact lens correction: CLRx $= (-10.62)$. Next, divide the CLRx by the spectacle Rx: $(-10.62/-12.50) = 0.8496$. Multiply this number times 100: CLVA $= 20/(100/0.8496) = 20/85$.

826. (B) The reading addition correction equals the apparent magnification required multiplied by 2.50. The apparent magnification required is $(20/50)/(20/85)$; therefore, $85/50 \times 2.5 = 4.25$ (power of the ADD). The reading distance needed $= 1/ADD = 1/4.25 = 0.235$ m $= 23.5$ cm.

827. (C) First, determine the amount of uncorrected ametropia present at the cornea. The amount is equal (but opposite in sign) to the power required in a contact lens; that is, (-13.91 D). Next, determine the power required in both the objective (spectacle lens) portion and the eyepiece (contact lens) portion of the +1.29x telescopic system; that is, for objective, $F_{spec} = [1.29-1]/[1.29(.017)] = +13.22$ and $F_{eyepiece} = -(13.22 \times 1.29) = -17.06$. Next, subtract the amount of the uncorrected ametropia (−13.91) from −17.09: −17.09−(−13.91) = −3.15. This amount (−3.15) represents the required contact lens prescription.

828. **(D)** Telescopes are still useful here. When prescribing a telescopic aid, cylindrical correction of 0.50 D or less may be omitted. Where corrected visual acuity is less than 20/600, the chances of treating patients optometrically are not good.

829. **(E)** Dim illumination is required for both of these conditions. In aniridia (without an iris), the effective pupil is quite large, allowing too much stray light to enter the eye. In albinism (congenital absence of pigment), the eye's retina is quite sensitive to bright light (glare).

830. **(C)** Minus power spectacle lenses minify. As minification increases, corrected visual acuity decreases. As a result, myopic patients requiring high prescriptions see better with contact lenses.

831. **(A)** Hemianopsia is defined as blindness in one-half of the visual field. It can occur in one or both eyes and involves either the superior/inferior or nasal/temporal retina. This technique allows optical images to be placed in the seeing portion of the retina.

832. **(C)** These results are based on a retrospective study of 318 low-vision patients. Those who complained of glare, light sensitivity, or photophobia were allowed to select their own filter. Of the 318 prescribed, 54 percent chose filter #101.

833. **(E)** Absorptive lenses are designed either to reduce or eliminate the intensity of certain wavelengths that enter the eye. If the intensity of incident light is reduced by the lens material by varying the color of that material, the lens is said to be a tinted lens. If it is reduced through the application of a thin film coat on the lens surface/surfaces, it is said to be a coated lens. Absorptive lenses should have all of these properties listed.

834. (E) All of these are correct. Rehabilitation training in the area of walking about (traveling) is done by orientation and mobility (O.M.) specialists. For more information, contact the American Foundation for the Blind.

835. (C) A bioptic telescope is a small diameter scope confined to the top portion of a lens carrier. The patient's Rx is incorporated into both the telescope portion and the carrier portion. The use of these scopes in driving is quite controversial.

836. (E) All of these are correct. These devices are available with different size monitors. These monitors allow brightness control as well as ability to reverse the print/background from black on white to white on black.

837. (A) Writing and typing are done easily under a television camera. Typewriter attachments are available for some, but not all, models. Other attachments to meet additional needs will become available in the future.

Sensory Anomalies of Binocular Vision/Strabismus

838. (E) Lens magnification depends on lens position. A rule of thumb for correcting refractive anisometropia with spectacle lenses gives 1.5 percent magnification per diopter, but approximately zero for a contact lens, because the back vertex distance is so small. Interocular retinal size differences in refractive anisometropia are introduced by spectacle lens corrections.

839. (E) Knapp's Law states that the retinal image sizes in axial anisometropes can be matched by a spectacle lens correction placed at the anterior focal plane of the eye. Also, approximate equality of retinal image size can be achieved by contact lens (CL) correction in refractive anisometropes. However, **aniseikonia,** which defines the perceived size ("ocular image") and not simply the retinal (optical) image size, may best be minimized by CL correction in all anisometropes because of retinal stretching in axial anisometropes. For example, an elongated myopic eye may, due to stretching, have a low density of retinal receptors at the posterior pole. In order to have an image cover the same number of receptors in this eye, it would have to be larger. Therefore, a CL correction for an axial myopic eye, which produces a larger optical image than expected in emmetropes, may create a neural image of about the same size (same number of receptors, ganglion cells, etc.). Because each retina may not stretch equally, or uniformly, the CL may not prove either accurate or general as an effective correction in axial anisometropia. Although Knapp's Law is a very useful rule of thumb for matching retinal image size in anisometropia, it cannot be used as a reliable predictor of aniseikonia, particularly with axial anisometropia (most cases).

840. **(B)** Sorsby was a British ophthalmologist. He studied a large population of anisometropes and found that virtually all anisometropias greater than 2 diopters were due to interocular differences in axial length. He was one of the first to use ultrasound to measure axial lengths.

841. **(E)** Amblyopia is not only associated with anisometropia, antimetropia (a special case of anisometropia), esotropia, and congenital cataracts, but is thought to be caused by these associated conditions. In general, amblyopia is found to occur with these and other abnormalities of binocular vision.

842. **(D)** Human strabismic amblyopes exhibit a wide variety of vision problems, but in general they are most pronounced for spatial vision tasks, particularly those involving fine detail targets. Interestingly, adding other targets in the proximity of the test target (e.g., a letter) has an exaggerated effect on the visual performance of these amblyopes (increased crowding). Clinically, color vision appears quite normal.

843. **(D)** Monocular fixation with the amblyopic eye of a strabismic subject is rarely accurate. Amblyopes generally exhibit unsteady fixation, and strabismic amblyopes often exhibit eccentric fixation. If the better eye is occluded, they do not experience diplopia.

844. **(E)** Clinically measured stereopsis in strabismic subjects is usually very poor or totally absent. Also, if nonstrabismic subjects were tested while they were incorrectly converged such that the

target plane was far from their horopter and outside of Panum's fusional area, they would also perform very badly on most stereo tests, because stereo acuity declines rapidly from its maximum at the horopter.

845. **(D)** The space eikonometer relies on stereoscopic depth perception in order for patients to detect the tilting planes. The instrument measures the monocular magnification that must be introduced in order to make different parts of the target appear to lie in the fronto-parallel plane. Stereo-blind patients cannot use this instrument.

846. **(A)** The after-images (AI) are created foveally during monocular fixation (other eye covered). Once orthogonal AIs are created, a normal or strabismic subject with normal retinal correspondence will see them both simultaneously crossing at the center where each filament was fixated. However, if the patient exhibits any ARC (harmonious or unharmonious) when viewing binocularly, one after-image will appear shifted with respect to the other. Most patients with eccentric fixation will not see both after-images crossing in the middle.

847. **(B)** The mirror symmetric oblique astigmatic correction will create a declination error. This will tilt the crossed lines in the space eikonometer about the horizontal axis (either top toward or top away). A declination error can occur whenever there are interocular differences in the meridian and/or magnitude of oblique astigmatism.

848. **(C)** Although an amblyope may have a visual acuity defined as equivalent to that of a normal uncorrected myope (e.g., 20/80), its scoring behavior on the acuity test is very different. Amblyopes tend to make errors over a wide range of letter sizes. They do not show an abrupt change from perfect scores to zero or chance scores.

849. **(C)** Nonconcomitant deviations can be due to any reduction in the efficacy of a particular extraocular muscle. Because the role of each muscle changes with the direction of gaze, the effect of a muscle problem will also change. For example, a weak right eye

medial rectus might lead to exotropia during leftward gaze, but the patient might be orthotropic with rightward gaze.

850. **(B)** In order to maintain orthotropia, a patient with paresis of an individual muscle must choose a direction of gaze that minimizes or eliminates the necessity for the paretic muscle to act. In general, a patient can achieve this by abnormal head posture such that the face is directed toward the diagnostic action field of the paretic muscle; that is, substituting head for eye movements. In the case of a paretic left eye superior rectus, which elevates, adducts, and intorts, the face would be up and to the right, and the head would be tilted toward the patient's right.

851. **(C)** Because angle kappa (angle separating the pupillary and visual axes) tests are typically performed monocularly, they are not generally used to determine tropias. Interocular differences in angle kappa are indicative (but not conclusive) evidence of monocular eccentric fixation, particularly if one eye is known to have amblyopia. When viewed from the fixation light, the first Purkinje image typically appears slightly nasal in the pupil. A nasal monocular eccentric fixation would shift the **pupil** nasally with respect to this catoptric image, and could reduce the clinical angle kappa measurement from +1 mm to +0.5 mm.

852. **(C)** Such a patient would report seeing a perfect cross. His or her ARC (manifest during the binocular test) and eccentric fixation (manifest during the monocular generation of the after-images) are equal. The after-image in the eccentrically fixating eye will be created 10° in the nasal retina. During binocular viewing, the HARC will make images 10° in the nasal retina appear to "correspond" (in terms of visual direction) to the fixation point imaged in the fovea of the nondeviating eye.

853. **(E)** Although not very accurate, the Worth test is an effective means of identifying eccentric fixation in amblyopia. Angle kappa is measured for each eye, and a difference between them indicates eccentric fixation. It makes assumptions about the relative location of the pupil and visual axes.

854. **(B)** A patient who fixates **nasally** rotates his or her eye nasally such that a point in the field that is nasal to the fixation target will

be imaged on the fovea, and therefore the fixation target is imaged on the nasal retina. With a nasally fixating right eye, the patient would see brushes 2.8 cm (4 degrees at 40 cm) to the left of the fixation point. This is the spatial projection of his anatomical fovea, which is the origin of the Hadinger Brush phenomenon.

855. **(A)** The Bagolini striated lenses provide two orthogonal light streaks that are the only two monocular stimuli in an otherwise "binocular" scene. An esotropic or exotropic patient with harmonious ARC and no scotoma will perceive both streaks in the appropriate direction, just as a normal patient. If the esotrope with ARC has a central scotoma, a gap will appear in the streak seen by the deviated eye. An esotrope without HARC will see two streaks that are decentered with respect to each other.

856. **(E)** There are two basic approaches to assessing the retinal point of fixation: (1) the perceived location of a fixation point relative to an entoptically viewed retinal landmark known to be concentric with the anatomical fovea (**C and D**) and (2) an instrument that projects a fixation target onto the retina and allows the clinician to observe it ophthalmoscopically and compare the image of the fixation target to the position of the anatomical foveal reflex (**A and B**).

857. **(B)** Although there may be interocular differences in the ocular images, patients with aniseikonia are often unaware of the differences or they experience distortions in depth, not size or shape. Metamorphopsia refers to abnormally perceived size and/or shape, and anisometropia defines an interocular difference in refractive error, which may or may not be accompanied by aniseikonia.

858. **(E)** Orthoptics is the treatment, by training and patching, of a wide variety of binocular vision disorders, including all of those listed. Orthoptic methods include patching, vergence exercises, suppression exercises, etc.

859. **(C)** Because of the plasticity of the developing visual system (best exemplified by animal studies of monocular deprivation), the very young patient undergoing patching therapy can suffer from "deprivation amblyopia" in the patched, previously normal

eye. Visual acuity must be checked frequently in the patched eye to avoid this outcome.

860. **(E)** If you can imagine it, someone has probably suggested it as a treatment of human amblyopia. This a a pretty good rule of thumb. However, several types of therapy have dominated treatment practices. Most prevalent is conventional patching (continuous or intermittent) of the nonamblyopic eye. Also, in an attempt to correct an eccentric fixation point, some amblyopes have their amblyopic eye patched. Another common technique is designed to stimulate the amblyopic eye with, for example, rotating gratings. No established techniques try to actively stimulate the nonamblyopic eye.

861. **(C)** Pleoptic therapies attempt to encourage foveal fixation in the amblyopic eyes of amblyopes by selectively desensitizing the area surrounding the fovea with a specially designed bright light source. The logic is simple. If the foveal center is the only functional part of the macula (the retina surrounding the fovea has been desensitized), then patients are likely to use their fovea, not the eccentric retinal point they may have been using.

862. **(C)** Because of the red and green filters in front of the eyes, the two green dots can only be seen by one eye, and the red dot only by the other eye. The white dot will be seen as a single dot of unstable color (red and/or green) by a normal individual for a total of four dots. However, the strabismic patient with NRC who is not suppressing will see the white dot as two dots, one red and one green, for a total of five. If, however, the patient is suppressing one eye, only two or three dots will be seen.

Anomalies of Eye Movements

863. **(E)** Esofixation disparities tend to occur when there is a bias to be less converged than necessary to be orthotropic. This bias is present when a patient cannot diverge in response to BI prism. It is also present in patients who have a pronounced esophoria.

864. **(C)** A prominent epicanthal fold gives the misleading impression that the eye is deviated nasally. This can give rise to the false

diagnosis of esotropia. Because the epicanthal fold is prominent in infants, esotropia can be incorrectly diagnosed.

865. **(D)** Perfect eye alignment during binocular fusion is referred to as orthotropia. However, when the fusion reflex is interrupted (e.g., in a cover test), misalignment of the eyes can manifest itself as a phoria. Some subjects keep their eyes aligned without the fusion reflex; these patients are orthophoric.

866. **(B)** The eso deviation increases on upward gaze with A pattern esotropia. This is not comitant esotropia. The converse happens with V pattern esotropia.

867. **(B)** A convergence insufficiency would create increased exophoria at near in a patient with a small exophoria at distance. It can also introduce an exophoria at near in a patient who is orthophoric at distance. Such a patient would be a candidate for orthoptic training.

868. **(D)** By alternately covering the right and left eyes, the clinician prevents binocular fusion, and thus cannot test for tropias. The clinician must rapidly move the occluder, but leave it in place over each eye for several seconds (alternation rate of 0.25 Hz). By watching the change in eye position when uncovered, the clinician learns of the deviation or misalignment present when occluded (a phoria).

869. **(E)** Because the Hirschberg test examines interocular differences in the positions of the catoptric images of the fixation light with respect to the image of the pupil, it assumes that the pupil and visual axis are not significantly misaligned (other than the typical angle kappa). This is a coarse technique for evaluating horizontal and vertical tropias only.

870. **(A)** Orthotropia can be maintained by adjusting head and gaze positions with lateral or medial recti palsies. Correct eye position is achieved by changing the gaze to a position that does not involve constriction of the palsied muscle. Combined with head rotation in the opposite direction, this strategy allows such patients to fixate objects binocularly. In this example, turning the head to

the right and gazing to the left allows the patient to bilaterally fixate an object directly in front of him or her.

871. **(E)** Because animals and humans cannot easily diverge their
eyes beyond that required for distance vision, bilateral base-in
prisms will place a distant target that is fixated by one eye into the
temporal field of the other eye. This is the same situation that exists with natural esotropia. One eye accurately fixates, and the fixation target is left in the temporal field of the deviating (esotropic)
eye.

872. **(C)** Unlike paralytic strabismus, which is usually nonconcomitant (noncomitant), concomitant strabismus remains stable irrespective of the angle of gaze or the fixating eye. This type of strabismus generally reflects some central neurological abnormality,
and not a problem with the extraocular muscles (e.g., paresis).

873. **(A)** A variety of forms of nystagmus exist, and two forms vary
dramatically with the direction of gaze. In one, the nystagmus is
present only when the patient gazes in the direction of the fast
component (first degree nystagmus), and a second type (second
degree nystagmus) occurs with gaze in the primary position *and*
in the direction of the fast phase of the nystagmus. Note: these
two types of nystagmus should **not** be confused with primary and
secondary nystagmus, which are quite different.

874. **(C)** In order for a point in object space to be imaged onto corresponding points in a patient with esofixation disparity, it must be
placed in front of the fixation plane. For example, both visual
axes intersect in front of the fixation target; therefore, an object
placed there will appear to lie in the same visual direction in both
eyes and will thus lie on the nonius horopter.

875. **(A)** An axis 90 magnifier, worn in front of the right eye, will
make the actual or physical fronto parallel plane (the far wall in
this example) appear tilted away from the person on the right
side. Of course, the apparent fronto parallel plane (AFPP), which
is the physical plane that appears to lie in the fronto parallel
plane, will be near on the right side and away on the left side.

876. (B) Axis 180 magnifiers of up to about 5 percent (or a little more) will "induce" a tilt (the induced effect) in the AFPP opposite to that produced by the same power axis 90 lens (which produces the geometric effect). In this example, the lens will make the physical fronto parallel plane appear to tilt toward the left eye (away from the right eye). Therefore, the AFPP is the opposite of this. A similar result would be obtained with an axis 90 magnifier in front of the RE.

877. (D) Flat prisms exhibit slightly more angular magnification at the apex than at the base. Therefore, when viewing through bilateral base-out prisms, the left field is magnified in the right eye and the right field is magnified in the left eye. From the simple laws of meridional magnifiers, the left field will appear tilted toward the left eye and the right field will appear tilted toward the right eye. Therefore, the fronto parallel plane will appear concave.

878. (E) Spherical afocal magnifiers magnify equally in both axis 90 and axis 180 meridians. It has been suggested that the failure to observe any tilts in the AFPP with low-power spherical magnifiers is due to cancellation of the geometric effect (caused by axis 90 magnification) and the induced effect (caused by axis 180 magnification).

879. (E) Optimal performance on a stereo acuity test can be impaired by virtually anything that disrupts the balance between the right and left eyes. Examples of this are monocular defocus, monocular suppression, and amblyopia. Also, the stereoscopic target must be imaged near to the horopter, which requires accurate convergence on the target. Clearly, there are many reasons why a patient may fail a stereopsis test.

Anomalies of Accommodation and Accommodative Convergence

880. (B) Binocular convergence can drive accommodation. The ratio of accommodation in diopters elicited by convergence, divided by the amount of convergence in prism diopters, is the CA/C ratio.

Because accommodation is impossible in presbyopes and unnecessary in myopes, the CA/C ratio is low (not high) in these individuals.

881. **(E)** Convergence of the eyes can be driven by an accommodative response. The ratio of prism diopters of convergence produced by a given amount of accommodation in diopters is the AC/A ratio (typically 3.5 prism diopters/diopter of accommodation). In order to maintain functional binocularity, myopes, who have to accommodate very little, tend to have a very high AC/A ratio.

882. **(D)** To compute the stimulus-based AC/A ratio, you must identify the amount of accommodative demand in diopters. In this example, it would be $(1/0.5 - 1/6) = 1.833$ D. However, the 6 meter distance is often approximated to optical infinity, and therefore the approximate accommodative demand becomes $(1/0.5 - 0) = 2$ D. This value (2.0 or 1.833 D) becomes the denominator in the AC/A calculation. Next, the amount of convergence without any binocular (disparity) input must be calculated from monocular measures. This becomes the accommodative convergence in prism diopters created by the change in accommodation. In this example, the subject was 1Δ exophoric at 6 m and 3Δ esophoric at 50 cm; that is, the change from 6 meters to 50 cm created 4Δ more convergence than the stimulus would demand. The accommodative convergence demand can be computed in prism diopters (which are angular units of displacement in cm/meter) by (PD/distance), using cm for the PD and meters for target distance. In this example, the convergence stimulus changed from 6/6 to 6/0.5 or $12 - 1 = 11\Delta$. A simple AC/A ratio calculation would give:

$$AC/A = (11\Delta + 4\Delta)/1.833 \text{ D} = 15\Delta/1.833 \text{ D} = 8.2 \ \Delta/D.$$

Clinically, the AC/A calculation is a little more complex. The denominator in this example would be 2, not 1.833, or it would be the dioptric power of a negative lens introduced to induce accommodation; e.g., a -2 D lens. Also, the accommodative demand would be calculated at the spectacle plane. Of course, the convergnce occurs by rotating the eye, and the average center of rotation is about 2.7 cm behind the spectacle plane. Therefore, the numerator in the accommodative convergence calculation becomes [PD/test distance + 2.7 cm)]. Clinically, the example used here would be calculated in the following way:

$$AC/A = [(6/(0.5 + 0.027)) + 4]\Delta/2 \, D = 15.4/2 = 7.7 \, \Delta/D$$

As you can see, these two methods only differ slightly, but the difference can become significant if the accommodative stimulus is large. It is clear from these calculations that the calculated AC/A ratio includes proximal (disparity) *and* accommodative convergence in the numerator.

883. **(E)** Anything that affects the accommodative or vergence amplitudes or ranges will affect the zone of clear, single, binocular vision. Also, Panum's fusional areas slightly extend the disparity zone of single vision.

884. **(A)** AC/A ratios are calculated clinically by measuring the phorias at two target distances and adding (or subtracting) these from the stimulus change in prism diopters, and then dividing this value by the change in the stimulus to accommodation in diopters. No measure of actual accommodation is made. This calculated AC/A ratio is referred to as the stimulus-based AC/A ratio.

885. **(C)** This question describes the gradient test to determine the stimulus AC/A ratio. The target distance remains constant, but, by introducing the +1D add, the accommodative stimulus decreases by 1D. With reduced accommodation, there will be less accommodative convergence (in this case 2Δ). In this example, the increase in accommodative stimulus from $1.5[(1/.4)-1]$ to $2.5 \, (1/.4)$ decreases the phoria by 2 prism diopters $[(-1) - (-3)]$. The AC/A ratio = $2/1 \, \Delta/D$.

886. **(D)** Because accommodative response tends to be less than demanded by the change in stimulus distance, the denominator of the response-based AC/A ratio will often be smaller than the dioptric change in the stimulus. Therefore, the response-based AC/A will generally be slightly higher than the stimulus-based ratio.

887. **(C)** A high AC/A ratio would tend to make a patient more esodeviated with increasing accommodation. Only **C** has this property.

888. (D) A patient who has an abnormally large AC/A ratio could be orthotropic (or nearly so) at distance and highly esophoric at near, and is described by Duane as having convergence excess. A patient who has a large exo-deviation at distance who becomes orthophoric at near also has a high AC/A ratio, but he or she is described as having divergence excess. Those with a low AC/A ratio can be described as having convergence insufficiency.

889. (B) Accommodative facility is tested clinically by examining the speed at which a patient can alternately increase and then decrease his or her accommodation. This is achieved by alternating ("rocking") between two lenses (e.g., +1.5 and −1.5 for a near target, or plano, and −2.5 for a distant target). The lenses are changed only when the image is brought into focus by the accommodative change. A normal patient should be able to achieve alternation rates of 20 per minute or more. Convergence facility can also be measured with a "prism-rock" test. A push-up test examines the **amplitude** of accommodation (and/or convergence).

890. (E) The Mallett test measures the amount of prism-induced disparity vergence necessary to eliminate the fixation disparity. This is **not** a direct measure of the amount of fixation disparity. This test can be used to prescribe prism for a patient's spectacle correction.

891. (A) Ogle showed that four general classes of fixation disparity behavior (I, II, III, and IV) could be identified in a population. Most subjects exhibited a sigmoidal function with increasing eso-fixation disparity with base-in prisms and increasing exo-fixation disparity with base-out prisms with a small zone near to zero prism power with little change in fixation disparity. He called this type I, and it seems as though approximately 60 percent of normals behave this way.

892. (E) Recent studies of prism adaptation by Schor have shown that prolonged viewing through prisms introduces changes in phorias and refractive states (due to accommodative "spasms"). These changes are thought to occur in the "tonic" control systems of both vergence and accommodation. Typically, under forced convergence, a patient would tend to be exophoric. This exophoria would tend to decrease over time due to adaptation and, after removal of the prisms, the patient would have a tendency to be overconverged (esophoric). Interestingly, adaptation to prisms can create adaptation of the accommodative system, and in this example the tendency would be to exhibit increased accommodation via convergence accommodation adaptation.

893. **(E)** The accommodative system can adapt. Adaptation can create increased accommodative responses after prolonged forced accommodations, or (through the convergence accommodation system) prolonged forced convergence. These increased accommodative responses can lead to "pseudo" myopia (otherwise known as hypertonic myopia).

894. **(C)** Clinically, we usually estimate the accommodative amplitude by the dioptric range that a patient can keep "in focus." Of course, in young people, this range will be determined largely by the amplitude of accommodation. The dioptric range of "clear vision" will generally be larger than the accommodative response because at either end of the range, targets will appear clear because of the "depth of focus" of the eye. It is important to realize that the depth of focus is not simply an optical phenomenon. It is affected directly by optics, and will be directly related to pupil diameter. However, the ability of the neural system to distinguish between in focus and defocused images will also determine the depth of focus. This additional range of clear vision has been referred to as psuedoaccommodation, and it can compromise the measurement of the apparent accommodative range in older patients.

Contact Lenses

895. **(A)** The strongest contraindication for a contact lens wearer is lack of motivation. A steep cornea or one with astigmatism greater than 2.50 D can be easily fitted with great satisfaction to the patient. Conjunctivitis of short duration is not a contraindication.

896. **(B)** Fluorescein solution can be kept free from *Pseudomonas aeruginosa* by autoclaving. The other chemicals are in the fluorescein solutions as preservatives, and as such are in too low concentration to be able to keep the solution free of *Pseudomonas* in the event of contamination.

897. (A) To loosen a "tight lens," one can decrease the optic zone diameter, increase the optic zone radius, and increase the lens thickness. Decreasing the lens thickness will tighten the lens.

898. (C) The amount of oxygen flow beneath a lens with each blink depends on the amount of tears exchanged with each blink, the frequency of blink, and the volume of the tear reservoir behind the lens.

899. (C) The silicon monomer to the methacrylate polymer in rigid gas permeable lenses provides oxygen permeability. The incorporation of the silicone monomer also makes the polymer more flexible.

900. (D) The methacrylate monomer, combined with the silicone acrylate type rigid gas permeable (RGP) lenses, provide good surface wetting characteristics.

901. (B) The addition of a fluorine monomer to silicone acrylate provides high oxygen permeability with good wetting characteristics, deposit resistance, and good stability not found in silicone.

902. (D) The advantage of T-butylstyrene in the fitting of patients with keratoconus is its dimensional stability. Thus, when fitting a keratoconic patient, one can design an extremely thin lens.

903. (D) The hydrogel lens will follow the contour of the cornea closely; therefore, the tear reservoir beneath the lens is very small as compared to the rigid lens. Thus, the amount of tears exchanged with each blink with a hydrogel lens is small: 1 percent.

904. (B) The amount of tears exchanged with each blink with a rigid lens is 16 to 19 percent. The rigid lens does not follow the contour of the cornea; as a result, there is a significant tear reservoir under the lens.

905. (A) The hybrid lens combines a rigid center of N-butylstyrene with a hydroxyethyl methacrylate peripheral skirt. This lens was designed to combine the excellent optical characteristics of the rigid lens with the comfort of the hydrogel lens.

906. (D) The concentration of hydrogen peroxide in soft lens care solution is 3 percent, stabilized with sodium stannate and sodium nitrate and buffered with phosphates.

907. (C) The neutralizer in the "Concept" hydrogen peroxide solution is sodium thiosulfate, whereas, in the AOSEPT system, the hydrogen peroxide is neutralized with a platinum-coated disc.

908. (B) Benzalkonium chloride is not used as a preservative in soft lens chemical disinfection systems. Benzalkoium chloride has the ability to bind in the soft lens and concentrate.

909. (A) Ultraviolet disinfection was found to damage many soft lens polymers too rapidly. The ultraviolet light is a short wavelength light of high energy, and may affect the chemical bond of the polymer.

910. (A) Hydrogel lenses whose water content is less than 45 percent are probably better for the slightly dry-eyed patient. There is a greater fluctuation of vision when a higher water content lens is used.

911. (D) Factors that favor protein deposits include thermal, disinfection, incomplete blinking, altered tear composition, tear deficiency, and chronic allergic and grant papillary conjunctivitis.

912. (A) In aphakic patients, more plus power is needed in the contact lens with respect to spectacle prescription because of the decrease in the plus power due to the effectivity distance.

913. (C) Poor wetting characteristics of a rigid gas permeable lens can produce bulbar conjunctival infection, palpebral conjunctival hypertrophy, and decrease in wearing time.

914. (D) Oxygen transmission through a contact lens is inversely proportional to lens thickness, but it is directly proportional to the water content of the material.

915. (C) Diffractive bifocal contact lens is a poor choice for visual tasks when ambient lighting is low. The concentric rings of the diffractive bifocal diffract the light such that two attenuated images are formed, instead of one sharp image.

916. (C) Prism ballasted bifocal provides the sharpest vision for both distance and near. There is a sharp transition between the distance and near portions of the lens.

917. (D) Prism ballast is the most effective method for stabilizing the rotation of a front toric hydrogel lens. The superior and inferior thinning of the lens margins works best when the astigmatism axes are 90 or 180 degrees.

918. (D) A rigid front toric lens would be the simplest contact lens design for this patient. The patient astigmatism of −2.50 D is due to residual astigmatism.

919. (C) Disposable contact lenses are not available in high astigmatic correction at this time. The disposable lens is extremely comfortable and convenient and is available in a wide range of minus and plus powers.

920. (D) Acanthamoeba keratitis is most commonly associated with daily wear soft lenses. One of the ways by which acanthamoeba contaminates the lenses is by the use of saline solutions made with salt tablets and tap or nonsterile water.

921. (B) Acanthamoeba keratitis in contact lens wearers has been traced to patients who were preparing their rinsing or storage saline solutions from salt tablets with tap or nonsterile water.

922. (B) The major disadvantage of monovision fitting is the adaption period, in which the patients experience headaches and fatigue. The monovision system is significantly less expensive than bifocal lenses, and easier to fit.

923. (A) Corneal infiltrates have been associated with hypoxia, toxicity, and hypersensitivity to solution preservatives, and debris entrapment under the lens.

924. (A) Acanthamoeba can contaminate contact lens care systems. Bacterial organisms may provide a food source that supports persistent contamination by acanthamoeba. It can adhere to contact lenses and penetrate the intact corneal epithelium.

925. (B) Benzalkonium chloride is effective against both the cystic and trophozoite forms of acanthamoeba.

926. (D) The patient has a corneal astigmatism of −1.75 D. In addition, the patient has residual astigmatism of −1.75 D, which negates the effect of the corneal astigmatism. A spherical soft lens should be the lens of choice.

927. (C) The patient has a corneal astigmatism of −1.75 D, but from the refraction there is also an astigmatism of −1.75 D, which means that all the astigmatism is due to the corneal toricity. The lens of choice should be a spherical, rigid contact lens.

928. (D) The patient with superior limbic keratitis may experience itching, photophobia, and foreign body sensation.

929. (A) 3 and 9 o'clock staining is caused by too much edge lift. Too tight a lens would produce a central staining pattern. Too much movement of the lens probably would not produce any staining, but the patient may complain of excessive movement.

References

1. Bailey IL, Hall A. *Visual Impairment, An Overview.* New York: American Foundation for the Blind; 1990.
2. Barron C. Bioptic telescopic spectacles for motor vehicle driving. *Journal of the American Optometric Association.* 6ℨ(1):37-41;1991.
3. Borish IM. *Clinical Refraction.* Vol I, 3rd ed. Chicago: Professional Press; 1970.
4. Borish IM. *Clinical Refraction.* Vol II, 3rd ed. Chicago: Professional Press; 1970.
5. Brooks CW, Borish IM. *System for Ophthalmic Dispensing.* Chicago: Professional Press; 1979.
6. Cline D, Hofstetter HW, Griffin JR. *Dictionary of Visual Science.* 4th ed. Radnor, Pa: Chilton; 1989.
7. Davson H, ed. *The Eye, Muscular Mechanisms.* Vol 3. New York: Academic Press; 1969.
8. Dowaliby M. *Practical Aspects of Ophthalmic Optics.* 3rd ed. New York: Professional Press Books; 1988.
9. Duane T, Jaeger E. *Clinical Ophthalmology.* Vol 1. Philadelphia: Harper & Row; 1983.
10. Duane TD. *Clinical Ophthalmology.* Vol I, rev. ed. Philadelphia: Harper & Row; 1990.
11. Epting JB, Morgret FC. *Ophthalmic Mechanics and Dispensing.* Philadelphia: Chilton; 1964.
12. Faye EE, ed. *Clinical Low Vision.* 2nd ed. Boston/Toronto: Little, Brown; 1984.
13. Fincham WHA. *Optics.* 6th ed. London: Hatton Press; 1951.
14. Fonda G. *Management of the Patient with Subnormal Vision.* 2nd ed. St. Louis: Mosby; 1970.
15. Fonda GE. *Management of Low Vision.* New York: Thieme-Stratton; 1981.

16. Gerstman DR. Multifocal Lens Decentration and Size as a Function of Reading Distance. *Journal of the American Optometric Association.* 55(8):575-579;1984.
17. Goss D. *Ocular Accommodation, Convergence, and Fixation Disparity: A Manual of Clinical Analysis.* New York: Fairchild Publications; 1986.
18. Griffin JR. *Binocular Anomalies: Procedures for Vision Therapy.* Chicago: Professional Press, Inc; 1976.
19. Grosvenor TP. *Primary Care Optometry.* 2nd ed. New York: Professional Press Books; 1989.
20. Grosvenor T, Flom M. *Refractive Anomalies.* Boston: Butterworth-Heinemann; 1991.
21. Hirsch MJ, Wick RE. *Vision of Children.* Philadelphia: Chilton; 1963.
22. Jalie M. *The Principles of Ophthalmic Lenses.* 3rd ed. London: The Association of Dispensing Opticians; 1977.
23. Jose RT. *Understanding Low Vision.* New York: American Foundation for the Blind; 1983.
24. Kanski JJ. *Clinical Ophthalmology.* 2nd ed. London: Butterworths; 1989.
25. Keating MP. *Geometrical, Physical, and Visual Optics.* Boston: Butterworths; 1988.
26. Maino JH, McMahon TT. NoIRs and Low Vision. *Journal of the American Optometric Association.* 57(7):532-535;1986.
27. Mandell RB. *Contact Lens Practice.* 4th ed. Springfield: Charles C Thomas; 1988.
28. Mehr EB, Freid AN. *Low Vision Care.* Chicago: Professional Press; 1975.
29. Moses RA, ed. *Adler's Physiology of the Eye, Clinical Applications.* 7th ed. St. Louis: Mosby; 1981.
30. Ogle KN. *Researches in Binocular Vision.* Philadelphia: WB Saunders Co; 1950.
31. Phillips AJ, Stone J, eds. *Contact Lenses.* 3rd ed. London: Butterworths; 1989.
32. Pickwell D. *Binocular Vision Anomalies.* London: Butterworths; 1984.
33. Schor CM, Ciuffreda KJ. *Vergence Eye Movements: Basic and Clinical Aspects.* Boston: Butterworths; 1983.
34. Stein HA, Slatt BJ, Stein RM. *Fitting Guide for Rigid and Soft Contact Lenses.* 3rd ed. St. Louis: CB Mosby; 1990.

35. Von Noorden GK. *Binocular Vision and Ocular Motility.* St. Louis: Mosby; 1980.
36. Woo G, ed. *Low Vision Principles and Applications.* New York: Springer-Verlag; 1986.

8

Perceptual Conditions

DIRECTIONS (Questions 930–964): Each of the numbered items or incomplete statements in this section is followed by answers or completions of the statement. Select the ONE lettered answer or completion that is BEST in each case.

Anomalies of Child Development

930. Children with normal vision who exhibit generally normal behavior but suffer from specific language problems (reading and/or writing) may be classified as having
    A. dyslexia
    B. dysnemkinesia
    C. dysphonesia
    D. diseidesia
    E. all of the above

931. Poor readers, in particular those who suffer from dyslexia, typically exhibit
   A. normal eye movements when reading
   B. abnormal saccades while viewing objects
   C. abnormal smooth pursuit movements
   D. reduced visual acuity
   E. none of the above

932. Children with cerebral palsy exhibit an unusually high incidence of
   A. strabismus
   B. optic atrophy
   C. high refractive error
   D. accommodative disorders
   E. all of the above

933. Which of the following ocular conditions occurs with an unusually high incidence in Down syndrome?
   A. infantile cataracts
   B. cataracts in young adults
   C. strabismus
   D. both A and C
   E. both B and C

934. Which of the following syndromes is commonly associated with mental retardation?
   A. Down syndrome
   B. cerebral palsy
   C. fragile X
   D. both A and B
   E. A, B, and C

935. A patient is considered to be *severely* mentally retarded if he or she has an IQ score of
   A. between 55–69
   B. between 40–54
   C. between 25–39
   D. less than 25
   E. none of the above

936. Cerebral palsy may originate
  A. prenatally, from a genetic disorder
  B. prenatally, from anoxia
  C. parinatally, from brain trauma
  D. postnatally, from infectious disease
  E. all of the above

937. Complete achromatopsia is
  A. an autosomal recessive condition
  B. a sex-linked recessive condition
  C. more common in males than females
  D. different from rod monochromacy
  E. present in about 3 percent of the population

938. An adult epileptic patient who, while appearing to remain conscious, exhibits generalized jerking of the extremities probably is most likely having a
  A. generalized tonic-clonic (grand mal) seizure
  B. absence (petit mal) seizure
  C. myoclonic seizure
  D. atonic (drop attack) seizure
  E. none of the above

939. Parents and siblings of dyslexic children are expected, on average, to have
  A. normal reading skills
  B. higher than normal rates of reading difficulties
  C. lower than normal rates of reading difficulties
  D. their reading skills genetically determined
  E. normal rates of reading difficulty

940. Reading improvements in children and adults with reading disabilities have been
  A. reported in patients with "scotopic sensitivity syndrome"
  B. reported if they read through broad-band colored filters
  C. reported by H. Irlen in 1983, using colored tints
  D. attributed to reduced glare in specific spectral regions
  E. all of the above

941. Migraine phosphenes can
  A. appear in the absence of visual stimulation
  B. appear as flickering "fortification scintillations"
  C. appear as arcs of "jagged lines," originating at the fixation point
  D. be accompanied by a "quarter moon" scotoma
  E. all of the above

942. The optometrist should be familiar with adaptive behaviors often developed by children with learning disabilities. Some of these behaviors are
  A. withdrawal: not participating in situations that can lead to failure or frustration
  B. regressive reactions: the child regresses to a less mature level of social and emotional development to avoid embarrassment
  C. "clowning around": the child rationalizes that he is not learning because he chooses not to learn
  D. all of the above
  E. none of the above

943. The practicing optometrist should be fully aware of the *Education of All Handicapped Children Act,* which recognizes eleven specific categories of "exceptionalities." Which of the following is considered an "exceptionality"?
  A. deaf-blind or visually handicapped
  B. orthopedically impaired or learning disabled
  C. hard-of-hearing or mentally retarded
  D. speech impaired or emotionally disturbed
  E. all of the above

944. The child with attention deficit hyperactivity disorder (ADHD) usually displays which of the following behaviors?
  A. inappropriate degrees of inattention
  B. impulsiveness
  C. hyperactivity
  D. all of the above
  E. none of the above

Anomalies of the Aging Adult

945. High frequency contrast sensitivity measured in older adults with healthy eyes can be lower than that of young adults because of
    A. reduced pupil size
    B. increased lenticular absorption
    C. higher retinal illuminance
    D. both A and B
    E. A, B, and C

946. Which of the following instruments is used to assess retinal function in cataract patients?
    A. visually evoked potentials recorded from the occipital lobe
    B. vistech contrast sensitivity test
    C. potential acuity meter (PAM)
    D. Pelli-Robson contrast sensitivity test
    E. brightness acuity tester (BAT)

947. Regarding oculomotor control in the aged,
    A. smooth pursuit of fast moving objects is less accurate
    B. fixation is less accurate
    C. saccadic latency is increased
    D. the range of eye rotation is decreased
    E. all of the above

948. Which of the following conditions is NOT a major cause of blindness in older people?
    A. multiple sclerosis
    B. glaucoma
    C. age-related maculopathy
    D. cataracts
    E. diabetic retinopathy

949. Which of the following conditions will produce excessive disability glare?
    A. nuclear sclerosis
    B. posterior subcapsular cataracts
    C. miosis
    D. pseudophakia
    E. both A and B

950. Since the aging adult tends to fatigue quickly, and may be somewhat hard of hearing, forgetful, and have a shorter attention span, errors in performance can be made during the course of any testing procedure; to avoid such errors the visual examination should
A. be scheduled during morning hours
B. utilize a trial frame and trial lenses to maintain a more normal environment
C. allow sufficient time for considered answers
D. utilize repeat visits when necessary
E. all of the above

951. Age-related macular degeneration (AMD) is one of the more common causes of permanent visual loss among older persons in the western world. A patient with AMD presents with which of the following signs and/or symptoms?
A. straight lines appear to be wavy/distorted; this symptom is best checked by utilizing the Amsler grid test
B. severe visual acuity loss that interferes with both reading and driving, thereby causing functional as well as economical disability
C. damage is confined to the macula area of the retina
D. peripheral vision remains good; individuals with "counting fingers" vision can still walk about comfortably and care for themselves
E. all of the above

952. Which of the following statements concerning the relationship between field of view (the visual field) and retinal sensitivity of the aging patient is correct?
A. Age gradually depresses the central isopters.
B. Age gradually depresses the peripheral isopters.
C. Isopters are not influenced by age in the healthy eye.
D. both A and B
E. none of the above

953. Hearing loss in older individuals can be a
A. conductive hearing loss, caused by excessive cerumen in the external ear canal
B. conductive hearing loss, caused by otosclerosis
C. sensorineural hearing loss, caused by atrophy of the organ of Corti

D. sensorineural hearing loss, caused by the loss of hair cells
E. all of the above

954. In order to effectively communicate with hearing impaired older patients who are using hearing amplification devices,
 A. simply shout and they will hear
 B. speak very quietly so that they are not "deafened" by the amplified signal
 C. try to remove all other sources of sound when you speak to them
 D. try to specifically amplify the vowels in your speech
 E. all of the above

955. Muscular rigidity, rhythmic tremors, a biochemical imbalance of the two neurotransmitters (acetylcholine and dopamine), a loss of cells in the *substantia nigra,* and medication with L-dopa are characteristics that accompany which of the following diseases found primarily in the elderly?
 A. Alzheimer's disease
 B. primary degenerative dementia
 C. Parkinson's disease
 D. muscular dystrophy
 E. multiple sclerosis

Anomalies of Color Vision (Congenital, Inherited)

956. The mode of inheritance of congenital red-green color deficiencies is
 A. autosomal, dominant
 B. autosomal, recessive
 C. sex-linked, dominant
 D. sex-linked, recessive
 E. autosomal, intermediate

957. Acquired color anomalies differ from hereditary color anomalies because, unlike inherited anomalies, they
   A. change over time
   B. exhibit anomalous Rayleigh matches
   C. produce altered anomaloscopic matches
   D. are bilateral
   E. exhibit displaced neutral points

958. The neutral point for a deuteranope is
   A. the wavelength which appears yellow
   B. the wavelength which appears the same as white
   C. approximately 500 nanometers
   D. approximately 532 nanometers
   E. both B and C

959. Which of the following color defects is encountered most often?
   A. protanopia
   B. deuteranopia
   C. protanomaly
   D. deuteranomaly
   E. tritanopia (congenital)

960. Which of the following characteristics is NOT commonly observed in a rod monochromat?
   A. Purkinje shift
   B. poor central acuity
   C. normal scotopic luminosity function
   D. absence of color vision
   E. photophobia

961. When adjusting the relative intensity of a spectral red (650 nm) and a spectral green (520 nm) combination in order to make hue matches with a spectral yellow (580 nm), a
   A. protanomalous trichromat will require more red
   B. deuteranope will require more red
   C. protanope will not accept the match of a normal trichromat
   D. deuteranomalous trichromat will accept the match of a normal trichromat
   E. deuteranomalous trichromat will require more red

962. Which of the following clinical tests specifically selects test colors that lie along the protanopic and deuteranopic color confusion lines?
A. Ishi Hara pseudoisochromatic plates
B. D-15 test
C. 100 hue test
D. none of the above
E. A, B, and C

963. The lighting used for clinical color vision tests is *unimportant* because the
A. colors are metamers
B. tests all use monochromatic stimuli
C. tests do not need any illumination
D. color of ink is independent of illuminant
E. none of the above

964. In which of the following professions might dichromacy be a significant impediment?
A. telephone engineer
B. lighting designer
C. train driver
D. buyer of fashion clothes
E. all of the above

Answers and Discussion

Anomalies of Child Development

930. (E) Unlike alexia, in which a person cannot identify or recognize letters or words, dyslexics can usually recognize letters but they have difficulty with words. There are several distinct types of dyslexia. Dysnemkinesia is a "motor" type of dyslexia in which reversals of letters and/or numbers occur during writing. This can often be treated with success. Dysphonesia is an "auditory" type of dyslexia in which there is poor phonetic encoding and spelling errors are often phonetically illogical. Dyseidesia is a "visual" type of dyslexia in which phonetically correct but visual illogical spelling errors will occur.

931. (E) As a general rule, dyslexics exhibit erratic eye movements during reading, with an excessive number of regressive saccades. However, they can have normal visual acuity, and they can have normal eye movements when tracking or saccading to nontext targets. However, this last observation (normal eye movements) may not be generalizable to all dyslexics and is currently somewhat controversial.

932. (E) Cerebral palsy is often associated with a number of vision disorders (estimates as high as 82 percent). These include, most often, refractive errors, strabismus, accommodative disorders, and also nystagmus, optic atrophy, muscle paresis, visual field defects, and eye movement control problems.

388

933. (E) Up to 60 percent of Down syndrome patients develop cataracts by early adulthood, and the estimate of strabismus incidence is about 40 percent. Other visual problems also occur in higher levels than observed in the normal population.

934. (E) Three of the major mental retardation (MR) syndromes are Down (16-27 percent of all MR), fragile-X (2–10 percent of all MR), and cerebral palsy (4.3 percent of all MR).

935. (C) The four classifications of level of mental retardation are assigned based on IQ scores: educable mentally handicapped (EMH) = 55–69; trainable mentally handicapped (TMH) = 40–54; severely mentally handicapped (SMH) = 25–39; profoundly mentally handicapped (PMH) = less than 25.

936. (E) Cerebral palsy is a classification of disorders that affect the motor centers of the central nervous system. Damage to these centers can occur before, during, or after birth from disease, anoxia, trauma, and genetic problems.

937. (A) Complete achromatopsia, or rod monochromacy, is present equally in males and females and has an incidence of about 0.003 percent. These patients exhibit a variety of vision problems, including photophobia and reduced visual acuity.

938. (C) A generalized tonic-clonic seizure (formally known as a grand mal seizure) has two phases; during the first (tonic), the patient becomes stiff, and during the second (clonic), there is rapid jerking of the body and the patient is unconscious during the entire seizure. An absence seizure (formally, petit mal) is characterized by a short (15 sec) loss of consciousness. Myoclonic seizure exhibits jerking of the extremities and generally lasts for less than 5 seconds, usually with a brief period of unconsciousness that can often go unnoticed. An atonic seizure (formally, a drop attack) is characterized by a paroxysmal loss of muscle tone, resulting in a fall.

939. (B) Dyslexia has been shown to run in families (parents and siblings of dyslexic children exhibit higher than normal rates of reading difficulties). However, there is no conclusive evidence that this familial association is genetically determined.

940. (E) In 1983, Irlen described a new "treatment" for reading disabilities. It was based on the notion that some reading disabilities result from increased glare and reduced contrast observed at photopic light levels. This condition, named "scotopic sensitivity syndrome" by Irlen, was "treated" by adding a colored tint to the patients' spectacles, and the specific tint that provided the biggest improvement varied from individual to individual. Clearly, the filters reduce retinal illumination and shape the spectrum of retinal irradiation from all broad-band sources. After considerable controversy and a number of studies, there is still no experimental evidence that the filters actually lead to an improvement in reading. Most studies and reports suffer from inadequate controls, and those that use controls tend to find a negative result.

941. (E) In some forms of migraine, phosphenes appear prior to the migraine attack. These phosphenes do not require visual stimulation but seem to reflect abnormal electrical activity in the primary visual cortex. Patients report seeing flickering jagged lines (fortification scintillations) that originate at the fixation point and travel in an arc into the peripheral field. The scintillations are often accompanied by a quarter moon scotoma.

942. (D) The optometrist's role is to ameliorate perceptual and visual dysfunction in children who have been identified as learning disabled (LD). At school, LD children often exhibit one or more of the behaviors listed in **A–C**. Vision problems can be quite prevalent in these children.

943. (E) All are included. The provisions of this act and its amendments require all states to provide handicapped children with a full range of programs and services that will enable them to receive free and appropriate education in the least restrictive environment.

944. (D) All of these activities (A–C) can be observed in ADHD children. Psychostimulants have been found to be effective in modulating the behavior of ADHD children. Although seemingly paradoxical, psychostimulants can have a salutary effect on hyperactive children.

Anomalies of the Aging Adult

945. (D) There are numerous pathologies present in older eyes that will reduce contrast sensitivity. However, reduced pupil size and increased lenticular absorption in healthy eyes will lead to reduced retinal illuminance, and high frequency contrast sensitivity and visual acuity are reduced by decreases in retinal illuminance. Reduced retinal illuminance can affect clinical acuity measures as well as complex behavioral tasks such as night driving.

946. (C) Any visual acuity or other vision test that employs a stimulus that must be imaged onto the retina by the eyes' optics will be susceptible to the optical image degradation effects of the cataract. Instruments that employ a localized, very narrow beam to "project" an acuity target into the eye can be directed by the clinician to get light onto the retina without hitting the cataract. The Potential Acuity Meter (PAM) is such a device that projects a letter chart through a very small zone of the pupil and it is used to asses retinal function unaffected by optical scatter from the cataract.

947. (E) In general, studies seem to indicate that oculomotor control in aged people is slower (increased latency). Also, it appears to be less accurate (saccades and tracking). The causes of these changes are not known.

948. (A) Although cataracts are now removed in the U.S. before serious visual disability develops, they are still a major cause of "blindness" in much of the world. In America, age-related maculopathy, diabetic retinopathy, and glaucoma are all major causes of blindness in the aging population. Although multiple sclerosis can severely degrade visual capability, many sufferers do not survive into late adulthood and, therefore, it is quite rare in older individuals.

949. (E) Any scatter source within the eye will create disability glare: the reduction in visual ability due to a bright light source present elsewhere in the visual field (e.g., the classic night driving problem: looking at a dimly lit street with oncoming headlights). Several conditions common to older people will create exaggerated disability glare; e.g., cataracts, nuclear sclerosis, corneal clouding, etc. Reduction in pupil size alone will not cause disability glare (but it can worsen disability glare if the person already has a PSC cataract). Also, pseudophakes have clear plastic IOLs that do not scatter large amounts of light.

950. **(E)** The geriatric patient can be a demanding test of the examination techniques of a practicing optometrist. The slowed reactions of the elderly require a slowed exam pace. It is helpful if the clinician exhibits extra patience and understanding.

951. **(E)** All. AMD patients can often walk about comfortably. However, reading presents a special problem to the aging adult with AMD. Although AMD patients may be able to walk, they should not drive.

952. **(D)** With aging the visual field normally undergoes a slow generalized depression. Sensitivity is reduced diffusely throughout all regions of the field as one grows older. Constricted isopters encountered during the visual fields test can be considered normal for older adults.

953. **(E)** Hearing loss in the elderly (presbycusis) can be due to a failure to conduct sound waves to the cochlea due to excessive buildup of wax (cerumen) in the external ear canal, or less common, due to changes in the structure of the bones in the middle ear (otosclerosis). However, it is more common for hearing loss to originate from senescent changes in the cochlea (inner ear) due to atrophy of the cochlea (organ of Corti) or, more specifically and more common, a loss of hair cells.

954. **(C)** Because most users of hearing aids frequently suffer from an inability to detect higher frequency sounds, the consonants, which contain most of the high frequencies, must be amplified. These individuals have trouble hearing speech because they tend only to hear the vowels. Hearing impaired individuals have trouble isolating the speech they wish to hear from all the other noises that also get amplified. They will be able to understand speech better if it is unaccompanied by other noises. Therefore, improved communication can be achieved by removing any other sources of sound.

955. (C) Muscular dystrophy or multiple sclerosis patients rarely survive into old age. Dementia in older patients can occur in both Parkinson's disease and Alzheimer's disease. However, the list of symptoms fits the profile of Parkinson's disease. Alzheimer's disease is an untreatable degenerative disease that is not as well understood as Parkinson's disease.

Anomalies of Color Vision (Congenital, Inherited)

956. (D) Both protanopia and deutranopia are inherited as sex-linked recessive traits. They are both present in about 1 percent of the male population, but in between 0.02 percent and 0.01 percent in the female population, respectively. Deutranomalous trichromacy is present in about 5 percent of the male population and in 0.4 percent of the female population. Protonomalous trichromats are present in about the same numbers as protonopes.

957. (A) B–E are found in both inherited and acquired color anomalies. However, inherited color anomalies exhibit stable color deficiencies over time. Only acquired color deficiencies change with time.

958. (E) All dichromats exhibit a neutral point, which is the wavelength that elicits the same response from the remaining two receptors as does an achromatic white. Therefore, this wavelength will be indistinguishable from white. Reports of the neutral point for deuteranopes vary between 495 and 510, with a mean near to 500 nm.

959. (D) Deuteranomalous trichromats are more common (about 4 to 5 percent of the male population) than deuteranopes, protanopes, or protanomalous trichromats (each present in about 1 to 1.5 percent of the male population). Tritanopes are very rare. Female dichromats are extremely rare.

960. (A) Because the monochromatic eye has only rods, there can be no Purkinje shift. An absence of color vision, poor acuity, and a functional blindness at very high light levels also accompany this condition.

961. (A)   Because both protanopes and deuteranopes are effectively monochromats above 520 nm, any combination of spectral red and spectral green will be indistinguishable from that of spectral yellow. Therefore, either type of dichromat will accept the hue match of a normal trichromat. However, just like normal trichromats, anomalous trichromats are effectively dichromatic at wavelengths above 520 nm, and they will see a change in hue from red to green as the relative intensity of the red and green light is varied. In contrast to normal trichromats, protanomalous trichromats require more red and deuteranomalous trichromats require more green in order to match spectral yellow.

962. (E)   The key to discriminating between a dichromat and a trichromat is that stimuli that are readily discriminable to trichromats are indiscriminable to dichromats. The color confusion lines define the confusable (and therefore not discriminable) colors. Most clinical color vision tests employ such colors, including the three listed here.

963. (E)   The reflected spectrum of any broad spectrum reflecting source (all inks) depends critically on the illuminant spectrum. Consequently, the colors of most objects and materials depend on the illuminant. In order for the test colors to lie on the color confusion lines, they must be illuminated with a standard calibrated source. Even slight changes in illuminant can introduce significant changes in colors. These changes can displace the colors used in clinical color vision tests from the color confusion lines of dichromats and render the tests worthless or at least compromised.

964. (E)   All of the professions listed make critical and sometimes life-threatening decisions based on the color of a paint, plastic, cloth, or light. Some professions require normal color vision, and they will not hire dichromats. The optometrist may be required to certify that a patient has "normal" color vision.

References

1. Boynton RM. *Human Color Vision*. New York: Holt, Rinehart and Winston; 1979.
2. Carpenter RHS. *Movements of the Eyes*. London: Pion; 1977.
3. Cline D, Hofstetter H, Griffin J. *Dictionary of Visual Science*. Radnor, Pa: Chilton Trade Book Publishing; 1980, 1989.
4. Cornsweet T. *Visual Perception*. San Diego: Harcourt Brace Jovanovich; 1970.
5. Duane T, Jaeger E. *Clinical Ophthalmology*. Vol 1. Philadelphia: Harper & Row; 1983.
6. Geering J, Maino D. The Patient with Mental Handicaps: A Primary Care Perspective. *The Southern Journal of Optometry*. 10:23–27;1992.
7. Grusser O, Landis T. *Visual Agnosias and Other Disturbances of Visual Perception and Cognition*. Vol 12 of *Vision and Visual Dysfunction*. 17 vols. Boca Raton, Fl: CRC Press, Inc; 1991.
8. Kart C, Metress E, Metress S. *Aging, Health, and Society*. Boston, Ma: Jones and Bartlett; 1988.
9. Maino D, Maino J, Maino S. Mental retardation syndromes with associated ocular defects. *J. American Optometric Association*. 61:707–716;1990.
10. Rosenbloom A, Morgan M. *Principles and Practice of Pediatric Optometry*. Philadelphia: JB Lippincott Co; 1990.
11. Rosner J, Rosner J. *Pediatric Optometry*. Boston: Butterworths; 1990.
12. Stein J. *Vision and Visual Dyslexia*. Vol 13 of *Vision and Visual Dysfunction*. 17 vols. Boca Raton, Fl: CRC Press, Inc; 1991.
13. Stolov W, Clowers M. *Handbook of Severe Disability*. Washington, D.C.: U.S. Government Printing Office; 1981.

9

Public Health

Epidemiology and Biostatistics

DIRECTIONS (Questions 965–976): Each of the numbered items or incomplete statements in this section is followed by answers or completions of the statement. Select the ONE lettered answer or completion that is BEST in each case.

965. A highly sensitive test, one that is good in detecting the condition it is testing for, has a low

    A. false-negative rate
    B. true-positive rate
    C. false-positive rate
    D. true-negative rate
    E. none of the above

966. Glaucoma is an effective subject for screening programs since it is a condition that is asymptomatic, prevalent within the population, and treatable. "Prevalence"
   A. is the same as "incidence"
   B. cannot be calculated for most diseases
   C. is the proportion of people who develop a given disease or condition in a specified period of time
   D. is the proportion of people who have a given disease or condition at a specified point in time
   E. is not of value to epidemiologists

967. Many clinical research projects utilize record reviews of established patients to study particular diseases, conditions, risk factors, etc. These types of studies are known as
   A. double-blind
   B. clinical trials
   C. retrospective
   D. longitudinal
   E. prospective

968. Statistical significance is generally interpreted as a result that would occur by chance less than 1 time in 20. In this instance, the corresponding P-value would be
   A. $P \leq .0005$
   B. $P \leq .005$
   C. $P \leq .05$
   D. $P \leq .5$
   E. $P \leq 5$

969. The square of the standard deviation is a measure of dispersion in a distribution of observations in a population or sample. This is known as
   A. validity
   B. reliability
   C. the correlation coefficient
   D. specificity
   E. variance

970. The ratio of the incidence of a disease or condition in exposed persons compared to the incidence of the same disease or condition in nonexposed persons is known as
A. analysis of variance (ANOVA)
B. confidence interval
C. odds ratio
D. relative risk
E. intrarater reliability

971. An optometrist performs an in-office record review by pulling every 14th chart off the filing shelves to obtain a sample population of 250. This technique is known as
A. systematic random sampling
B. stratified sampling
C. simple random sampling
D. cluster sampling
E. interval sampling

Environmental Vision

972. The amount of light that is being reflected or emitted per area from an object in a given direction is known as
A. illuminance
B. radiation
C. luminance
D. photometry
E. specular reflection

973. Which of the following factors may pose an occupational/industrial risk to the eyes?
A. excessive smoke, dust, or powder
B. excessive radiation, including lasers
C. chemical vapors and spray
D. flying particles or objects
E. all of the above

974. The nonprofit organization that coordinates the voluntary development and maintenance of standards for protective eyewear is
   A. CIE
   B. OSHA
   C. ANSI
   D. IES
   E. ASCII

975. A 23-year-old male patient who is emmetropic and monocular presents to you for acute care due to a metallic corneal foreign body. Your treatment and management of this patient includes
   A. removal of the corneal foreign body
   B. evaluation to rule out globe penetration
   C. a careful history to determine the nature and projectile speed of the foreign body
   D. counseling about protective eyewear
   E. all of the above

976. Which of the following factors affects the lighting requirements of elderly patients?
   A. reduced retinal sensitivity
   B. reduced contrast sensitivity
   C. acquired miosis
   D. reduced media transmission
   E. all of the above

Health Care Organization

DIRECTIONS (Questions 977–983): Each set of matching questions in this section consists of a list of up to ten lettered options followed by several numbered items. For each item, select the one best lettered option that is most closely associated with it. Each lettered heading may be selected once, more than once, or not at all.

   A. PRO
   B. HCFA
   C. Medicare
   D. Quality Assurance (QA)
   E. PPO

F. VSP
G. PSRO
H. HMO
I. Medicaid
J. IPA

977. A system to study structure, process, and outcome of health care, with the goal of guaranteeing that the highest level of care is being delivered, is known as _____.

978. A government-sponsored program, established under Federal Title XIX to provide health care to financially needy members of the population, is _____.

979. A comprehensive, prepaid health plan that organizes and provides care for a voluntarily enrolled group of persons for a prenegotiated, fixed periodic payment is known as a(n) _____.

980. A nationwide independent health plan that provides for vision care services delivered by a panel of doctors is _____.

981. The federal agency responsible for developing health care policies and procedures and that also provides technical assistance to recipients, providers, intermediaries, and other governmental agencies is _____.

982. A prepaid health care plan that utilizes a limited or preferred group of providers and hospitals who deliver contracted care at discounted or reduced fees to third-party payers, employers, or insurers is a(n) _____.

983. Title XVIII of the Social Security Act enacted the federal health care program to provide care for those over the age of 65 known as _____.

Answers and Discussion

Epidemiology and Biostatistics

965. (A) If a test has high sensitivity, it does not often falsely give a negative result in patients who actually have the disease. Thus, a highly sensitive test has a low false-negative rate. The rate of false-negative responses is assessed in many types of automated perimetry to help determine patient reliability during testing.

966. (D) Along with incidence, prevalence is a measure of morbidity. It is used by epidemiologists to evaluate disease patterns and to make future projections. The incidence of a condition refers to the number of new episodes arising in a population over an estimated period of time.

967. (C) Retrospective studies are those undertaken after the clinical observations have been made. The goal is to identify the factor or factors that resulted in a certain effect or outcome. Many epidemiological studies are retrospective in design.

968. (C) P-value is the probability of obtaining a result as extreme as, or more extreme than, the one actually observed based on chance alone. A null hypothesis assumes that there is no difference between the two populations from which two study groups are derived. If this theory is tested and calculations indicate that there is a probability of less than 5 percent that the observed difference between the two groups or a larger difference could have arisen by chance, then the difference is viewed to be statistically significant.

969. (E) Variance is the square of the standard deviation. Standard deviation is a measure of the scatter of observations around their arithmetic mean. Standard deviation is the most frequently used statistic for measuring the degree of variability in a set of outcomes.

970. (D) The relative risk or risk ratio is usually calculated when a group of patients with the risk factor and a group without the risk factor are first identified and then followed through time to determine which patients develop the disease. Thus, it is a measure of the relative risk of a given condition developing from exposure to an identified risk factor. The statistical abbreviation for relative risk is "RR."

971. (A) The sampling interval utilized in systematic random sampling is determined by dividing the number of items in the sampling frame by the desired sample size. If the sampling interval is 14, then each 14th record is pulled. The term sampling frame refers to all the elements in a population from which the sample is drawn.

Environmental Vision

972. (C) The luminance of an object, which affects its perceived brightness, is determined by the density of light falling upon it (illuminance), the percentage of light reflected from the object, and the angles from which the object is illuminated and viewed. Luminance is expressed in candela per square meter (cd/m^2). It is a photometric unit of measure.

973. (E) Industrial vision pertains to the protection of the eye in the workplace from all of the listed factors. Doctors of optometry play important roles in the field of industrial vision. Prescribing and recommending protective eyewear for the occupational setting is a prominent component of this area of eye and vision care.

974. (C) The American National Standards Institute (ANSI) develops standards that reflect the consensus recommendations of manufacturers, consumers, and government agencies, as well as the scientific, technical, and professional communities. Standard

Z87.1 pertains to Occupational and Industrial Eye and Face Protection. Standard Z80 pertains to FDA Requirements for Eye Glasses and Sunglasses.

975. (E) In addition to treating the acute problem, this patient needs protective eyewear to help prevent a recurrence of eye injury. Polycarbonate spectacle lenses currently provide the most protection from potential eye injury. Patients who are potential candidates for spectacles with polycarbonate lenses include children, monocular patients, athletes, and those with special occupational needs.

976. (E) All of the listed factors result in the outcome that older patients require a higher level of illumination for a given visual task than do younger patients. Doctors of optometry frequently counsel patients on lighting set-ups. Depending upon their visual status, elderly patients may also benefit from higher plus adds and other optical and non-optical devices for the visually impaired.

Health Care Organization

977. (D) Quality assurance is an important part of the planning and delivery of health care services, including optometric services. Health care reform efforts will likely bring quality assurance initiatives into renewed prominence. Quality assurance programs include components of provider credentialing and outcome measures.

978. (I) The Medicaid program is administered by the individual states, under federal guidelines. Eye and vision care delivered under a Medicaid program is typically subject to a variety of guidelines. For example, the frequency and type of examination may be specified, along with the types of materials that can be dispensed.

979. (H) Health Maintenance Organizations (HMOs) are a type of managed care model. They are organized to provide comprehensive care while controlling health care costs. HMOs have been in existence since 1929, and they remain as a successful alternative for prepaid health care plans.

980. (F) The Vision Service Plan (VSP) was founded by optometrists to fill the vision care void in many employer health care plans. From its beginning as individual state programs, VSP has emerged as the nation's largest provider of vision care. VSP is an example of a preferred provider organization (PPO).

981. (B) The Health Care Financing Administration (HCFA) was established in 1977. It also oversees the Medicare and Medicaid programs. Optometric services are included in the Medicare program as well as in most Medicaid programs.

982. (E) Preferred Provider Organizations (PPOs) are a type of managed care program. PPOs tend to allow some freedom of choice for the consumer from among the panel of providers. PPOs are growing in number and popularity.

983. (C) The Medicare program provides benefits for persons over the age of 65. Medicare also provides services to those under the age of 65 who are blind, disabled, or have certain chronic diseases. Optometrists obtained parity as physician providers in the Medicare program in 1986.

References

1. Dawson-Saunders B, Trapp RG. *Basic and Clinical Biostatistics.* Norwalk, Ct: Appleton & Lange; 1990.
2. Mahlman HE. *Handbook of Federal Vision Requirements.* Boston: Butterworths; 1982.
3. Newcomb RD, Marshall EC, eds. *Public Health and Community Optometry.* 2nd ed. Boston: Butterworths; 1990.

10

Clinicolegal Issues

Licensure and Governmental Regulation

DIRECTIONS (Questions 984–1000): Each of the numbered items or incomplete statements in this section is followed by answers or completions of the statement. Select the ONE lettered answer or completion that is BEST in each case.

984. The Food and Drug Administration (FDA) tests and approves
   A. ophthalmic medications
   B. contact lenses and contact lens solutions
   C. spectacle frame materials
   D. spectacle lens materials
   E. all of the above

985. State boards of optometry
   A. set licensure requirements for new graduates, reciprocity, and licensure by endorsement
   B. execute legislated mandates for the profession
   C. handle complaints and disciplinary actions against optometrists
   D. monitor continuing education requirements
   E. all of the above

986. Which of the following statements is true regarding your care of contact lens patients?
   A. Informed consent is important as it pertains to the risks associated with extended wear lenses.
   B. Routine care aspects of contact lens patients (eg, tonometry and routine dilated fundus evaluation) must not be overlooked.
   C. Consent from a parent or guardian must be obtained before fitting a minor with contact lenses.
   D. Periodic follow-up examinations are important for all contact lens wearers.
   E. all of the above

Ethical Considerations

987. Ethical considerations in providing care to patients dictate that the
   A. needs of the doctor be placed uppermost
   B. needs of the patient be placed uppermost
   C. type of insurance coverage determines which procedures are performed
   D. needs of the staff be placed uppermost
   E. None of the above; ethics have no place in contemporary optometric care.

Patient Records

988. You examined a 44-year-old female patient five years ago. She stops into your office without an appointment. She has decided to change to another eyecare provider and is interested in obtaining the record of her prior initial, comprehensive examination with you. The most appropriate action on the part of your office staff in response to her request is to
   A. refuse her request, since it has been more than 3 years since you examined her
   B. give her the original examination record
   C. give her a copy of the examination record
   D. give her a copy of the examination record following her written release
   E. send the original record only to her new doctor

989. In the course of examining a patient, you have inadvertently made an incorrect record entry. The most appropriate way to correct this error is to
   A. use a pencil for record entries so that mistakes may be easily corrected
   B. strike the entry, using a single pen line with initialing and dating alongside
   C. use "white out" to correct the entry
   D. use an ink eraser to correct ballpoint pen entries
   E. use a ballpoint pen to completely obliterate the incorrect entry

990. At the conclusion of your examination of a 23-year-old male patient, you have determined that he needs a spectacle correction for myopia. What are the Federal Trade Commission (FTC) requirements for release of the final spectacle prescription to the patient?
   A. A copy of the prescription is given only if the patient requests it.
   B. A copy of the prescription is given only if he orders spectacles from you.
   C. A copy of the prescription is given only if it represents a significant change from his previous prescription.
   D. A copy of the prescription must be given to the patient at the conclusion of the examination.
   E. A copy of the prescription is given only if his spectacles are needed to renew his driver's license.

991. You have diagnosed a 62-year-old patient as having ocular hypertension. You recommend a three-month follow-up. Appropriate patient management in this case includes
   A. a verbal explanation of your findings to the patient
   B. a record entry documenting the need for follow-up in three months
   C. preappointment of the patient
   D. written recall notification
   E. all of the above

Confidentiality of Patient Information

992. One of your patients has been involved in an automobile accident and is being sued. The plaintiff's attorney has telephoned you for information on your patient's visual status. Your most appropriate response is to
   A.   request a written patient release before giving examination information
   B.   deny having examined the patient
   C.   refuse to speak with the attorney
   D.   immediately give needed information over the phone
   E.   telephone your attorney

993. You examined a 37-year-old male patient for a comprehensive evaluation. A week later a woman calls to ask you questions about the examination results. It is most appropriate that you
   A.   immediately discuss the examination results with her
   B.   ask her why she wants the information
   C.   obtain the patient's permission to discuss the examination results with her
   D.   ask about their marital status
   E.   ask her when she last had an eye/visual examination

Professional Liability

994. The standards for competent eye care delivery by optometrists have continued to evolve for a variety of reasons. Which of the following statements accurately describes the current "standard of care"?
   A.   routine pupillary dilation for patients of all ages
   B.   vigilant attention to all aspects of ocular health findings for contact lens patients
   C.   after-hours access to you or an appropriate provider substitute for emergency care
   D.   complete and thorough record keeping
   E.   all of the above

995. Which of the following patient types is an appropriate candidate for polycarbonate spectacle lenses?
A. a pediatric patient
B. a monocular patient
C. a law enforcement officer
D. a racquetball player
E. all of the above

996. One of the paraoptometric personnel in your office inadvertently induced a corneal abrasion in a patient for whom he or she was inserting a contact lens. If the patient sues for malpractice, which of the following statements best describes this situation?
A. You are not liable, since you did not cause the abrasion.
B. You are not liable if the cornea heals.
C. You are liable for the errors of your staff members.
D. You are not liable if the patient does not pay his/her bill.
E. You are liable only if the patient is a minor.

997. A 72-year-old patient calls an optometrist's office complaining of a sudden monocular loss of vision. The receptionist schedules the patient for a routine examination in two weeks, at which time it is determined that vision is irreversibly lost due to temporal arteritis. Based on the above, what needs to occur in this office?
A. proper staff training so that acute/emergency eye care visits are scheduled appropriately
B. the addition of an associate to reduce waiting time for routine appointments
C. increase the number of incoming telephone lines
D. restrict the practice to only the examination of patients 70 years of age or less
E. incorporate a computerized appointment system

998. What is the greatest area of liability for doctors of optometry?
A. professional liability from inappropriate treatment
B. vicarious liability from support staff
C. professional liability from failure to diagnose
D. personal liability from parking lot accidents
E. professional liability from spectacle materials

Evaluation of Disability

999. The usual definition of legal blindness is
  A. 20/200 uncorrected visual acuity or 20 degrees of visual field in the worse eye
  B. failure to pass the vision test for a driver's license
  C. 20/200 best corrected visual acuity or 20 degrees of visual field in the worse eye
  D. 20/200 best corrected visual acuity or 20 degrees of visual field in the better eye
  E. 20/200 uncorrected visual acuity or 20 degrees of visual field in the better eye

1000. Optometrists may be called upon/required to
  A. report suspected child abuse
  B. certify legal blindness
  C. report a patient's inability to meet vision requirements for driving
  D. certify that a patient qualifies for disability benefits
  E. all of the above

Answers and Discussion

Licensure and Governmental Regulation

984.(E)   All of the listed items are regulated by the FDA. This regulation is provided for in the Federal Food, Drug, and Cosmetic Act, including the 1976 Medical Service Amendments for devices. The FDA is responsible for enforcing laws to protect the public against harmful drugs, foods, cosmetics, medical devices (including ophthalmic materials, spectacles, and contact lenses), and radiation products.

985. (E)   All of the listed items fall under the realm of state licensing boards. These boards are established by professional practice acts to ensure that practitioners meet certain minimum practice standards. Unless the licensing board dictates otherwise, a practitioner must hold a valid state license in the state in which he or she wishes to practice.

986. (E)   All of the statements are important aspects of clinical care for contact lens patients. Education of the patient is important to advise him or her of the responsibility of wearing contact lenses. This includes proper handling and wearing of the lenses, as well as the importance of regular professional examinations.

Ethical Considerations

987. (B)   Placing the needs of the patient uppermost is central to ethical optometric practice irrespective of practice setting. The American Optometric Association (AOA), as well as many state affiliate associations, have established recommended Codes of Ethics. The Optometric Oath adopted by the AOA and the Association of Schools and Colleges of Optometry (ASCO) also emphasizes that the needs of the patient be placed uppermost.

Patient Records

988. **(D)**   A patient has a right to a copy of the examination results. A written release should be signed by the patient before record copies are given. The patient should not be given the original examination record.

989. **(B)**   Proper techniques must be utilized to change incorrect record entries. The technique described allows for interpretation of the data entry change. It is not appropriate to alter past record entries.

990. **(D)**   Effective with the July 13, 1978 ruling of the FTC, a copy of the spectacle prescription must be given to the patient. This prescription copy must be given at the conclusion of the examination whether or not the patient requests it.

991. **(E)**   All of the listed items constitute effective and important aspects of thorough, quality patient management. It is important that the office procedures and staff be organized to provide for effective patient recall. Each patient should be told of the recommended follow-up/re-examination interval, based upon the outcome of the examination.

Confidentiality of Patient Information

992. **(A)**   In the example given, information should not be released to the attorney without a written release from your patient. Once the written request is received, along with a signed patient release, it is important to provide the information requested. If the patient was given specific instructions about driving restrictions, this information should have been documented in the patient record at the time of examination.

993. (C) To protect patient confidentiality, information about examination results must not be given without the adult patient's permission. This even applies to family members of the patient. It is very helpful to keep family members abreast of the examination findings, but you must have permission from the patient to do so.

Professional Liability

994. (E) All of the statements describe various aspects of current "standards of care." It is very important that all health providers keep abreast of standards of care for various conditions and examination types. Clinical care guidelines are documents currently under development to help delineate appropriate patient care protocols.

995. (E) All of the listed patients are candidates for polycarbonate spectacle lenses. In these instances, polycarbonate lenses are recommended to maximize eye protection and to minimize the risk of spectacle lens breakage. It is very important that patients are clearly told the options for spectacle lens materials when they select eyewear.

996. (C) As a result of vicarious liability, optometrists are responsible for errors of their staff members. It is very important that all staff members be fully trained to avoid errors as best as possible. This applies to front desk and reception personnel as well as staff members who have direct patient contact.

997. (A) Staff members must be properly trained to appropriately schedule patients with acute eye care needs. It is very helpful/recommended that staff members who handle incoming patient telephone calls have a checklist-type form in order to readily identify those patients who have acute/emergency eye-care needs. The optometrist's patient appointment schedule must have sufficient flexibity to accommodate same-day appointments as needed, or an alternative care source must be arranged.

998. (C) Professional liability from failure to diagnose is the most vulnerable area of malpractice for optometrists. Thus, it is very important that the optometrist be familiar with established examination protocols and standards of care to help avoid this possibility. If findings are equivocal or uncertain, arranging for a second opinion from a colleague or another eye-care provider can be helpful.

Evaluation of Disability

999. **(D)** 20/200 best corrected visual acuity or 20 degrees of visual field in the better eye constitutes legal blindness in most states. Through low vision and vision rehabilitation evaluation, a number of optical and nonoptical aids may be of assistance to the legally blind patient. In this manner, daily living and occupational skills can be maintained.

1000. **(E)** Although requirements vary from state to state, optometrists have responsibilities in all of the listed areas. It is helpful for optometrists to become familiar with the social service agencies in their communities as well as established state agencies. In this manner, reporting of any of the listed items can be readily accomplished when the optometrist is called upon to do so.

References

1. Classe JG. *Legal Aspects of Optometry.* Boston: Butterworths; 1989.
2. Elmstrom G. *Advanced Management for Optometrists.* Chicago: The Professional Press; 1974.
3. Elmstrom G. *Advanced Management Strategies for Optometrists.* Boston: Butterworths; 1982.
4. Newcomb RD, Marshall EC. *Public Health and Community Optometry.* 2nd ed. Boston: Butterworths; 1990.
5. Rosenwasser HM. *Malpractice and Contact Lenses: An Updated Edition.* Boston: Butterworths; 1991.

Printed in the United States
4182